P9-CEY-631

UNITED STATES
LAMBERT CONFORMAL CONIC PROJECTION
Copyright by C. S. HAMMOND & Co., N.Y.

SCALE OF MILES

0   50   100   200   300

Capitals of Countries
State and Provincial Capitals
International Boundaries
State Boundaries
Provincial Boundaries

APPROXIMATE ELEVATIONS

10,000 ft.
5,000 ft.
2,000 ft.
1,000 ft.
500 ft.
Sea level
Depression

Longitude 90° West of Greenwich

GEOGRAPHY
OF THE WORLD

For Young Readers

CONSULTANTS:

Robert Leifels, Ed.D.
Assistant Superintendent of Schools
Uniondale, New York

Robert Burns, M.A.
Professor of Education,
Truro Normal School
Truro, Nova Scotia, Canada

Dugald Sarty, M.A.
Former English Teacher,
Montreal High School
Montreal, P.Q., Canada

Margot L. Wolf
Design and Production

GEOGRAPHY
OF THE WORLD

For Young Readers

Written by Paul J. Gelinas, M.A., M.Sc., Ed.D.,
   Supervising Principal, Union Free Schools, District 2,
   Suffolk County, Long Island, New York

Assisted by Robert Scharff, M.A.

GROSSET & DUNLAP • Publishers • NEW YORK

Foreword

The book you are about to read is the story of an exciting adventure. It is also a book about an important science.

The adventure is a trip around the world, with visits to strange and wonderful places . . . cities and towns and villages with narrow, crooked, crowded streets through which perhaps a bull, a donkey or an ox might saunter, or a motorcycle might come rasping; quiet, rolling farms, sheltered by vast mountains capped with snow; sandy deserts under blazing-hot skies; dim forests into which the sunlight trickles in tiny drops, like rain.

This is the sort of adventure that you could *really* have. The trip would take you a few weeks, or months, at most. It would have taken your grandfather years. It might have taken *his* grandfather a lifetime. The Greek sailor-warrior Odysseus has been told about and sung about for thousands of years because he made a trip less than one-tenth as long. This means that everyone in the whole world has "come closer" to everyone else, through faster means of travel.

The science in this book is the science of geography. It is the study of how and where various kinds of people live; how they earn their living; how they govern themselves or are ruled by others; how they trade; how they make war, and why. Geography is not an *exact* science. Physics and chemistry have simple rules that let us predict just how things will behave when we mix them or separate them, heat them or cool them. But geography has no rules that tell us just how people will behave, or how nations will behave. Nevertheless, the more we know about different kinds of people living in different ways, the better we can guess what will happen in the world in the forthcoming years, the years in which you will have to run the world. It is because everyone in the world *is* getting closer to everyone else that you, in order to be a good citizen, will have to be a bit of a geographer.

Donald Barr, Headmaster
The Dalton School, New York, N.Y.

Library of Congress Catalog Card Number: 65-20031

PICTURE CREDITS

The publisher gratefully acknowledges the cooperation of the sources listed below in furnishing the nearly 500 pictures used to illustrate this book.

Key to picture position: t—top; c—center; b—bottom; l—left; r—right. Combinations: tl—top left, etc.

American Museum of Natural History: 94, 213 t, 333, 365 b, 376 b.
American President Lines (Palmer Pictures): 50, 69, 77, 98, 150 tl, 317 tl, 337.
Arabian American Oil Co.: 121, 133, 303.
Armour & Co.: 32, 33 tr.
Australian News and Information Bureau: 78, 79, 81, 82 b, 83, 84, 85, 86, 87, 88, 89 b, 90, 91, 92, 93, 94, 95, 96, 97.
N. W. Ayer & Son: 329 b.
Edmund Barrett: 18 tc, 22.
Belgian Government Information Center and Tourist Bureau: 256, 258, 259 cr, 322, 323, 331, 339.
British Information Service: 232, 234, 236 b, 237, 238, 240 t, 241, 247, 252, 253, 296, 321, 325 t, 327, 329 tl.
British Overseas Airline Corporation (BOAC): 105, 235 t, 240 b, 309, 330 b, 332.
British Travel Association: 236 t, 239, 242, 243, 245, 246, 250, 251, 255.
Brooklyn Children's Museum: 57 r.
Burlington Route: 40.
Rafaello Busoni: 58, 59, 70 l, 82 t, 89 tr, 144, 145 r, 157 b, 195, 264 tl, 284 tl, 298, 299, 343, 344, 346, 360.
California Mission Trails Association: 47 b.
Casa De Portugal: 290, 291, 292, 293, 294.
Chicago Association of Commerce: 30 l.
Danish National Travel Office: 228 l, 231 t.
Desert Sea News Bureau: 45 t.
Dodge City Chamber of Commerce: 38 l.
Firestone News Service: 335, 345 tr.
The Fragrance Foundation: 274.
French Government Tourist Office: 261, 262, 264 bl, 265 cr, 266, 267 t, 268 t, 269 r, 270, 271 b, 272, 273, 275, 297, 300 tr, 301, 336.
Ewing Galloway: 102 t, 107 t, 118, 134 b, 142 t, 143, 208, 210, 219, 222, 224, 226, 229, 231 b, 278, 284 cl, 356 bl, 375 t, 379, 380.
German Tourist Information Office: 184, 186, 187, 188, 189, 190, 191, 192, 193, 195.
Government of India Information Service: 101 tl, 116.
Government of India Tourist Office: 107 b, 110, 112, 114, 115, 119.
Grace Line: 347, 359 tr, 361 tr, 361 b, 362, 363 r, 369.
Israel National Tourist Center: 124 t, 125 r, 131 tr, 131 br.
Israel Office of Information: 122, 124 l, 125 l, 126, 127, 128, 129, 130, 131 l, 132.
Italian State Tourist Office: 150 tr, 151 t, 151 br, 153, 155, 156, 157 t, 159 t, 160, 161, 163, 164, 165, 166.
Japan National Tourist Organization: 56, 63, 68.
Japan Travel Information Office: 54, 55, 57 t, 60 r, 61, 64, 65 tr.
Kansas Industrial Development Commission: 37 t.

Jo Kotula: 11, 12, 13, 29, 53.
Library of Congress: 20, 23, 26 tl, 109 t.
MASSIE — Missouri Resources Division: 36 tl, 37 b.
Maxwell House Coffee: 352.
Metropolitan Museum of Art: 136, 140 b, 312, 313, 319.
Moore-McCormack Lines, Inc.: 348, 349 t, 351, 354.
Museum of Primitive Arts: 333.
National Archives: 17.
National Capital Parks: 18 l, 21.
National Park Service: 18 b, 25, 41, 46 bl.
Netherlands Information Service: 196, 200, 201, 204, 207.
Newport News Shipbuilding: 340.
Norwegian National Travel Office: 211, 212, 213 r, 214, 215, 216, 217.
Panama Canal Official Photo: 373.
Pan American World Airways: 60 l, 65 b, 67, 71, 101 r, 113, 117, 265 bl, 267 r, 285 tr, 289 br, 289 r, 324, 349 r, 350, 355, 356 tl, 357, 358, 359 b, 363 b, 365 t, 365 c, 367, 370, 371, 375 r, 376 tl, 377.
Pennsylvania State Dept. of Commerce: 26 bl, 28.
Philippine Airlines: 72.
Philippine Tourist and Travel Association: 74, 76.
Redwood Empire Association: 48 b.
Reno Chamber of Commerce: 44, 45 br.
Rockefeller Center, Inc.: 8.
Royal Danish Ministry for Foreign Affairs, Press Department: 229 tl, 231 rc.
Royal Greek Embassy Press and Information Service: 134, 137 r, 139, 142 c, 142 b.
Sabena Belgian World Airlines: 259 tr.
Sacramento Chamber of Commerce: 47 t.
San Francisco Chamber of Commerce: 49.
Santa Fe Railway: 31, 33 b.
South African Tourist Corporation: 320, 326.
Spanish State Tourist Office: 278 br; 282, 283, 284 t, 284 br, 286, 287.
Springfield Illinois Chamber of Commerce: 34.
Springfield Ill. Division of Parks (Hedrich-Blessing Photos): 35.
Standard Oil Co. of N. J.: 27, 36, 38 t, 39, 198, 199, 202, 259 tl, 263, 265 tr, 269 t, 277, 300 tl, 306, 345 br.
Swedish National Travel Office: 208, 223, 225.
Swiss National Tourist Office: 170, 171, 172, 173, 174, 175, 176, 177, 179, 180, 181, 182, 183.
Trans World Airlines (TWA): 46 t, 132, 137 t, 141, 145 b, 146, 289 bl, 307, 310, 311, 315, 316, 317 r.
Union of South Africa Government Information Service: 329 r, 330 l.
UNATIONS: 102 l, 103, 108, 109 r, 111, 333, 361 cr, 368.
U.S. Department of Agriculture: 30 r.
Utah Tourist and Publicity Council: 42, 43.
Wine Institute: 48 t.
Margot L. Wolf: 152, 203, 205, 271 r.

Contents

CHAPTER 1

Our Trip Around the World

Have you ever wished that you could take a trip around the world? If you have, come join us as we prepare for such a journey.

We plan to start our journey from the capital city of the United States, Washington, D. C., cross the country to the Pacific coast, and then visit the lands and meet the people of Asia, Australia, Europe, Africa and South America. We want to find out how men, women, boys and girls live in various places and why they live as they do; also, to see some of the animals, trees, mountains, deserts, rivers, lakes, buildings, museums, and various points of interest throughout the world.

To help us plan our trip, we visit a friend who himself has traveled far and wide for many years as a news reporter and writer. He suggests a route that will include the places we want to see and traces it out for us on a series of maps. He explains that explorers use maps, and since, in a way, we too will be exploring, maps will help to guide us. A collection of maps of countries of the world in book form is called an "atlas," so named after the ancient Greek god Atlas

9

who, according to legend, was so strong that he could hold the world on his shoulders.

Men have been making maps for hundreds of years, but in the early days, when the world was supposed to be flat, it was thought that if a ship sailed too far out on the ocean, it would fall right off the edge of the world. Later on, brave explorers like Christopher Columbus and Ferdinand Magellan helped prove that the world was round. Actually, it was Magellan's pioneering round-the-world voyage which first showed this to be a fact. On September 20, 1519, five small ships under his command set sail westward from the port of Sanlúcar de Barrameda, Spain. Although Magellan himself was killed by savages on a Pacific island some nineteen months later and four of his ships were turned back or lost, one kept sailing on. It finally arrived back where it had started from, on September 6, 1522 — the first ship to go completely around the world.

There is a model of the world, called a "globe," in our friend's house. Looking at it, we see that it is round like a ball, and by turning it, it is possible for us to see all the places we are going to visit on our trip. The earth on which we live rotates just as the globe does — by spinning on its "axis." (If we were to imagine a solid rod or stick running through the earth from top to bottom, the rod would be called the "axis.") The tips of the earth's axis are called poles — the North Pole at the top of the globe and the South Pole at the bottom.

The rotation of the earth on its axis is what causes night and day. If the earth did not turn, one side of it would always face the sun for constant daylight; the other side would always be in darkness. But since the earth *does* rotate on its axis, every part of it faces the sun for a measurable period of daytime and then is turned away from the sun for a measurable period of night. It is important to remember that the word "day" can mean the daylight hours, or it can mean the time taken for one complete rotation

10

through daylight and night, which is 24 hours. In addition, the earth as a planet moves around the sun. The planet Earth takes 365¼ days, or one year, to move once around the sun.

When speaking of north in our travels, we will mean in a direction going toward the North Pole; and when speaking of south, we will mean in a direction going toward the South Pole. In addition to the directions of north and south, there are also east and west. (Here is a simple rule for telling directions: By facing north, our back is to the south, east is to the right, and west is to the left.) There are also "in-between" directions: northeast, southeast, southwest, and northwest. The names, in this case, already indicate what the directions mean: northeast is between north and east, southeast between south and east, and so on.

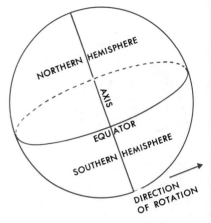

The equator is halfway between the two poles and divides the earth into the Northern and Southern Hemispheres.

The seasons are caused by the angle of the sun's rays and the changing lengths of day and night. The Northern Hemisphere receives direct rays in summer and slanted rays in winter. In June the rotating earth receives more sunlight (longer days) above the equator than it does below. The two hemispheres have opposite seasons: when it is summer in New York, it is winter in Sydney, Australia.

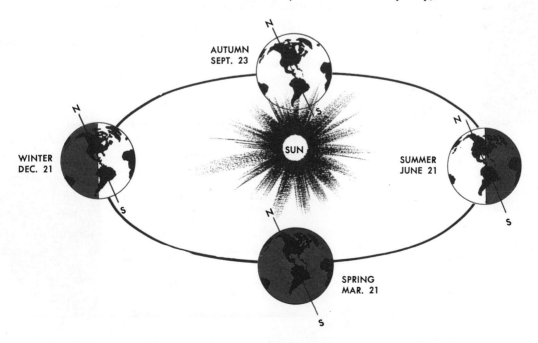

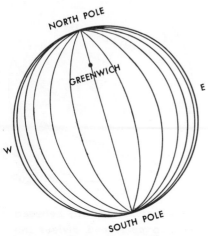

The meridians of longitude are north-south lines on maps and globes which pass through both poles. Greenwich, England, is on the zero meridian.

Looking closely at the globe, we see a line, called the "Equator," that runs around it exactly halfway between the North Pole (the point farthest north on the earth) and the South Pole (the point farthest south on the earth). The equator is not a real line on the earth. No one has ever seen it, and no one ever will. It is not like a line drawn down the middle of a road. It is just a line drawn on globes and maps to help people locate places. The same is true for all of the other lines drawn around the globe. They are not actual lines on the earth.

The equator divides the earth in two equal halves, called hemispheres. A sphere is anything round, like a ball, and hemi means "half." The earth, as we know, is also shaped somewhat like a ball. The earth, then, is a sphere, and half the earth is a half-sphere, or a hemisphere. The half of the earth north of the equator is called the Northern Hemisphere. The southern half — the Southern Hemisphere.

A careful look shows us that there are lines on the globe drawn parallel to the equator. These are the lines of latitude which mark the distance of a place north or south of the equator, measured in degrees. The equator is considered to be at zero degrees (0°) latitude, while the North Pole is at 90° north, and the South Pole is at 90° south. The lines between the equator and the pole on each hemisphere range from 0° to 90°. For instance, the parallel marked 40, north of the equator, is 40° north latitude; the 40th parallel, south

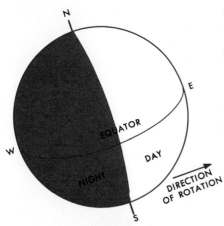

On or about March 21 and September 23, each year, the sun is directly above the equator, and night and day are 12 hours long everywhere in the world.

On June 21 there are 24 hours of daylight in the North Pole region and 24 hours of darkness at the South Pole.

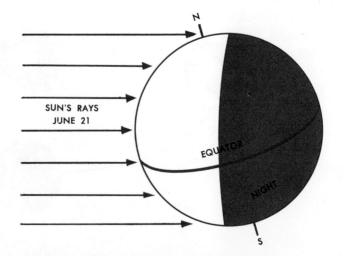

SUN'S RAYS
JUNE 21

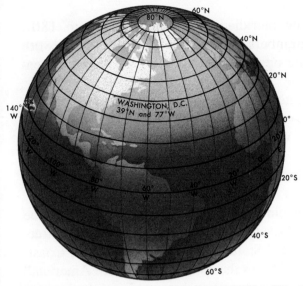

Globe with lines of longitude (in color) and parallels of latitude (in black). Washington, D. C. is located at about 39° north latitude and 77° west longitude.

of the equator, is 40° south latitude. Each numbered line goes completely around the globe, so one could travel completely around the world and still stay on the same latitude line.

For this reason, a place that is 40° north latitude could be in the United States, in Europe, or in Asia. To pinpoint the location of a place exactly, there is a need for other imaginary lines which determine its location east or west. These lines, which run from pole to pole, are called meridians. By naming one of them the zero meridian, we can count east or west from it to get the longitude of any spot on the globe. Longitude indicates how far east or west of the zero meridian a point may be.

Our newsman-friend says, "Some ancient map-makers put the zero meridian just west of Spain. Later, people in the various countries of the world chose their own favorite location. Italian map-makers ran their zero meridian through Naples, Italy. Frenchmen chose Paris, while Americans picked Washington, D. C. In 1884, however, most geographers agreed to count meridians east and west of an imaginary line that they drew through Greenwich, England, a suburb of London. Going west from the zero meridian line

13

at Greenwich, the meridians are numbered up to 180°. Corresponding numbers go east up to 180°. The 180th meridian is on the opposite side of the world from Greenwich."

Our friend points to a place on the globe and says, "The starting point of your trip is located about 39° north and 77° west. In other words, the position of Washington, D. C., on earth is about 39° north latitude, or 39° north of the equator; and it is 77° west longitude or 77° west of the zero meridian."

He goes on, "From the nation's capital, which is on the East, or Atlantic, Coast, you will travel in a westerly direction across the United States to the West, or Pacific, Coast. That is how you will cross the continent of North America."

As our friend points out our route on the globe, we see that all of the continent of North America is north of the equator, and thus is in the Northern Hemisphere. Canada is the largest country in North America, north of all the United States except Alaska. Mexico is south of the United States. Central America, Greenland and the islands of the West Indies are also in North America. The North American continent is attached to South America by a slender strip of land called the Isthmus of Panama.

Looking at the globe, we also notice that two great oceans separate North and South America from Europe, Asia, Africa and Australia: the Atlantic Ocean east of the Americas, and the Pacific Ocean west of them. An imaginary "split" running north and south through these oceans divides the earth into an Eastern Hemisphere and a Western Hemisphere. Starting our trip in the United States, we are in both the Northern and Western Hemispheres. When visiting South America, we shall be in both the Southern and Western Hemispheres. When in Europe, we shall find ourselves in both the Northern and Eastern Hemispheres. Australia is in both the Southern and Eastern Hemispheres.

From the West Coast city of San Francisco, our plans

are to fly across the Pacific Ocean to Japan. "This country," our friend points out, "is an island group in Asia." Again looking closely at the globe, we notice that the continent with the shortest name is the largest continent on the earth. Asia is larger than North America and South America together.

"After your visit to Japan," our friend continues, "your next stop could be the continent of Australia. While it is the smallest continent on earth, Australia is the only one occupied by a single country. In other words, Australia is both a country and a continent. On your way there, you would cross the equator. Since Australia is in the Southern Hemisphere, the seasons of the year are just opposite of ours. That is, the Australian people have winter when we in the United States are having summer, and summer when we are having winter."

Pointing to the globe again, he says, "From Perth, Australia, you could fly to Calcutta, India. In this way you would re-cross the equator and the airplane would take you back to the continent of Asia. While it may seem odd to go out of the way to visit Australia, I can assure you that you will find this country and continent one of the strangest in the whole world." We can hardly wait to visit Australia to find out exactly what our friend means by this statement.

Rotating the globe slightly, our friend suggests that from India we can go west to Israel and then on to Greece. Greece is on the continent of Europe, the second smallest in size. But unlike the smallest continent which has only one country, Europe has 33 countries. Some of these countries of Europe, such as Liechtenstein, Monaco, Andorra, Vatican City and San Marino, are so small that they appear only as dots on the globe. For our proposed journey through Europe, our friend lists 14 countries for us to visit. He explains that many of our ancestors first came from these European nations, as did the traditional ways of living — our language, our form of government, our ideas of freedom, many of the foods we eat, and even the kinds of clothes we wear. While visiting these countries, we will also want to go to museums, art galleries, cathedrals and attend interesting and special events, if there is time.

From Portugal, the last country we plan to visit in Europe, we will head south to the huge continent of Africa. It is the second largest continent in size, so big that the United States would fit into it about three times. A camel ride on the Sahara Desert, a boat trip down the Nile, an auto safari into lion country, and a visit with a tribe of pygmies are all "musts" while in Africa, our friend tells us. With these and the many other exciting things to do, it is no wonder that we are looking forward to our journey in Africa.

From Africa we shall cross the Atlantic Ocean and visit the continent of South America. There we shall explore part of the Amazon River by river steamer, get to know something about Brazil's jungle, its rubber plantations, its coffee plantations, and Brasília, its capital. We shall see Rio de Janeiro's harbor from Sugar Loaf Mountain, then go on to view Argentina's pampas and the Andes Mountains. Chile, Bolivia, Peru, Ecuador, Panama, the Canal Zone and Mexico are also to be included in our itinerary.

After seeing how our neighbors in South and Central America live, we will arrive back at our starting point, Washington, D. C. The entire journey around the world will take about six months. On our trip we shall visit all the continents except one — Antarctica. Our friend jokingly remarks that except for a few scientists and explorers who are studying the continent, the only residents of Antarctica are penguins. No one lives there as a matter of choice, because it is too cold.

We will have to take clothes for both warm and cold weather, since our plans call for travel in the tropical, polar, and temperate regions. When near the equator, we will be in the tropics, while near the North Pole in Norway and Sweden we will be in a polar region. When we are in an

16

area between polar regions and tropical regions, we will be in temperate regions. The United States, of course, is in a temperate region, with four seasons of the year called spring, summer, fall, and winter.

In the tropics the weather is warm the year around, while in the polar region it is usually cold. In the temperate region, however, the temperature will depend on the season of the year. Our trip will start in the spring, but since we live in the Northern Hemisphere, it will be fall in the countries in the temperate regions of the Southern Hemisphere. When returning home in the fall, the Southern Hemisphere will be having its spring season. Thus, our journey is going to call for a year-round supply of clothes.

Before leaving on our journey, we must have a health certificate which states that we have received inoculations ("shots") against such diseases as cholera, typhus and typhoid. We must also apply for a passport, a document issued by the Department of State which certifies that we are United States citizens and, further, requests that other governments provide us with all lawful aid and protection. Even in the few countries which do not require a passport for visitors' entry, this document is most useful as evidence of our nationality and proof of identity.

We are now ready to set forth on our adventure of a trip around the world.

This is the U.S.S. Bear in the "frozen desert" of the Bay of Whales, greeted by the "natives" of Antarctica, the penguins. Antarctica is the only continent we will not visit during our trip.

The impressive Capitol Building in Washington, D. C.

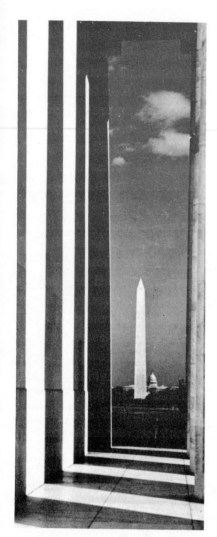

The Washington Monument, seen through the pillars of the Lincoln Memorial. Behind it is the dome of the Capitol.

Jefferson Memorial.

18

CHAPTER 2

Across A Big, Beautiful Land

We are in Washington, D. C., and ready to leave on the journey around the world. Suitcases are packed with a variety of clothes for our travel adventure. After checking into the accommodations reserved for us, we discover that we have some leisure time. We decide that it would be a good idea to take advantage of this opportunity by visiting the nation's capital. To do this, we board a sightseeing bus conveniently waiting outside the hotel.

As the bus travels through the business district of Washington, our capital tour-guide informs us that the government of the United States had no specific location in its early days. The place of convention moved about quite frequently. Before 1790, Congress had met in various other cities and states. At last, in that year, the lawmakers decided that the federal government needed a permanent home which would not be in any one state. The site for the seat of government would be known as the District of Columbia.

"After many places were considered," our guide says, "Congress chose a plot of land along the shores of the

UNITED STATES

Largest country on the North American continent. **Area** • 3,619,623 sq. m. (including all territories and possessions). **Population** • 189,375,000. **Language** • English. **Government** • Democratic, based on Constitution as supreme law. There are three branches of government, the executive (President), the legislative (Congress) and the judicial (Supreme Court). Each branch balances the other in power and can check the other if they seem to use their power unfairly or unwisely. **Monetary Unit** • U.S. Dollar ($). **Chief cities** • New York, N. Y.; Chicago, Ill.; Los Angeles, Cal.; Philadelphia, Pa.; Detroit, Mich. (all have a population of more than one million people in the city proper); Baltimore, Md.; Houston, Texas; Cleveland, Ohio; Washington, D. C. (capital); St. Louis, Mo.; Milwaukee, Wis.; San Francisco, Cal.; Boston, Mass.; Pittsburgh, Pa.; Buffalo, N. Y.; Minneapolis, Minn. (with a population over one million including the suburbs). **Religion** • about 60% Protestant, 35% Roman Catholic, 4% Jewish, 1% other religions. **Mountains** • Mt. McKinley in Alaska (20,320 ft.) is the highest. Mt. Ranier in the State of Washington follows with 14,410 ft. **Rivers** • the Missouri and Mississippi Rivers (over 2,000 miles) are the longest. **Lakes** • the Great Lakes (Lake Superior, Huron, Erie, Ontario), with parts in Canada, and Lake Michigan, and the Great Salt Lake, belong to the largest lakes of the world.

19

Potomac River, because this location was almost in the center of the long strip of thirteen states that then made up the nation. The original District of Columbia, or D. C., for short, was on both sides of the Potomac River, in Maryland and Virginia. But in 1846 Congress voted to give back the Virginia land, and thus the seat of federal government is now on land that formerly belonged to Maryland. Government offices were moved in 1800 to the city that was named for the country's first president. Today the city of Washington occupies the entire area of the District of Columbia."

The first stop of the tour is at the Capitol Building, meeting place of the Congress. Built on a little hill now known as "Capitol Hill," this large building has a beautiful alabaster dome, 288 feet high, on top of which stands a statue created by Thomas Crawford and called the Goddess of Freedom. We climb a broad flight of steps at the Capitol's east entrance — the traditional site and setting for the inauguration of the President every four years.

Through two big bronze doors, we come directly into the great Rotunda, the large circular hall directly below the Capitol dome. After we look at the important historical

View of the Main Building of the Library of Congress in Washington, D. C., showing the newer Annex in the background.

paintings around this room, the guide calls attention to the dome. An immense painting, the "Apotheosis of Washington," by Constantino Brumidi, fills the dome's ceiling. We are told that the artist took eleven months to complete this masterpiece. Next, the guide demonstrates the famous "whispering gallery." When he goes to the other side of the dome and whispers, we hear him clearly, some 95 feet away. From the dome's windows the city of Washington is spread out below us in all its beauty.

Leaving the Rotunda, we enter the south wing of the Capitol, passing many offices, until we see the large square room, or chamber, where the House of Representatives meets. From the visitor's gallery, or balcony, it is possible to see and hear Congressmen as they discuss or debate the fine points of pending legislation. Later, in the north wing of the Capitol, we listen in the Senate gallery to the discussions of the Senators. A guard gives us a keyed floor plan of the Senate Chamber by which it is possible to identify any Senator who may be speaking. We can see by this diagram just where the two Senators from our home state sit. (The House of Representatives and the Senate together are known as the Congress and make the laws. Members of Congress are elected by the people.)

To the southeast of the Capitol is the Library of Congress — the largest library in America — containing two copies of every book or publication copyrighted under the laws of the United States. (The word "copyright" means that no one else has the right to copy any part of the publication or print it without the author's or publisher's permission.) The Library of Congress also has many of the nation's important documents, as well as books and publications from all over the world. A world-famous collection of original scores, both vocal and instrumental, of the great immortals of music (Haydn, Bach, Wagner, Beethoven, and many others) is contained in a large music library. Here, too, is the greatest collection of American

The statue of Abraham Lincoln in the Lincoln Memorial, sensitively created by the sculptor Daniel Chester French.

21

folk songs — hillbilly songs, cowboy songs, Negro spirituals, prison songs, songs of working people — songs that record the life of the people.

Directly to the north of the Library of Congress, and facing the Capitol, is the Supreme Court Building, regarded by many as Washington's most beautiful building. Entering the building, we walk through Memorial Hall, which exhibits statues of famous American jurists, past several offices, and then go into the courtroom of the Supreme Court. On the platform at one end of the room we see the chairs reserved for nine justices. Questions involving state laws and their possible conflict with the United States Constitution are decided by these justices. Individuals — the humblest and the most powerful alike — have legal access to this court when they have reason to believe that the lower courts have made a wrong judgment. But the decisions reached in this courtroom are final; the Supreme Court is supreme in our land.

Riding down Pennsylvania Avenue, we see government

The entrance to the Supreme Court Building in Washington, D. C. proclaims its motto on the cornice: "EQUAL JUSTICE UNDER LAW."

A sketch of the first egg rolling on the White House lawn (the building can be seen in the background) appeared in 1887 in Leslie's Magazine.

buildings everywhere. They include the Departments of Commerce, Labor, Post Office, and Justice. The Archives Building is along this thoroughfare, too, and America's greatest documents, including the Constitution, the Declaration of Independence and the Bill of Rights, can be seen in its exhibition hall. Continuing along Pennsylvania Avenue, we reach the White House, home of American Presidents since 1800. There are many stories as to how the home of the Presidents came to be called the White House. One story is that the gleaming white sandstone from which it was built gave the White House its name. President James Madison made the official title Executive Mansion in 1818, but most people still thought of it as the White House. Finally, in 1901-02 President Theodore Roosevelt decided to make the popular name the official one. By act of Congress it has been called the White House on all official documents and stationery ever since.

The Executive Mansion is indeed a big house, with 132 rooms, a private theater, a gym, a swimming pool, several elevators and four entrances. Tourist visitors enter the White House by the east door and are permitted to visit part of the ground and first floors, but not the private

The State dining room of the White House as it looked during President William McKinley's term of office.

23

family rooms of the President. We see where the President entertains and where he transacts much of the important business of the nation. Of all rooms, the East Room is the most beautiful. It is like the great hall of a palace, with giant sparkling chandeliers and decorations of white and gold. Special receptions, musicales, and other entertainments are held in this room, where once the wife of John Adams hung her washing. In all fairness to Abigail Adams, it must be understood that this room was empty when she used it as a drying room. It was not completely furnished until the 1830's — long after she and her husband had left the White House.

There are many statues of famous Americans in Washington, but the three memorials for three great Presidents — Washington, Lincoln and Jefferson — are the most interesting. The first one we visit is the Washington Monument, a structure near the Potomac River which looks like a giant finger, some 555 feet high. After taking an elevator to the observation deck at the top, we walk down the 898 steps to the ground. Returning to our sightseeing bus, we consider how like George Washington's character this great monument is. Both the man and the monument express great simplicity and enduring solidity.

About a half-mile away is the Lincoln Memorial. Within this white marble building is a huge statue of President Abraham Lincoln seated in a great armchair. On the wall in back of the statue and above his head is written:

IN THIS TEMPLE

AS IN THE HEARTS OF THE PEOPLE

FOR WHOM HE SAVED THE UNION

THE MEMORY OF ABRAHAM LINCOLN

IS ENSHRINED FOREVER

On the north and south walls are imprinted passages from Lincoln's two most famous speeches, the Gettysburg Address and his Second Inaugural Address. As we look at the statue again before leaving the Memorial, Lincoln's deep-set eyes seem to look right into our eyes and even beyond — across the great lawns, beyond even the dome of the Capitol, into the future when men the world around may truly be as Lincoln dreamed: brothers.

Our tour continues with a visit to the Jefferson Memorial, which is near the Potomac River. Within a gleaming white-domed building stands a large bronze statue of the third President of the United States, author of the Declaration of Independence. Since it is spring, the lovely blossoms of the Japanese cherry trees can be seen all around the Tidal Basin near the Memorial. These lovely trees were originally a gift from the city of Tokyo in 1912.

On the Virginia side of the Potomac, a stop is made at Arlington National Cemetery, largest national burial ground in America. In this cemetery are buried many thousands of servicemen (and women) from every state in the union. Here, too, is the grave of President John F. Kennedy and the Tomb of the Unknowns. Our guide tells us that after World War I, four unidentified American soldiers were brought from four French battlefields to Châlons-sur-Marne. There Sergeant Edward Younger, an American soldier, made a selection by placing a white rose on one of the coffins, and this unknown soldier became the symbol of

The Tomb of the Unknowns in Arlington National Cemetery.

An aerial view shows why this building is called the Pentagon (which means five-sided). It is headquarters for the U. S. Department of Defense in Washington.

all the nation's war dead. On Armistice Day (now known as Veterans Day) in 1921 he was buried in a white marble tomb bearing the inscription: *Here rests in honored glory an American soldier known but to God.* Two more unidentified bodies of United States servicemen, taken from the battlefields of World War II and the Korean War, were subsequently buried in adjacent graves on Memorial Day, 1958. A sentry paces solemnly back and forth before the Tomb of the Unknowns, his rifle over his shoulder, as we wait to observe the changing of the guard. Honor guardsmen are ever on duty, day and night, at the Tomb.

We see and visit many other interesting sights in Washington — the National Art Gallery, the Department of Justice Building where the Federal Bureau of Investigation (FBI) is located, the buildings of the Smithsonian Institution, and the Bureau of Engraving and Printing Building, where every day more than 100 million stamps and over four million pieces of paper money are produced by giant printing presses. Finally, after a most interesting tour of Washington, we return to our hotel.

Next morning, we put our bags in the trunk of a rented automobile and head out into traffic. As we move forward, there is a pleasurable thrill of anticipation in the realization that we are starting to cross a continent. Our destination is San Francisco, on the first part, or leg, of our trip around the world.

A look at a road map tells us that the road we want to follow is numbered Route 70, so we watch for signs that read "70." The signs lead us where we want to go. We head northwest out of Washington into Maryland.

At Frederick, Maryland, we enter Route 15 and follow the same road north that the Confederate Army took on its way to Gettysburg, Pennsylvania, where the most famous battle of the Civil War, or War between the States, took place. Most of the afternoon is spent visiting the significant areas of this three days' battle, which was the turning point of the war. Many statues and memorials to fighting units are in evidence. We see where President Abraham Lincoln delivered his immortal Gettysburg Address when dedicating the National Cemetery, and recall the famous words inscribed on the walls of the Lincoln Memorial in Washington, D. C. The gas flame of the Eternal Light Peace Memorial, first lit in 1938, burns in memory of the brave soldiers of the Blue and the Gray who died at the Battle of Gettysburg. It brings back a memory of another Eternal Light flame which we saw at Arlington National Cemetery, burning at the grave of President John F. Kennedy.

After an overnight stay in a motel near Gettysburg, we start out early next morning, heading westward on the Pennsylvania Turnpike. A turnpike is a road upon which motorists pay a charge or toll for its use. We have to pay to drive on the Pennsylvania Turnpike, but since there are no traffic lights, or required stops, we are able to save a great deal of time.

On our westward drive we notice that the flat lands are changing into hills and, a little later on, into mountains. These are the Appalachian Mountains. Great coal resources

Pittsburgh, Pennsylvania, the "steel city," seen from across the Monongahela River.

lie beneath these mountains, and mining towns can still be seen in the valleys between ridges. The first oil well in the United States was drilled in the Appalachian region in 1859. Pennsylvania wells are still producing oil.

Along the Pennsylvania Turnpike, we see a sign that reads "Pittsburgh Exit," and it prompts us to take a look at the "Steel City of America." We remember from our studies in school that Pittsburgh became a steel center because it was close to great deposits of coal, beds of iron ore and limestone rock. All of these substances are necessary in the manufacture of iron and steel. Today, however, the iron deposits of Pennsylvania no longer furnish enough ore for the mills of Pittsburgh. The major part must come from other states. A great deal of it comes from mines in Minnesota and Upper Michigan, transported by Great Lakes ships to terminals on Lake Erie. From there the ore goes by railroad to Pittsburgh.

The business district of Pittsburgh, we discover, is concentrated at the point where the Monongahela and the Allegheny Rivers join to form the Ohio River. (On our road map we see that the Ohio River joins the Mississippi River farther west.) The area around this point is called the "Golden Triangle" and was the site of Fort Pitt, "Gateway to the West" in the early 1800's. A small brick blockhouse, the only remaining building of the original fort, stands at the junction of the rivers in Golden Triangle Park. East of the Golden Triangle is the University of Pittsburgh, its main building a towering structure of 42 stories. It has often been said that Pittsburgh has the only university with a "skyscraper campus."

Driving back toward the Pennsylvania Turnpike, we pass several big steel mills that make rails for railroad tracks, beams for tall buildings and bridges, and many other items of steel and iron. There are other factories along the way which manufacture glass, aluminum, paints and chemicals.

West from Pittsburgh on the Turnpike, the hills gradually

Fort Pitt Blockhouse at Pittsburgh in Allegheny County, Pennsylvania, is the only building of the original fort that remains.

28

PACIFIC TIME

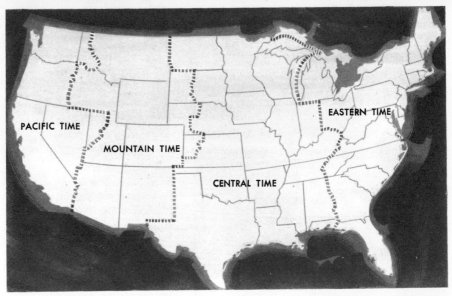

PACIFIC TIME

MOUNTAIN TIME

EASTERN TIME

CENTRAL TIME

MOUNTAIN TIME

become smaller. Then the land becomes comparatively flat. We see by signs that we have entered the state of Ohio and that the road is the Ohio Turnpike. Most of the land is used for farming. The main crops are corn, winter wheat, soybeans, oats, hay, tomatoes and apples. There are farms, too, that raise cattle, hogs, and sheep, and dairy farms supply milk and other dairy products to the big industrial cities in Ohio, like Cleveland, Akron, Columbus and Cincinnati. A wide range of products is manufactured in these cities, including rubber goods, machine tools, glass, paints, electrical equipment, flour, cereals, clay products, farm equipment, textiles, business machines and chemicals. A sign along the Turnpike boasts that seven Presidents of the United States were born in Ohio. We remember that in only one other state have more Presidents been born. Eight Presidents, so far, have come from the state of Virginia.

When stopping to pay the toll at the Ohio-Indiana border, we are reminded that after thirty miles we will be entering a new time zone. We turn our watches back one hour. Going across the United States, we will pass through four different time zones. While in Washington, D. C., Maryland, Pennsylvania and Ohio, we have been on Eastern Time. For the next part of our journey, we will be on Central Time.

American Standard Time zones: The time is one hour earlier in each zone to the west. At 3 o'clock Eastern Standard Time it is 2 o'clock Central Time, 1 o'clock Mountain Time and 12 o'clock Pacific Time.

CENTRAL TIME

EASTERN TIME

29

There are newer and better means of transportation, but the ancient ox cart is still a part of Indiana's countryside.

Molten iron is poured from a giant ladle at one of many steel mills in Gary, Indiana.

Why are there different time zones?

We know that the earth makes a complete revolution on its axis every day. Because of this rotation, the sun seems to rise in the east and move across the sky, setting in the west. Thus, every minute of the day, somewhere on our earth, the sun seems to be coming up. Somewhere, too, at this very moment, the sun appears to be setting. But since the earth rotates from west to east, as we know it, the eastern part of the United States receives the day's sunlight "before" the western part of our country. In other words, dawn comes to Washington, D. C., before it comes to Pittsburgh. And the sun rises in Pittsburgh, Pennsylvania before it does on the Ohio-Indiana border. If every part of the country had the same time simultaneously, the sun would rise in some places at, say, six o'clock in the morning, and in locations farther west at seven, eight, or nine o'clock. To compensate for this difference, it was decided in the year 1883 to divide the mainland of the United States into four parts, or zones, and to standardize the time for all the cities and towns within each zone.

Going across Indiana, there is little apparent change in scenery from that of Ohio. It is the same flat, almost tree-

30

less farm land. The farms themselves are the same kind as those seen in Ohio and the same type of modern machinery is used. But as we near the western part of the Indiana Turnpike, we see the huge oil refineries at Hammond, and the steel mills at Gary. Hammond and Gary are really a part of Greater Chicago, along the southwestern shore of Lake Michigan. The city of Chicago, in Illinois, is our next stop.

We decide to park our automobile and take a sightseeing bus for a tour of the so-called Windy City. Our bus ride starts from the very heart of Chicago, called the Loop. This part of the city was given its name because the elevated railroad that winds around the main business district forms a great loop. We first drive along Michigan Avenue near the lake front, adjacent to Chicago's beautiful Lake Shore Drive. To the west are some immense buildings, including the famous Merchandise Mart, the world's largest commercial building, and the Conrad Hilton Hotel, the world's largest hotel. To the east is Grant Park and the deep blue waters of Lake Michigan.

World-famous Michigan Avenue in Chicago is studded with skyscrapers that house some of the most important corporations of the United States.

Our guide tells us that Lake Michigan is one of five Great Lakes — and the only one that lies wholly inside the United States. "All the other lakes," he explains, "form a borderline between Canada and the United States. Of these lakes, Lake Superior is the largest, as well as the deepest, Lake Erie the shallowest, and Lake Ontario the smallest. Lake Huron has the longest coastline. All together, the lakes form the greatest connected area of fresh water on earth, and Lake Superior is larger than any other freshwater lake and bigger than any salt-water lake except the Caspian Sea in the Near East. A ship can leave Duluth at the extreme western end of Lake Superior and travel through the five lakes and the St. Lawrence Seaway to the Atlantic Ocean. Iron ore, wheat, coal, meat and machinery can go by ship to many parts of the world."

Chicago is the second largest city in the United States

31

This is a birds-eye view of live-stock pens and runs at the Union Stockyards in Chicago.

and the world's greatest transportation center. More trains buses and trucks enter and leave Chicago with passengers and cargo than from any other city in the world. It also has two large airports and is the largest single port on the Great Lakes. In addition to being a transportation center, this city is also the industrial capital of middle America. There are steel mills, railroad car plants, and factories that make farm machinery in Chicago. It is second only to New York City in the number of companies that publish magazines, newspapers and books. The largest mail-order firms have their main offices in Chicago.

One of the points of interest to see is the Water Tower, the only structure of the business district that survived the Great Fire in 1871. It was part of the pumping system which brought lake water into the city. The Great Fire is one of the most important events in Chicago's history, and it all supposedly began with Mrs. O'Leary's cow.

In the early days of Chicago before 1871, people lived mainly in small wooden houses. In one of these houses on De Koven Street lived the Patrick O'Leary family. They kept a cow in a shed in the back yard. The legend prevails that some member of the family visited the cow by the light of a lantern to get some milk, and that the animal, who did not like to be disturbed, kicked over the lantern; and thus started the Great Chicago Fire.

Whether or not this is true, it is a fact that a fire started on De Koven Street. In a few minutes all of the neighboring wooden buildings were in flames. A strong wind helped the fire leap from street to street. Sheets of flame rose into the sky and sparks sailed on the wind. All night and day the conflagration raged, and when it was finally stopped, three and a third square miles of the city lay in ashes. But Chicago's people had courageous spirits and they set to work at once to rebuild their city. Help poured in from all over the country, and out of the ruins grew a bigger and finer city of steel and stone.

Going along Michigan Avenue, our bus passes by or near the Art Institute, the Natural History Museum, the Aquarium, and Soldier Field, where many important football games are played. Farther south we turn off Michigan Avenue and enter Union Stockyards, the largest in the world. Stockyards are places where cattle, hogs, and sheep are sold to meat-packing companies. These companies, in turn, sell the meat which they get from the animals to local meat markets, where it is sold to consumers.

Looking about the stockyards, we see miles of railroad tracks and streets which are used to bring livestock from farms in the Midwest. There are also thousands of small pens where cattle, hogs and sheep are kept until they are sold. When they are bought by meat-packers, they will be killed to make meat, lard and many by-products. These by-products include glue, leather, bone meal, fertilizer, medicine, and other useful things. Our guide says, "Every bit of the cattle, hogs, and sheep is used but their moos, squeal and baas." We also learn that Chicago has become a great meat-packing center because it is not far away from the farms and ranches that raise the cattle and the farms where the feed is available, plus the fact that it has many ways of shipping both the animals and the meat.

After a pleasant two-day stay in Chicago, our trip proceeds toward St. Louis, Missouri. There are large corn fields everywhere. As a matter of fact, Illinois and Iowa are noted as the two greatest corn states. The states in this region of the country are said to be in the "Corn Belt."

Inside a meat packing plant in Chicago, where a large number of "franks" are made.

Miles of steel tracks lead to and from the many railroad stations of Chicago. (This is Dearborn Station).

Abraham Lincoln's New Salem Village is restored to its original condition.

Abraham Lincoln's Tomb and Monument in Oak Ridge Cemetery, Springfield, Illinois.

Most of the corn grown here is fed to farm and ranch animals. Some of it, however, is used to make cereal.

We stop to have lunch at Springfield, the capital of the state of Illinois. This city was for many years the home of Abraham Lincoln. After eating, we visit the house where he lived prior to his election to the Presidency of the United States. Near Springfield is the little village of New Salem, where Lincoln lived for six years and where he grew to manhood. He arrived in New Salem in the summer of 1831 at the age of twenty-two. This village gave him his first experience in community living, in getting along with people. Here his neighbors were close by for the first time in his life. (Up to this time in Lincoln's life he had lived in the wilderness country where he met few people.) There was companionship in good talk — discussions in the stores, at the grist mill, in the cabins. There was civic pride in the community, and folks "did" for each other. Half the women in town fed young Abe and mended his pants and shirts, in return for baby-sitting, cutting logs, or telling a good story. One man taught Lincoln grammar, another taught him surveying, while still another helped him with arithmetic.

Here in New Salem Lincoln tried many ways of earning a living — farm work and woodcutting; store clerking and store keeping; mail-handling and surveying. He learned that he was no businessman. But he knew he would rather work with his head than with his hands and muscles. From New Salem he marched away, a Captain of Volunteers, to fight in the Black Hawk War, and returned to enter politics. Elected to the state legislature, he began to study law during his spare time, and by 1837 he had become a lawyer. The six years that Lincoln spent in New Salem almost completely covered the town's brief history. The community was growing and thriving when Lincoln arrived in 1831, but in 1839, just two years after he had left for Springfield to practice law and advance himself to the Presidency, the majority of its residents had moved to nearby Petersburg. Thereafter New Salem declined rapidly. In about 1885 the last log cabin in the town crumbled to the ground. But today New Salem has been almost completely rebuilt so that it looks as it did in Lincoln's time. We see the Rutledge Tavern where Lincoln lived, the cooper shop where he studied at night by the light of the fireplace, the store where he worked, and we mail postcards to our friends back home from the post office where Lincoln was postmaster.

About two hours after leaving New Salem, we see "Old Man River," the mighty Mississippi. This river, combined with the Missouri, is one of the longest in the world. Its basin extends from western Pennsylvania to Montana, covering about two-fifths of the entire United States. (When water is carried off the land by a river, we say that the river drains the lands. Land that is drained by a river and its branches, or tributaries, is called a "river basin.") The Mississippi River really cuts the mainland of the United States into two parts, but the two parts are not of equal size. The part west of the Mississippi is about twice as big as the part east of the river. We cross the Mississippi by bridge, from Illinois into Missouri, at St. Louis.

St. Louis, the chief city of Missouri, is the largest city in the basin of the Mississippi River, situated almost midway between the upper and the lower Mississippi Valley. Its river traffic handles a great variety of products, including cotton and tobacco from the South, meat and wheat from the West, corn and wheat from the North, coal from Illinois, and the zinc, iron, coal, lead, glass and leather products of Missouri. St. Louis was one of the early trading posts in the Mississippi Valley and still is a great fur market. It is also a great lumber center, and its manufactured products include clothing, chemicals, shoes, automobiles, beer and drugs. It is a meat-packing center, too.

Passing through the beautiful farmlands west of St. Louis, we realize a vast debt of gratitude to Thomas Jefferson and

70-foot-high statue of Chief Black Hawk in Oregon, Illinois.

35

A modern Tom Sawyer and Huckleberry Finn watch a departing stern-wheeler on the Mississippi River.

Large tractors are used for plowing and harvesting the grain fields of Kansas.

other men who bought this land from France in 1803. This transaction, known as the Louisiana Purchase, included the territory from the Gulf of Mexico to the Canadian border, and from the Mississippi River westward to the Rocky Mountains. It doubled the size of the United States at that time and included complete control of the Mississippi River, which, with the coming of the steamboat a few years later, contributed greatly to the development of the country.

Much of our trip westward will be on land obtained from the Louisiana Purchase.

After a short visit to two cities having the same name — Kansas City — one in Missouri and the other in Kansas, our drive continues across the prairie plains of Kansas. (A prairie is a wide, nearly level, and almost treeless stretch of land.) Kansas is a state halfway between oceans and one of the richest wheat-producing regions in the world. The farms are large and the farmers use the most modern machinery. We see large tractors being used to plow the fields, while others are employed in the planting of seed. In late summer, when the golden ripe wheat is ready for harvesting, a large machine, called a combined harvester and thresher, cuts the head of wheat from the stalks, knocks the grains of wheat from the head, and then cleans and bags the grain — all in one continuous operation. Trucks then carry the bagged wheat to grain elevators where it is graded, weighed, and generally stored. Actually, grain elevators on

railway sidings are the principal structures on the Kansas skyline. Later a Western farmer tells us that settlements in the so-called "wheat states" of Kansas, Nebraska and South Dakota are ranked as one-, two-, or three-elevator towns. A one-elevator place will be just a railway shed and general store serving a wide countryside, but by the time a town has acquired *three* grain elevators, it will have a Main Street and even a drug store with a soda fountain and a post office. From the elevators the grain is shipped by train to flour mills or to ports where ships can take it to other countries. Kansas leads the nation in wheat production.

North of Hanover, Kansas is the original Pony Express station, unaltered by time or man.

Riding along past the grain fields, we suddenly see a sign that reads: "To Dodge City." Our interest is immediately aroused, since we have watched many TV programs with stories of events that were supposed to have happened in this town. Dodge City is really a small town, but one with a great deal to see. It marks a frontier between the farming and the major cattle-raising sections of the United States. During the 1870's and 80's, millions of longhorn cattle were driven along the cattle trails from Texas to Dodge City. They were then loaded on railroad cars for shipment to Chicago and to other cities in the Midwest and East. Life on the trail was seldom easy. Ten or twelve cowboys would handle an average herd of 2,500 to 3,000 heads of cattle. A good day's travel was about 12 to 15 miles. Cowhands had to be constantly on guard against a stampede, especially at night. Stormy weather, with thunder and lightning, were most dreaded. It is little wonder that when their job was finished after a month or so on the trail, cowboys wanted to "bust loose." Because of this, "Dodge" became famous as "the wildest little city in America." As the railroad went farther west, however, cattle trails to Dodge City were no longer used. It became the quiet little town that it is today. Yet it could be easily imagined even now that somewhere behind the low buildings there might lurk ghosts of adventurers bent on daring cattle-rustling raids.

A statue commemorates the Pony Express.

37

Cattle branding requires all the skills of a professional cowboy.

The famous cowboy statue on Boot Hill, Dodge City.

We walk down Front Street, the scene of many gun fights, once considered the roughest and most notorious street in the West. Bat Masterson and Wyatt Earp were among the few who were able to bring law and order to Front Street. We stroll down the Board Walk and tour through the old stores, the Long Branch Saloon (only soft drinks are served there now), and the Beeson Museum, to view personal effects and items used by famous Dodge City citizens of the past. We see the cowboy statue that marks the site of Dodge City's "Boot Hill." We ask one of the sheriff's deputies why many of the early Western cemeteries were called "Boot Hill." He explains that most of the burial grounds were located on hills and most of the unfortunate cowboys "died with their boots on."

A short while after departing from Dodge City, the wheat fields of Kansas are left behind. Ahead are the endless stretches of prairie land used for cattle grazing. Rolling hills, cliffs, and big boulders bring to mind stories of stagecoach hold-ups and the early days of the romantic West seen in motion pictures and on televison. Actually, we have been following the old Santa Fe Trail ever since leaving Kansas City. As we drive along perfect roads through this rugged country, our thoughts go back to the hardy pioneers who blazed the trail when there was little to guide them and little to make their labor easier. Those courageous Americans were the men who built up our country, and we feel a deep respect for their character and determination as we cross the land that they made ours.

Occasionally we see a cowboy or two looking after herds of cattle out in the rangelands, as the fields are called in this part of the country. They ride on horseback and wear leather boots, blue jeans (called "levis") and ten-gallon hats. Cowboy costumes are very practical and necessary in riding through the roadless prairies with underbrush of briars, and across fields in the scorching sun. They wear neckerchiefs to keep the dust from their faces. The cow-punchers, as cowboys are often called, stay with their herds all the time they are on the range. They sleep and eat in camps near the herds, too. They return to the ranch only for supplies. Theirs is a hard, lonesome and dirty job.

We see some oil wells as we drive through western Kansas. The oil is pumped from underground to the surface and then sent by pipeline to a refinery where it is converted to gasoline and other oil products. The gasoline we are using in our automobile might well have come originally from under the ground we are driving over!

Huge towers dominate the site of an oil refinery in western Kansas.

Heading west in Colorado on Route 160, we know that we are coming to the Rocky Mountains, because the road goes up and up. We again set our watches back an hour, since we are now on Rocky Mountain time. It is not hard to guess how the state of Colorado received its nickname, "the roof of North America." Driving onward, we see a sign that reads: "Continental Divide." The Divide forms the crest of the continent and separates streams, rivers and watersheds that flow toward the Atlantic Ocean from those that flow into the Pacific Ocean. That is, on the Atlantic side of the Continental Divide, all streams and rivers flow toward the Gulf of Mexico and the Atlantic Ocean. On the Pacific side they flow into the Pacific Ocean. The Continental Divide in the United States generally follows a delineation along the highest points of the Rockies.

The Rocky Mountains are much higher and rougher than the Appalachians we crossed earlier on our trip and there are many snow-capped peaks. Trees are in evi-

Bear Lake with the Rocky Mountains in the background.

dence only below the level known as the timberline. In some of the valleys we find sheep ranches. The sheep spend the summer high in the mountains and are brought back to the valleys prior the winter months. In the spring the ranchers shear the wool from the sheep and sell it. It is then made into cloth, blankets, and many other products.

Colorado, like most Rocky Mountain states, has rich mineral resources. Gold, copper, lead, zinc and silver are found in the mountainous regions. Three-fourths of the world's supply of molybdenum, a metal used in hardening steel, comes from Colorado. The state also possesses rich deposits of uranium. With so many raw materials and natural resources available, Colorado quite naturally has become one of the leading manufacturing states west of the Mississippi. Chief among its products are iron and steel, lumber products, textiles and processed meat.

We stop at Mesa Verde National Park in Colorado, an area where cliff-dwelling Indians of long ago (often called the "little people" because of their small size) built their homes in the high canyon walls. These homes were communal dwellings, or as they might be called today, apartment houses. Some of them were several stories high and housed hundreds of people. They were built under the protecting cliffs of the mesa, or plateau. We visit the Cliff Palace, which contains more than 200 rooms where the Indians lived, plus 23 kivas (underground places of worship) and many small storage rooms. It has eight levels, and was once the home of at least 400 Indians. A park ranger tells us that the cliff dwellers who lived at Mesa Verde are somewhat of an enigma. Who were they? Where did they come from? Where did they go? Some day archaeologists may be able to answer these questions.

From Mesa Verde National Park, our journey heads northwest toward Salt Lake City, the largest city in Utah, and its state capital. On the way, we pass breathtaking views of canyons, weird rock formations, erosion-carved natural bridges, huge caves, deserts, forests — but not many people. Upon entering the Valley of the Great Salt Lake, however, we observe many fine farms with fields of alfalfa, oats, wheat, sugar beets, corn, and neat rows of vegetables. While this area now looks good for farming, it did not appear so to the first settlers. At that time it was simply a desert valley surrounded by barren mountains, containing a huge blue lake with a crusty rim of white salt. Irrigation and hard labor, however, accomplished wonders. (Irrigation is the bringing of water to dry ground by ditches or canals from nearby streams. Land so watered is said to be irrigated.)

Salt Lake City is a city with beautiful public buildings, homes and wide, clean streets. It was settled by a religious group known as Mormons, members of the Church of Jesus

Breathtaking views of canyons and weird rock formations make the trip a special experience.

Square Tower House, an ancient "apartment house" of 60 rooms, is one of the best-preserved of the ancient cliff dwellings in Mesa Verde National Park.

Sea Gull Monument in Salt Lake City, Utah.

Christ of Latter-day Saints. We see their Temple and hear an organ recital in the big Tabernacle. So magnificent are the acoustics in this latter building that when all is quiet a pin dropped at one end can be plainly heard some 200 feet away, at the other. Temple Square, in the center of the city, contains several monuments of general interest, but perhaps the most unusual one is the Sea Gull Monument, which pays significant homage to a bird.

A policeman tells us the story of why the monument was put there and why the sea gull is Utah's sacred bird. He says, "During the winter and early spring following the arrival of the Mormons in the Salt Lake Valley, these pioneers planted five thousand acres of grain to insure food not only for themselves but also for the large group of colonists who were expected to come that summer. The grain grew very well with the help of irrigation and everything looked promising for an excellent crop. Then one day in the spring of 1848 word was brought from the outlying fields that great hordes of crickets were eating the grain. The farmers fought to stop the crickets. They tried burning the insects. They tried drowning them. They used every resource at their command, but still the crickets came, leaving behind barren spots of desert where only shortly before there had been a people's hope for bread. It was a very bad situation. These colonists were in an isolated outpost, with no means of communication other than slow ox teams."

The policeman continues: "With their own strength exhausted, the Mormons lifted their voices in prayer. Then they heard the cries of sea gulls flying from the west. At first they thought it another impending foe to complete the destruction already begun. But the gulls settled on the fields and began eating the crickets, and continued to do so until the grain was cleaned of them. Through the help of the gulls, a good portion of the crop was saved and the pioneers were able to survive the following winter."

42

We decide to drive out to the Great Salt Lake for a swim. We walk offshore until the water is somewhat higher than our knees and then we settle back in the water. Five to seven times as salty as the ocean, the lake supports reclining people like a soft mattress. We cannot sink. It is even difficult, where the water is much above the waist, to keep one's feet on the bottom. It is possible to remain in a sitting position on the surface, and when a person floats, it is an amusing sight to see how much of him remains above water. The Great Salt Lake is so salty that no fish can live in the water. Bathing in it is an experience not easily forgotten.

Salt continues to season our trip as we put the lake behind us and follow a straightaway across the Great Salt Desert. As far as the eye can see, ahead and on each side, an expansive stretch of solid salt reaches out before us. It is as white as snow, and as smooth and level as a frozen lake. Stopping the automobile, we get out and scrape some of the ground salt with a knife. The crystals taste exactly the same as the kind used on food. Actually, the Great Salt Desert and Lake are the remains of ancient Lake Bonneville. Thousands of years ago, this inland sea was almost as large as Lake Michigan. The old shoreline of Lake Bonneville is visible high up on the surrounding hills.

Near Wendover, Utah, we observe the Bonneville Speedway, also called Bonneville Salt Flats. On this 100-square-mile stretch of desert, the salt is as hard as concrete, and automobile-racing drivers have set many international speed records here.

Upon leaving Utah, we enter the state of Nevada, setting our watches ahead another hour — we are now in the

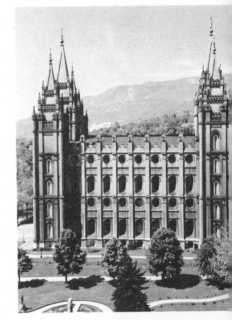

Mormon Temple, cathedral of the Church of Jesus Christ of Latter-day Saints, on Temple Square in Salt Lake City.

The Great Salt Desert.

Reno, Nevada, the "biggest little city in the world," at night.

Six legs are high in the air. Two of them belong to the rider of the bucking bronco.

Pacific Time Zone. The atlas reveals that Nevada is the seventh largest state in the United States, yet it has the least number of people of any state, except Alaska. Nevada is a state filled with mountains. Between these mountains there are dry desert valleys. The valleys are not very wide, but many of them extend north and south for fifty miles or more. The state's limited water supply allows irrigation of only a small amount of land. For this reason, most of the farmland is used to raise sheep and cattle. Even where irrigation is possible, hay for winter feeding of the animals is the chief crop.

Just outside of Elko, Nevada, we stop to attend a rodeo. This popular Western entertainment consists of one thrilling event after another. In one of them, the bucking-bronco contest, the wildest and most high-spirited "outlaw" horses are used. The horses are driven from the corral into small confining wooden pens called chutes. A cowboy sitting on the fence of one of these chutes saddles a horse, and the rider also mounts it from there. As soon as the rider is in the saddle, the gate is opened and out rushes the horse, leaping into the air with all four feet, spinning around in circles, and bucking wildly. Riding a highly trained horse, another cowboy, called the hazer, races alongside to keep

44

the bucking horse from rubbing his rider against the fence. After ten seconds of this wild performance, the judge's pistol-shot is heard and the bronco-rider may then leap from his wild horse to the back of the hazer's horse, while the "outlaw" gallops off down the field. Ten seconds does not seem a long time to stay on a horse's back, but many cowboys are tossed off long before. The bulldogging (steerwrestling) and steer-roping events are exciting, too.

Back on the road, we pass several completely empty, or ghost, towns. These are old mining towns that were deserted when the nearby ore ran out. It was gold and silver mining which first made Nevada important. We stop at Virginia City, the most famous mining town of the 1870's. Its Comstock Lode was one of the richest deposits of gold and silver ever discovered. At one time Virginia City had 150 saloons, 6 churches, 4 banks, 1 opera house, plus the most celebrated newspaper in the West. The *Territorial Enterprise* had on its staff Samuel L. Clemens, who first signed a story with the by-line Mark Twain, which was to become immortal. (We remember that Samuel L. Clemens, or Mark Twain, wrote *Tom Sawyer* and *Huckleberry Finn.*) But today this city is a ghost town. Only a very few people live here. We walk through the streets and

Chief Thunderface, a full chief tribal medicine man of the Paiute Indians, is from Pyramid Lake Reservation, only 30 miles from Reno, Nevada.

45

Death Valley from Dante's view, Telescope Mountain in left background.

Giant redwood tree in Muir Woods.

visit many of the landmarks that still stand, including Piper's Opera House and the Consolidated Virginia Mine.

Mining and smelting of ores is still Nevada's biggest business. But today, copper, manganese, tungsten, mercury and zinc are mined more widely than silver and gold.

From Virginia City, our tour takes us to Reno and then through the Sierra Nevada Mountains into California, the most populated state in our country. California is also the longest state in the United States. If we could physically transfer California to the Atlantic coast of the United States, it would extend almost from New York to Florida. In addition, California has Mount Whitney — the highest mountain in the United States, except for several peaks in Alaska. Curiously enough, less than a hundred miles from Mount Whitney is the lowest place in the United States, Death Valley.

On our way down the Sierra Nevadas, we take a side road to Coloma, California, and the site of Sutter's saw-mill, where James W. Marshall discovered gold. News of the discovery brought thousands of gold-seekers to California in the famous "gold rush of 1849." These people

46

were called "forty-niners." Though a few of the forty-niners found gold, the majority did not. Many of these people stayed in California and became farmers or businessmen.

Back on the main road again, we come to California's capital city of Sacramento. In addition to being the capital, this city is an important center for the shipping of fresh fruits and vegetables, as well as the home of large canning and food processing plants. This city also received its start during the gold-rush days.

Westward from Sacramento, the road winds into the Central Valley of California which has an abundance of fruit orchards, vineyards and fields of growing vegetables. Since two days remain before we are due to board a plane for the next part of our trip, there is time for a visit to Muir Woods. Here there are many giant redwoods, the largest trees in the world. One of them is 246 feet tall.

It is only an 18-mile drive from Muir Woods to San Francisco, the end of our transcontinental journey. We have now crossed the entire North American continent by way of the mainland of the United States. It was a case of "seeing America first." An alternative automobile route might well have been one that would have taken us through the southern part of Canada on the Trans-Canada Highway, a 4,860-mile-long road that stretches from St. John's, Newfoundland, in the East, to Victoria, British Columbia, in the West. Canada, our neighbor to the north, is also a big, wide beautiful land, and its people share with us a similar way of life, although its government is somewhat different. Most of its citizens are concentrated along the northern border of the United States, a circumstance which may account in part for our common interests and close ties, but we also share a common background. Almost all Canadians can trace their ancestry to Europeans — in the main, they are of British and French descent. Indeed, throughout the province of Quebec, in parts of the Maritime Provinces and Manitoba, and in northern Ontario, French is the language used. English is

California's State Capitol Building in Sacramento.

Mission Santa Barbara, the "Queen of the Missions" in California, was founded December 4, 1786.

47

Cellar of one of many California wineries.

A Chinese New Year's procession in San Francisco's Chinatown.

spoken everywhere else — and it is generally understood in all parts of the country.

North of the 200-mile-wide strip that parallels the United States border and which includes most of Canada's population is a vast region of forests, lakes and scenic splendor containing immense amounts of natural resources. Ten provinces (comparable to states in the United States) and two territories make up the entire country. So expansive is Canada's land, extending northward past the Arctic Circle to the polar ice pack, that it amounts to the second largest country in the world! (Only the area of the Soviet Union is greater.) Its coastline — approximately 60,000 miles overall — is indisputably the longest one in the world for a single nation. A trip through this exciting and picturesque country will have to await another time in — hopefully — the not-too-distant future.

We enter San Francisco by way of the Golden Gate Bridge, one of the most beautiful suspension bridges to be seen anywhere. From this bridge we can see one of the world's longest bridges, the 8¼-mile long San Francisco-Oakland Bay Bridge, as well as enjoy a fine view of the greatest natural harbor in the world.

Along the San Francisco waterfront, ships from many nations are seen berthed at the docks or anchored in the harbor. Fishermen are observed returning with their catches. While down on the waterfront, we visit Fisherman's Wharf and eat at one of the famous seafood restaurants. We also visit Chinatown, the finest, biggest, and most interesting Oriental colony in the United States. But the most impressive sight is San Francisco's hills and its steep streets. We board a cable car to take us up Telegraph Hill, one of the highest hills in the city, but before we start, we watch the conductor push the cable car around on a wooden turntable. Then we "hold on for dear life!" As the conductor clangs the bell, the car swings around curves and speeds down some of San Francisco's forty-two hills.

Aerial view of San Francisco showing the approach and a portion of the San Francisco-Oakland Bay Bridge in the foreground. In the background, right, is the famous (former) U. S. Penitentiary on Alcatraz Island; on the left, in the background, is Golden Gate Bridge.

Back in our automobile again, we drive out to Golden Gate Park, the playground of San Francisco, there to enjoy a swim in the Pacific Ocean. From the Park, we go back to our hotel and arrange for the return of our rented car. In the morning we are to be taken to the San Francisco International Airport to wait for our airplane flight.

Ahead, over and beyond the Pacific waters, is the next leg of our journey around the world.

49

JAPAN

Crescent-shaped archipelago off the Pacific East coast of Asia. **Area** • 140,680 sq. m. **Population** • 95,899,000. **Language** • Japanese. **Government** • Empire (under new constitution, in force since May 1947). **Monetary unit** • Yen (= about 0.27½ U.S. $). **Chief cities** • Tokyo (capital), Osaka, Nagoya, Yokohama, Kyoto, Kobe (all with more than one million people, Tokyo with over 10 million the largest city in the world). All are on Honshu, the largest Japanese island. **Religion** • Shintoism and Buddhism (some Roman Catholics and Protestants). **Mountains** • about 50 active volcanoes including Fujiyama (12,389 ft.), the highest peak of Japan. **Rivers** • none of the many rivers are of great size and they are too swift for navigation.

Japanese farmwomen on their way to the village. Snow-capped Mount Fuji is in the background.

CHAPTER 3

Mountains in the Ocean

"Announcing the departure of jet-flight number 481 for Tokyo, Japan! Seven-thirty A. M.! Passengers now loading at Gate Number 3. All aboard, please!"

These words, coming through the loudspeakers in the air-terminal building of the San Francisco International Airport, are the ones for which we have been waiting. Arriving at Gate Number 3, we see that our giant jet airliner is already there, and we go aboard. Our suitcases and bags have already been brought to the plane's freight compartment, where they will remain during the flight. Our tickets, health certificates and passports have also been checked.

At seven-thirty, the "FASTEN SEAT BELTS—NO SMOKING" signs flash on, and the door of the plane through which we entered swings shut. Engine number one is started and we hear a low rumble. Soon all the jet engines are running, and the rumble builds up as our pilot applies more and more power in his final test of the engines.

Looking out the window, we discover that our airplane has started to move. On the runway, it gains more speed . . . and finally, we are in the air! As the aircraft climbs rapidly, the rumble of the jets fades to a low "whoosh." In a few minutes the familiar landmarks of San Francisco, such as the Golden Gate Bridge, are far below and far behind. We are above the clouds and heading due west toward Honshu, largest island of Japan, the next destination on our journey around the world.

Now we sit back in our seats and watch a motion picture as the jet speeds across the Pacific Ocean. Many hours later, our pilot announces, "It is now Monday, the 31st of May. In a few minutes it will be Tuesday, the 1st of June. We will be losing a whole day."

The stewardess explains that our plane is about to cross the International Date Line. When we cross this line, we change days. The day west of the line is always one day ahead of the day east of the line. Because the earth rotates once in a day, as we learned earlier, the side facing the sun has sunlight, while the side opposite has night. When it is noon in one place, it is midnight halfway around the earth. Since the earth keeps on rotating all the time, the sun appears to be coming up somewhere every minute of the day, and at that same minute halfway around the earth, the sun seems to be going down. In order for people to get a "new" day, an imaginary line had to be drawn. The International Date Line is that line and it marks the place on earth where each day starts. It was purposely chosen to be in an area where very few people live — in the middle of the world's largest ocean.

Our stewardess tells us that the International Date Line basically follows the 180th meridian, except that it was arranged so that it would not cut through certain Pacific Ocean island groups, leaving one or two islands on one side and the rest of the group on the other side. If this had not been done, the date on one island would have been a day earlier than the calendar date on the neighboring island. By looking at the map, we are able to verify that the International Date Line was bent as a matter of convenience.

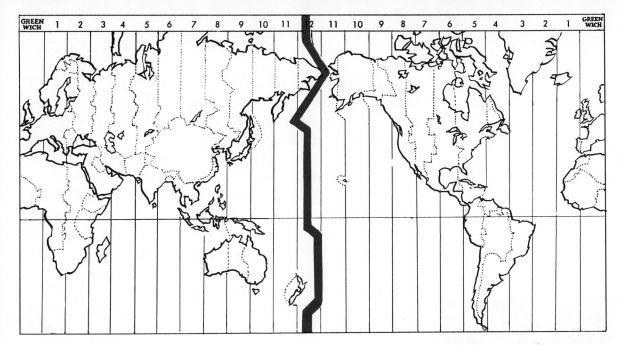

World time chart, divided into 24 one-hour zones, each 15 degrees longitude wide. The colored line that follows the 180th meridian for most of its distance is the International Date Line, which jogs from it at several places to avoid cutting through the eastern tip of Asia and some of the island groups.

The stewardess explains further, "Since the earth rotates once, or 360°, every 24 hours, it rotates 15° in one hour. Therefore, each time zone covers about 15° on the earth, with a difference of one hour from time zone to time zone. Since it is 5 P. M. here at the date line, it is 5 A. M. at Greenwich, England, which is halfway around the earth." Our stewardess gives us a map that shows the time zones of the world. It will serve as a good reference for us on the rest of our journey.

She also gives us a handsome certificate that states that we are members of the International Date Line Club. It reads: *Know ye all by these presents that on the 31st day of May in the year 1965 you were flown by an airplane across the International Date Line at 46° latitude, 180° longitude while en route from San Francisco to Tokyo. Therefore being well qualified, you are hereby accepted into the select company of the International Date Line Club. Given under my hand and seal.* (Signed) *William E. Frank, Captain and Grand Pilot, I. D. L. C.*

Some time later, the pilot awakens us from a nap when his voice comes over the loudspeaker saying, "We will land at Tokyo International Airport in ten minutes. Please fasten your seat belts."

As the stewardess walks up the aisle to make sure that we follow instructions properly, she suggests that we look out of our window. "Soon," she tells us, "Mount Fuji, the highest mountain in Japan, will come into view."

Suddenly it is so. Though the lower part of the mountain cannot be seen because it is below the clouds, the snow-covered peak shines in the sunlight. The snow in its volcanic crater is known as "The Eternal Snow," since, apparently, it never melts. Mount Fuji is a beautiful sight, and one that we shall remember for a long time.

As our airplane comes down out of the clouds, we find ourselves over Tokyo Bay. Ahead is Tokyo, Japan's capital and the largest city in the world. When our plane lands, we shall be on Honshu, the largest of the four main Japanese islands. The other main islands, which are located in the western Pacific off the coast of Asia, are Hokkaido to the north of Honshu, and Shikoku and Kyushu to the south. The four islands, which are really the visible areas of a partially submerged mountain range, are dotted with short, shallow, rocky rivers, and with lakes and natural hot springs. A jagged coastline forms many beautiful bays, inlets, and fine harbors. Together with some five hundred islets, Japan's four main islands are smaller in area than the state of California, yet crowded with six times as many people.

The far northern point of Hokkaido lies in the same latitude as Minnesota, southern Maine or northern Oregon. The far southern part of Kyushu, the southernmost island, is situated about in the latitude of New Orleans, Houston or northern Florida. Japan's climate is very much like that of the areas in the United States which lie in comparable latitudes. The climate near Tokyo is similar to that of New York City or Washington, D. C., though in the mountainous central and northern sections of Honshu there is usually enough snow for long seasons of skiing.

Grand Image of Buddha in bronze at Kamakura, Japan. Constructed in 1252, the statue is 42 feet, 6 inches in height and weighs 103 tons.

54

Ainus, aborigines of Japan,
still live on Hokkaido in the
northern part of the country.

After arriving at the airport, we get into a small taxi-cab which will take us to a hotel in the heart of the city. Japanese taxi drivers, like many other cabbies throughout the world, have acquired a reputation for recklessness. Our driver shows us how they got that reputation by driving speedily through the crowded streets. We swerve around motor scooters and bicycles whose riders are transporting various things. We pass slow-moving streetcars and just miss several horse-drawn carts. There are few lights or policemen to direct the heavy vehicular traffic at busy city intersections. Furthermore, the Japanese attitude toward street traffic is somewhat different from ours. Instead of looking both ways before crossing, the Japanese pedestrian usually depends on the sound of a vehicle's horn or bell to warn him of danger. The constant car-horn blowing by Japanese motorists is something to which we will have to get accustomed, for the safety of ourselves and others. After many close calls, we finally arrive at the modern hotel where we will stay while in Japan's capital city.

After a short visit to our rooms, we go out for a walk. The city of Tokyo is a mixture of the ancient and the new. There are tall office buildings of steel and concrete, modern stores, motion-picture theaters and large factory buildings. In the side streets there are many little shops and family factories where craftsmen live, work and sell their wares. Most of the people we see on the streets dress as we do in the United States. Some women and a few men, though, wear kimonos, which are loose robes tied with sashes. For shoes, they wear wooden clogs which make a "clack-clack" sound as they walk along the streets. People seem to be very polite. Friends bow to each other when they meet.

Ahead of us, as we walk along Uchiborio-Dori Avenue, is the Imperial Palace. Here the Emperor of Japan and his family have made their home in the castle of Edo for about a hundred years. We cannot visit the palace or its gardens because they are open to visitors only on special days, such as the Emperor's birthday and New Year's Day, but we can stroll about the beautiful Imperial Palace Plaza, which is in

Below (left), part of the Imperial Palace in back of the moat and (right) the Diet Building, both in Tokyo.

Two Japanese women wearing traditional costumes are a marked contrast to the modern Tokyo buildings in the background.

Japanese doll. Nothing is missing in the historic dress, not even the paper umbrella.

front of the main entrance. The palace and the gardens around it are surrounded by a wide moat filled with water. (A moat is a wide, deep ditch which in medieval times was an obstacle around a palace or castle that was intended to discourage enemy soldiers from attacking.) Just beyond the moat is a high stone wall.

A few minutes' walk from the Imperial Palace Plaza takes us to the National Diet Building, which houses Japan's lawmaking body, just as the Capitol Building in Washington, D. C. houses our own legislative branches, the Senate and the House of Representatives. Like our Capitol Building, too, it is white. Eighteen years were necessary for its construction.

After lunch in a charming restaurant, we take a bus to Ueno Park. We enter through a gateway which the Japanese call a torii. This is a simple crossbar arrangement which is seen all over Japan at the entrance to every Shinto shrine. (Shintoism is one of two major religious faiths of Japan — Buddhism is the other — and a shrine is a sacred place or object.) This shrine was built in memory of Ieyasu, founder of the Tokugawa shogunate. (A shogunate is a military dictatorship.) In the seventeenth century Ieyasu declared that his capital would be Tokyo — it was then called Edo. When the Emperor of Japan overthrew the Tokugawa shogunate in 1868, the name was changed to Tokyo, meaning "eastern capital," as opposed to Kyoto, the western capital. Later, the Emperor of Japan made it the national capital, and made Edo Castle the Imperial Palace.

Strolling about the beautiful garden, we notice over three hundred oddly shaped stone and bronze lanterns which line the approach to a five-story-high pagoda (a sacred building). These lanterns were gifts of noble lords. One of the lanterns is known as a "spook lantern." There is a charming little superstition related to this large lantern. It is believed that if a child hops on one leg all the way around the base, the wooden clog (shoe) that is left behind will be taken away by an unseen spirit.

Leaving Ueno Park, we hear the beating of wooden clappers, a drum, and a horn, which announces the daily visit of the children's theater or paper show. After selling candies to the children who want a "front seat," the storyteller sets up a wooden frame and entertains the children with fairy tales, fables, and historical legends. As he talks, he slips paper drawings in and out of the frame to illustrate the story.

Torii and bronze lanterns in a typical Japanese landscape.

58

*Sumo wrestlers in
starting position.*

At night, there are many things we can do. If we wish
to go to the theater, Japan offers a variety — Noh, Kabuki,
puppets, light opera, and musical revues, as well as Japanese and American movies. Japan's oldest dramatic form
is the classical Noh play. This dates back to the fourteenth
century and has changed little since then. It deals with a
religious or historical subject. Two or three brightly cos-
tumed actors dance, gesture in pantomime, and don various
masks that show age, characters and emotions, while a
chorus chants the story to music.

Kabuki, Japan's traditional popular drama, is also centuries old, but is more like our own drama. It, too, combines
music and dancing with acting, and its costumes and settings
are beautiful. Female parts in the Kabuki are always played
by male actors.

If we wish to see a sporting event, we can attend an
exhibition of sumo wrestling. Compared to wrestling as we
may know it, the rules of sumo are much simpler. At the
start of the match, the two wrestlers toss salt into the air
as a token of amity, and then squat facing each other at
close range. Then they finally leap "into grips." The match
ends when any part of a wrestler's body, aside from
his feet, touches the floor, or when a wrestler — or even
one foot — is forced out of the ring. A match seldom lasts

more than two or three minutes. Sumo wrestlers are usually giant men weighing from 250 to 400 pounds and standing taller than six feet.

It has been said that sumo wrestling is to Japan what baseball is to the United States, but the Japanese like our national sport, too. In Tokyo there are several baseball stadiums and they have their own leagues. An American big-league team plays against Japanese teams each fall in Tokyo, as well as other cities in Japan. Japanese boys, and sometimes girls, play baseball on almost any land space available.

When it is time for us to leave the capital city, we board a train at Tokyo Station, one of the largest and busiest railway stations in the world. Here almost every ten minutes during the day trains leave for destinations all over Japan. There are about ninety trains daily. A Japanese boy helps us place our suitcases on an overhead rack and we settle back in our comfortable seats.

About twenty minutes after leaving Tokyo, our fast electric train comes to a stop at the city of Yokohama. The conductor tells us that this city is the fourth largest city in Japan, but that it was only a tiny fishing settlement in 1854 when Commodore Matthew C. Perry of the United States Navy came here and demanded that the nation open its ports to American trade. Up to that time, Japan

Japanese girls wear different costumes in different regions. These are girls from Yase.

This is a scene from a Kabuki play.

had been isolated from the rest of the world by the shoguns (military dictators). These rulers allowed no one to build a ship which could travel on the ocean. No Japanese person was permitted to visit a foreign country. Foreign missionaries were kept out of Japan. But Perry's visit resulted in a treaty with the United States, and world traders soon opened offices in Yokohama. Looking out of our train window, we see ships from all over the world, coming in and out of Yokohama harbor, or berthed at its docks.

After leaving this city, we start to enjoy the rural scenery of Japan. The first farms we see are those that grow rice. Rice is a favorite food of the Japanese; they raise more of it than any other grain. The rice plants grow in flooded fields. They are irrigated by water which flows down in ditches from the mountains. While most of the rice fields, or "paddies," as they are called, are on the lower, flatter lands because they are easier to flood, some of the sloping land is terraced. In addition to giving the farmer more land to use, these terraces keep the water from running off to lower areas too quickly. A terraced hillside in appearance is much like a wide stairway.

61

The railroad conductor further informs us that most of the farmers sow the rice seeds in the wet mud of a small field which is called a seedbed. When the young plants are several inches high, they are transplanted by hand from the seedbed into the flooded paddy.

The growing rice plants look much like a field of growing wheat. The plants remain green until the rice grains start to ripen. When the rice is nearly ripe, the fields are drained. The stalks then turn to a golden brown as the grain forms in the heads, much as does wheat. The matured rice is cut with a sharp knife, tied into small bundles, and dried on poles erected near the paddies. Small machines are used to knock the rice grains from the stalks. This work is called "threshing." The grains are then sent to market.

We ask the conductor if any of the farms in this area raise other crops. He replies that wheat, millet, corn, barley, radishes, sweet potatoes, peas and soy beans are grown on the higher ground. "But," he continues, "Japanese farmers have few farm animals. Because there is so little good farm land, farmers must use it to grow food for people rather than to feed cattle. Pasture land is poor, as the hills are overrun with wild, tough, coarse bamboo grass that cuts the mouths of cattle. Most farmers," he explains, "raise some chickens and ducks. Their tools and farm equipment are of the simplest kind when compared to that used in your country. Not all the farmers own an ox or a horse to pull a plow. Planting, spreading fertilizer, weeding, irrigating, and harvesting are generally done by hand. Every member of the family works hard to make a living from their small farm."

As our express train continues southwestward, it goes through many tunnels. Some of them are short, while others are so long that it takes almost ten minutes for the train to pass through. Each time the train comes out of a tunnel, there is a new view of steep beaches, of mountains, and fields dotted with mandarin orange, persimmon and plum

62

trees. As the train goes past the village of Yoshiwara, we see Mount Fuji again. Because of the many people who want to climb this mountain, a special railroad station has been built. One of the Japanese passengers says, "Climbing it is a tough job and we Japanese have a proverb: 'He who fails to climb Fuji in his lifetime is a fool; he who climbs it twice is a bigger fool.'" Many Americans climb it each year, though they can reach the top only during the summer months when the peak has the least amount of snow.

On the terraced hillsides near Shizuoka are many rows of small bushes which we are told are tea plants. In the springtime, women pick the young leaves and put them into baskets. Most Japanese tea is put into firing machines immediately to keep it from fermenting. This method of

63

making the tea ready for market allows the tea to keep the green color of the leaves. While much of the tea crop is used in the Japanese homeland, a large quantity also finds its way to the United States.

Still farther along on our railroad trip, we see fields of a different kind of low trees. Our conductor explains that these are mulberry trees, the leaves of which are fed to silkworms. Many farmers near Toyohashi raise silkworms. They buy the eggs, and when the larvae are hatched, the mulberry leaves are fed to the growing worms. The farmer and his family spend a great deal of time picking leaves because silkworks have a tremendous appetite and eat at least their own weight in leaves each day. In about five weeks, the silkworms are ready to spin their cocoons. From a small hole in each silkworm's lower lip comes a gluelike fluid which quickly hardens into silk thread when air touches it. The worm spins this thread around itself to form an oval-shaped covering, or cocoon. The farmer sells the cocoons to a textile factory.

If nothing were done to the cocoon, a moth would hatch in it and would break its way out. But at the factory the cocoons are dipped in hot water or steamed to kill the insect inside. Then the silk thread from the cocoons is wound onto small reels. A thread from a single cocoon may be 2,000 feet or longer. The threads can then be woven into lustrous silk cloth.

An attentive audience listens to the twangs of a koto, traditional Japanese musical instrument whose 13 strings are plucked with the fingers.

After a four-hour ride from Yokohama, our train stops at the city of Nagoya. While we do not get off the train, our conductor informs us that Nagoya is famous for its pottery and chinaware. Usually when someone refers to "china" we think of the beautiful ceramics which were originally made in the land of China. Four hundred years ago the Japanese visited the ceramic centers of China and persuaded some of the expert potters to come to their country. The best clay for making pottery was found near Nagoya, and the city became Japan's china center. If we were to walk along almost any street, we would see rows of clay teapots drying in the sun, revolving potter's wheels and clay-kneaders treading up and down on small boards, mixing the material used for various ceramic pieces.

A short while after leaving Nagoya, our train crosses the Nagara River where at night may be seen one of the most unusual sights in the world — cormorant fishing. Cormorants are large, long-necked birds that are trained to fish. Fishing parties in small boats, each equipped with a dozen or more cormorants with twelve-foot cords tied around their necks, set out to fish about nightfall, except when the moon is bright. A blazing flare in a large iron cradle swinging from a rod at the bow of each boat serves to attract whole schools of small fish — a kind of smelt called "ayu." When these fish come near the boats, the birds dive and catch them. The fishermen then pull back the cormorants that

Mother and child, both kimono-clad, during morning house-cleaning.

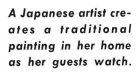

A Japanese artist creates a traditional painting in her home as her guests watch.

have caught some fish. The birds are unable to swallow fish . because of the tight cords around their necks.

The fishing industry is very important to this island country. Because comparatively few cattle are raised in Japan, fish generally takes the place of meat in Japanese menus. Actually, the Japanese catch and eat more fish than the people of any other country. Fishing fleets go out into the North Pacific Ocean for sardines, cod, bonito, salmon, herring, shark, mackerel, and tuna. Some Japanese fishermen even make the long voyage to the Antarctic to catch whales. Whale oil and meat help to supply food which the people of Japan need.

Shellfish such as crabs, shrimps, lobsters, and crayfish make up a valuable part of the fishing industry, too. An unusual part of the oyster business is the production of cultured pearls. Mr. Ishii, a passenger on our train, tells how cultured pearls are grown: "First, the baby oysters which are found swimming freely in coastal waters during the spring are collected and placed in wire cages. These baby oysters are placed in selected spots on the ocean bottom for three years. At the end of this time the 'amas,' or diving girls, plunge to the bottom of the sea to bring up these three-year-old oysters. The oysters are then taken to a nearby factory where the shell is carefully opened by a skilled worker, and a very tiny bead is placed inside."

Mr. Ishii continues his story by saying, "These oysters are put back into the wire cages and the cages are returned to the ocean bottom. The tiny bead inside the oyster shell is so uncomfortable to the oyster that it covers it with layer upon layer of a smooth, lustrous substance. After about seven years, the oysters become full-grown and the shell is opened again. The tiny bead that was placed there has now become a lustrous pearl, a fine 'gem of the ocean.' Before pearls were produced by this method, they were formed only by chance and were very hard to find. Today, almost all the pearls in the world come from my country."

66

Geisha girls pause to chat in Kyoto, Japan. The Toji Pagoda is seen in the background.

The next stop our train makes is at the inland city of Kyoto, the capital of Japan from 794 to 1868. As our train enters the city, we see many shrines, temples and palaces with beautiful gardens. Kyoto is also known as a city of festivals. Almost every day is a day of festival in Japan, according to Mr. Ishii. There are parades in which musicians, jugglers, floats, men on highly ornamented horses, boys with kites, and dancing and singing girls take part. Two of Japan's annual holidays honor even the children. On March 3, the Peach Blossom, or Dolls', Festival reminds young girls that they must be as peaceful and gentle as peach blossoms. On this day the girls entertain their friends and show off their dolls. Many of the dolls are handed down from one generation to another. Most of these dolls are family treasures, but each little girl has two of her own. Later, when she marries, she takes them to her husband's home.

On the day of the Boys' Festival, May 5, every family with sons puts up a long bamboo pole in front of their home. From this pole one paper flag in the shape of a carp is flown for each son. (The eldest boy — always the most important child in a Japanese family — has the largest one.) These colorful paper-fish flags swell in the wind and seem to swim like real fish. The boys learn that their parents want them to be as strong and brave as the carp, which

Diving for oyster shells is a task that belongs to the hardy women of fishing villages who learn their trade while still very young, and so feel equally at home at the rocky seashore or under the waves.

struggles upstream past the waterfalls. The boys are given miniature figures of ancient warriors and toy weapons. The Boys' Festival is centuries old, and it is designed to remind boys of the manly virtues of bravery and strength.

As soon the train pulls out of Kyoto Station, the five-storied pagoda of Daigoji Temple, highest of its kind in Japan, is seen above the roofs to the left. Some time later we arrive at Osaka, the second largest city in the country. The giant steel mills, chemical plants, textile factories, electrical appliance and electronic plants, and camera factories that we see as the train passes through, have helped make Osaka Japan's most important industrial city.

As our train pulls into the railway station at Kobe, Mr. Ishii asks us to visit him at his home. We gladly accept, and travel with him by taxi. Driving along, we notice that nearly all Japanese homes are small one-story bungalows, or at most, two-story houses. Generally, they are built of unpainted wood and have tile or corrugated-iron roofs.

On arriving at Mr. Ishii's home, we see that a small garden surrounds his home. This garden reminds us of the small potted "gardens" sold by florists in the United States — with miniature trees, bridges, and shrine. Every rock and every plant in his garden is placed in a special way which is supposed to bring the house good luck. It is in the garden that we meet Mrs. Ishii and the two children — Taro and Mariko. Introductions and greetings follow a ritual of low bows. The bowing begins when we meet and tends to continue as long as we exchange questions and answers.

We learn that the Japanese leave their shoes outside the door to protect floors. This is important, since the family sits and sleeps on the floor. Shoes would track in dirt and soon wear out the *tatami* (straw mats) that cover the floor. It would be as ill-mannered for us to walk on the *tatami* in our shoes as it would be for us to put our feet on an American host's sofa. So when going into Mr. Ishii's home, we take off our shoes before entering it.

A shrine is carried through the streets during one of many religious festivals.

Inside, we find a combination living room, dining room, and bedroom — with very little furnishings to be seen. However, by placing simple cushions on the *tatami,* the room becomes a living room. The same cushions placed around a low table (about a foot high) make it a dining room. At night the table is removed and *futon* (sleeping quilts) are placed on the floor. One or more of these makes a mattress, while other quilts are used as covers. A block of wood, or a cloth cover, packed tightly with rice straw, serves as a pillow. (Most Japanese do not use beds.) At one end of this room we find a *tokonoma* — a small recess in the wall. Here are displayed a selection of decorations, usually a hanging scroll, a flower arrangement, and a classic painting or some other object of art. Mrs. Ishii, like most Japanese women, is an artist at flower arrangements, in which the position of each blossom and twig has a special meaning.

Mr. Ishii invites us to dinner. We are offered damp towels with which to wipe our hands and face before the meal. As we kneel at the low table, the whole meal is placed before us at once, so we can tell right away what is in store for us. First, we drink fish soup from small lacquered bowls. Then we eat thin slices of radishes, turnip, cucumber, and pickles. The main course is tempura, which is shrimp dipped

Bonsai, the art of dwarfing trees, is an age-old Japanese gardening technique. Trees a couple of hundred years old and yet no higher than a foot have been produced by artificially controlling their growth.

Many Japanese homes have beautifully landscaped gardens.

Serving tea is an important ceremony in Japan.

Using chopsticks for eating, instead of a knife and fork, is a knack to be learned.

in batter and fried in oil to a golden brown. It is served with rice and *nori,* or seaweed. Everything is placed in small bowls, rather than plates; this makes eating with chopsticks easier. With a little practice we soon learn how to hold the bowl in our left hand and use the chopsticks with our right. With our dinner we drink tea from little cups having no handles.

After eating, we talk to Taro and Mariko about school. Instead of learning to write twenty-six letters of the alphabet, as we do, the Japanese boy or girl must learn more than one thousand symbols for different sounds. The Japanese language has no alphabet and actually contains several thousand such symbols, or word signs. These are made with a brush instead of with a pencil or a pen. Japanese students study our language, too. All children in Japan attend school through the first nine grades. For those who wish to continue their education, there are senior high schools, colleges and universities.

As we leave, the Ishii family bids us "Sayonara," which means "Good-by — but come back again." Returning to Tokyo, we board the jet airplane saying, "Sayonara, Japan, sayonara . . . Hello, Australia, hello."

71

PHILIPPINES

Group of some 7,000 islands and rocks, the most important being Luzon, Mindanao, Samar, Negros. **Area** • 115,600 sq. m. **Population** • 30,331,-000. **Language** • Filipino, a new language based on Tagalog, a Malayan dialect; there are about 87 different dialects spoken, but also English and Spanish. **Government** • Republic.

Monetary unit • Peso (= about 0.50 U.S. $). **Chief cities** • Manila, Quezon City (capital), Cebu, Davao. **Religion** • mostly Roman Catholic. **Mountains** • Mt. Apo (9,690 ft.), highest. **Rivers** • Cagayan (220 m. long) is the longest. **Lakes** • largest, Laguna De Bay and Taal.

Mayon volcano, towering 7,943 feet above Legaspi on Luzon Island, is the most active Philippine volcano.

CHAPTER 4

The Land Down Under

STOPOVER PHILIPPINES

"We shall be landing in the Philippines in a few minutes," the stewardess announces. "There will be a four-hour wait before this plane takes off for Australia. For those passengers who would like to do some sightseeing, a bus will be available for a tour of Manila."

Since we want to take this tour, we decide that it would be a good idea to learn a little about the Philippines by looking at our atlas. The Philippine Islands lie off the coast of Southeast Asia. Though there are more than seven thousand islands making up the Filipino's country, most of the population is concentrated on only eleven of them. The Philippines' total land area is slightly larger than the state of Arizona.

The islands have abundant rainfall, warm weather, and gentle winds. There are three seasons here. The hot season is from the beginning of March to the end of June, followed by the rainy season from early July to the end of October. The cool season is from the beginning of November to the end of February. April and May are the hottest months, and

73

August and September are the wettest. During the latter months, tropical storms called typhoons are common and often do great damage.

We learn that the island's soil is rich and fertile. Because of this, farming has been the country's most important occupation. The chief crops are sugar cane, corn, rice, coconuts, fruits and vegetables. Also, some of the most valuable timber in the world is to be found in the Philippines, coming from such important trees and plants as bamboo, hemp, mahogany and ebony. There are tropical fruits, such as bananas, papayas, mangoes and breadfruit. In addition, there is untold wealth deep under the fertile soil. Deposits of gold, silver, iron, copper, chromite, manganese, lead, coal and petroleum are hidden among the green mountains and valleys of the Philippines.

Our jet plane lands at Manila Airport on the island of Luzon. The sightseeing bus is indeed awaiting us, and we are among the first to enter it. As it moves toward the city, the guide tells us some of the history of the Philippines. Ferdinand Magellan, the first world traveler, is given credit for "discovering" the Philippines in 1521. (It was here that he was killed during the first journey around the world.) The islands had been known to the Chinese, Indonesians and

An aerial view of Manila's City Hall.

Ancient Banaue rice terraces are a source of wonder to modern engineers.

Malays centuries before, but in the sixteenth century the islands were made known to the Europeans, who promptly claimed them. Actually, the islands were named in 1542, after King Don Felipe — Philip II — of Spain. From 1565 until 1898 they were under Spanish rule. Then, when the Spanish-American War ended with an American victory, the Philippines became a territory of the United States. In 1935 the island became autonomous with Manuel L. Quezon as the first president. When World War II started, the Japanese occupied the country. They were driven out in February, 1945 and full independence came in 1946. The Philippines are now a republic, and Quezon City (named after their first president) is the capital.

We enter the city on Dewey Boulevard, named for the American naval hero of the Spanish-American War. This boulevard skirts the Manila Bay shoreline and waterfront. Manila has a fine harbor and is a leading Far Eastern shipping port. Many factories that process Philippine products such as coconuts, sugar, minerals and hemp — used in making rope and string — are found here.

Our first stop is at historic Luneta Park. It was here that Philippine patriot José Rizal was executed by the Spanish in 1896 for his efforts to gain freedom for his countrymen. A monument to Rizal now stands in the Luneta, where

A Moro couple from Mindanao, Philippines, garbed in picturesque Mohammedan costumes.

Moro testing the blade of his kris. The Moros are the non-Christian Filipino inhabitants of Mindanao and Sulu, the two southernmost islands of the archipelago.

Inside San Augustine Church in Intramuros, Manila.

he is buried, and where his memory is honored in solemn and patriotic ceremonies every December 30.

Beside the park are the ruins of the ancient Spanish walled city of Intramuros. Shortly after the first Spanish settlers arrived here in 1571, they enclosed themselves within two and a half miles of high wall. Over the years Manila spread out beyond the walls of Intramuros, but inside them the stately Spanish capital remained, a city within a city. During World War II, the old city was almost completely destroyed, except for two historic landmarks. One is the old Spanish Fort Santiago. While visiting this fort, we view the cell in which José Rizal was imprisoned before his execution and the dungeons where other Filipino heroes were wrongly imprisoned and tortured. In the center of Fort Santiago we find a modern monument over the grave of the Philippines' Unknown Soldier of World War II, with an eternal light burning before it.

The second landmark is the San Augustine Church, built in 1599 — the oldest stone church in the Philippines. This church has survived five severe earthquakes and the World War II fighting with only minor damage. It was in the vestry of this historic church that the commander of the Spanish forces in the Philippines signed the order surrendering to the Americans in 1898.

Philippine cart drawn by a carabao.

The modern business and shipping districts are across the Pasig River from Intramuros. This new section of the city is like any large city in the United States. Listening to the Filipinos talk, it can be noted that a good portion of them speak English. We are told that the Filipinos are a people of several languages and dialects. The native languages, of which there are nine, differ so greatly that people of one region find it difficult to understand people of another. Hence, English serves as a common language. School instruction is usually in English, one of the three official languages of the country. The native Tagalog, and Spanish, are also official languages.

Upon saying "paálam" ("good-by" in Tagalog) to our guide, and his reply of "bumisita po kayo uli" ("please come again"), we reboard our airplane. Then, after a couple of hours of being airborne, our pilot announces over the loudspeaker: "We have just crossed the equator. In the name of old King Jupiter, I appoint you members of the royal court of Jupiter Rex. Since on airplanes, as well as on steamships, this is an event to remember, your stewardess will give you a certificate to prove that you have crossed the equator." When we arrive back home, this certificate, and the one from the International Date Line Club, will be framed and hung on the wall for all to see.

AUSTRALIA

The smallest continent of the world and at the same time it is the largest island. **Area** • 2,948,366 sq. m. **Population** • 10,916,000 (excluding full-blooded aborigines, which are estimated at 40,081). **Language** • English. **Government** • Independent member of British Commonwealth of Nations; while technically a kingdom with the same sovereign as England, it has a parliament and government of its own which selects the Governor General representing the crown. **Monetary Unit** • Australian pound (= 2.24 U.S. $ in 1965). **Chief Cities** • Sydney, Melbourne, Brisbane, Adelaide, Perth, Canberra (capital). **Religion** • majority Protestant (chiefly Anglican); over 20% Roman Catholic. **Mountains** • Mt. Kosciusko (7,305 ft.), the highest peak in the so-called Australian Alps. **Rivers** • Murray River (the only Australian River which carries water all year round) and its tributaries, the Darling River and Murrumbridgee River. **Lakes** • Mackay, Amadeus, Eyre (in central region) are usually dry.

Federal Parliament House at Canberra, National Capital of Australia.

As the plane nears Australia, we look at a map of the continent. When it is held upside down, we see that Australia seems to look very much like the United States. Though Australia is almost as large in area as our country (excluding Alaska), its entire population is only fifty per cent larger than that of New York City. Because Australia lies in the Southern Hemisphere, the seasons are just the opposite of ours. It is still late spring back home, but it is the latter part of autumn in Australia. On the whole, Australia's summers are warm, winters are mild, and there is usually plenty of sunshine. The northern portion of the island continent is located nearest to the equator; thus, Australians think of the north as their hot or tropical region. On the other hand, "going south" in that country means going to the cooler section. Because it is south of the equator, Australia is sometimes referred to as the country "down under."

A view of the eastern end of Ayers Rock in Central Australia.

Australia is a land of unusual things. Some of the rivers flow inland, instead of to the sea as most rivers do, and many of these disappear in the sands of the desert. Sea shells and salt-water marine fossils are found thousands of miles from the coastline, evidence that the sea once covered this land area in a bygone age. Near the center of the continent, the world's largest rock, Ayers Rock, can be found. Rumors of Australia reached Europe at the time of Jesus Christ, and the new land soon appeared on maps as *Terra Australis*. Spanish and Dutch explorers confirmed the existence of the strange land in the early seventeenth century. The Latin *Terra Australis* (which means southern land) developed into the modern name of Australia.

Australia is the only continent whose borders do not touch other countries. It is occupied by a single nation. The Commonwealth of Australia is made up of six states and two territories. Five states are on the mainland. They are

Western Australia, South Australia, Victoria, New South Wales and Queensland. The sixth state is Tasmania, an island off the southern coast. The territories are the Northern Territory and Capital Territory. The latter contains the capital city, Canberra, and like Washington, D. C., it is not a part of the state in which it is located.

Our stewardess informs us that the Australian government is a mixture of both the British and the American systems. First of all, it is a federation, or a combination, of six states — roughly similar to the American system of fifty states. There is a federal government with a Parliament, a House of Representatives and Senate, which is similar to and chosen somewhat on the same order as the United States Congress. It is responsible for making laws concerning defense, foreign affairs, trade and commerce with other nations. A Prime Minister from the majority party is appointed to perform tasks similar to those of our President. He is the leader of Australian government until he loses the confidence of Parliament or there is a new election.

Australia is a British dominion, a member of the British Commonwealth of Nations, but this does not mean that Great Britain owns or rules Australia. The Australians govern themselves as a separate nation. At the same time, there are certain traditional ties with Great Britain which the Australians value. The Queen, on the advice of the Australians, appoints a Governor-General as *her* personal representative, not that of the British Government. In addition to these ties, the British and Australian Governments exchange high commissioners, much the same as other countries exchange ambassadors.

Except for frozen Antarctica, Australia was the last continent to be occupied by white men. Less than two hundred years ago, it was practically a vacant land, inhabited by only a few hundred thousand natives — the Australians call them "Abos" (for Aborigines) — living about the same way they did in the Stone Age. The Abos' skin is very dark,

Australian aborigines live their daily lives under conditions that harken back to the Stone Age. (Above) The village council. (Below) They perform the dance of Mana, the shark, during a tribal religious ceremony.

Arunta man, Australia, hardening his boomerang in the fire.

Young native with his pet pig.

their hair is black and wavy. They are skillful hunters. For weapons they use stone hatchets, wooden spears and a throwing stick, or boomerang, which they make from a flat curved piece of wood. If the boomerang misses its mark, it will circle through the air and come back to the thrower, and the Abo can try again.

The aborigines at one time lived all over the continent, but they are now found in the central part of Australia. In their own way of life, Abos wear little or no clothes and generally have no houses. They wander over the country in small bands of twenty or thirty. When they camp for a time, they make rough huts out of branches or grass. Abos are a good-natured, happy people, kind to their children and pets, and respectful to the older members of the tribe. They have special places where they dance, and sometimes many of them gather there for what they call their "corroborrees." Maybe we will see some Abos while we are in Australia.

We are told that our airplane will land in Sydney, the chief city of New South Wales. We will return to Sydney, but first we fly to Darwin, the capital of the Northern Territory. When we reach Darwin, we see the small airplane that is going to take us on part of the journey within Australia. We also see an airplane of the famous Flying Doctor Service landing and bringing a patient from "outback" — a word used by Australians to describe the interior portion of their country — to the hospital in Darwin. Our stewardess tells us that the flying service, begun in 1928 with one plane, today flies hundreds of missions of mercy a year. A two-way radio keeps each isolated settlement in touch with Flying Doctor headquarters. When a serious accident or illness is reported, a doctor is flown to the scene immediately. In addition, each ranch or isolated settlement has a medicine cabinet filled with drugs. For a simple illness, the doctor may simply say, over the radio, "Take one of Number 9 pill every four hours."

Early the next morning we take off in the small airplane and head southeast. From the plane's window, the land below seems exceptionally barren. Here and there are a few small trees, and we occasionally see herds of cattle grazing below. Our pilot tells us that beef cattle are raised in both the state of Queensland and the Northern Territory. The ranches in Queensland are rather small, while those in the Northern Territory are large. The largest ranch in the Territory covers more land than the state of Vermont. Grass grows slowly here because the country is quite dry. The cattlemen in this region are trying to improve the grass crop so that they can raise more cattle on less land.

"We Australians call our cowboys 'stockmen' and a ranch is a 'station,'" says our pilot. "A herd of cattle is known as a 'mob' and the mob is taken to market by 'drovers.' Since the cattle may have to be driven hundreds of miles on foot to slaughterhouses or railroad stops, the drovers usually follow a Travel Stock Route, along which special grazing and watering areas have been set aside to allow the cattle to stop and feed." He continues, "We export large amounts of beef and hides to England and to other European countries."

Several other small airplanes can be seen in the air. Our pilot says, "Airplanes are the most important means of quick transportation to people in the 'outback' country because it is not unusual to find cattle stations a hundred miles apart. Roads are poor or nonexistent, and railroad stops are few and far between." Our pilot explains that radio also plays an important part in the lives of the people of

Cattlemen of the Northern Territory are as skillful at their work as are their American counterparts, the cowboys.

the outback. Children often get their school lessons by means of a radio program called the "School of the Air." The teacher asks questions and receives answers from pupils by means of a two-way radio. Tests and homework are mailed to the teacher and she returns them marked and corrected. "How would you like to go to school like that?" asks our pilot.

Approaching the coastal region, the ground below us becomes greener, and in a few minutes we are flying over a thick forest. Our plane soon lands at Cairns and there we board a glass-bottomed boat for the famous Great Barrier Reef. Our first questions to the guide are: What is the Great Barrier Reef and how was it started? He tells us that the Great Barrier Reef is the biggest coral structure in the world and that it stretches for 1,250 miles (almost the same distance from New York City to Miami, Florida) along the northeast coast of the Australian continent. Up to five miles wide, the Reef is closest to the coast at its northern end and a hundred miles out in the Pacific Ocean at its southern extremity. Immediately beyond the Reef, the ocean bottom is more than six thousand feet deep. During storms many ships have been wrecked on this coral shelf.

According to our guide, this huge coral reef is estimated by scientists to be some thirty million years old. And it all

Part of the Great Barrier Reef in Australia.

Brisbane is the semitropical capital of Queensland.

started as a tiny sea animal known as a polyp! The polyp protects itself by forming a skeleton of lime which, if examined closely, can be seen to resemble a tiny sac. A coral reef is formed by the constant increase of these limy skeletons which harden and, by a continuous building process, grow into many beautiful shapes. Flourishing coral colonies are usually found only in warm climates and where the sun's rays can penetrate to the depths of the crystal-clear sea.

We see hundreds of varieties of coral in all sorts of shapes and sizes here on Great Barrier Reef. The colors of the underwater coral range from the lightest blue to a brilliant yellow, often with shades of lavender, purple, crimson, pink, green, and lemon. Fancy shapes catch the eye and add to the beauty of the Reef. Among the many sea creatures seen through the glass-bottomed boat are giant clam shells, ribbon fish, electric eels, sting-rays, garfish, sea-snakes, flying-fish, sea urchins, scallops and thousands of brilliantly colored tropical fish.

Staying overnight in Cairns, we get on board our small plane again and head south toward Brisbane, the third largest city of Australia. After several hours of flying along the coast, the city and suburbs of Brisbane come in sight. This city is the capital of Queensland and extends for several miles along both sides of the curving Brisbane River. The river must be deep since several ocean-going ships are

Sugar cane cutters in the Mackay district of Northern Queensland.

85

docked at the wharves. The main business center occupies a bend of the river, which is spanned by several large bridges. On the outskirts of the city we can see plantations that grow oranges and avocados. We are not going to visit Brisbane, but our plane needs gasoline to continue its trip into the interior of Australia, so we make a landing.

Airborne again, we see many small farms, since this is the region (between Sydney and Brisbane) where almost every needed crop can be raised. Dairy farms supply all the milk, butter and cheese that the Australians need. The chief field crops are potatoes, corn, oats, barley, alfalfa and wheat. Orchards in the area also yield rich harvests of apples, pears, peaches and plums. Our pilot informs us that north of Brisbane, pineapples, papaws, bananas, tobacco, cotton and sugar cane are grown.

As our plane flies westward toward the outback country, we go over the mountains of the Great Dividing Range. All the major rivers of Australia have their sources in these mountains. Most of the rivers flow toward the near coast and empty in the ocean, but a few of them, as we have already noted, flow down the mountain slopes toward the interior, where they disappear into the parched desert soil. There are several huge dams and reservoirs on many of these interior rivers, and the water is used to irrigate the land west of the Great Dividing Range. Once past the mountains, our airplane flies over thousands of acres of vineyards and orchards that were wastelands prior to World War II.

Farther westward, wheat fields are in view as far as the eye can see. This region reminds us of the wheat fields of Kansas, and Australian farmers use the same modern machinery as their United States counterparts. In the region around Dubbo, where our plane is to land, we also see many sheep ranches, or stations. Almost one-third of all wool grown in the world is grown on this continent. Actually, Australia has many more sheep than people. In some years there are more than fifteen sheep for every person. In years

Termites, often called "white ants," are represented by 116 described species in Australia. This is a mound built by the "magnetic white ants" of Northern Territory, which still puzzle scientists.

86

of drought the flocks are smaller. Woolgrowing is Australia's chief industry, and wool is its most valuable export.

Most of the sheep, our pilot tells us, are a breed known as merino. This kind of sheep came from Spain, the country that first raised the breed. There was a Spanish law against sending any merino sheep from Spain, but a few of them were smuggled out of the country and sent to Australia. The climate and the grass in this country seemed to be ideal for the merinos and the sheep began to produce a better quality of wool — and more of it — than they did in Spain. Today merino sheep are also raised in the United States, Great Britain and South America.

Another animal that was brought into Australia from Europe was the rabbit, but their rapid increase was not appreciated because they soon began to eat valuable grasslands needed by sheep. They damaged the grasslands to such an extent that many farmers attempted to build rabbit-proof fences around grazing lands, but the fences did not prove to be too successful, and as a last resort, some of the rabbits were caught. After giving these rabbits a disease that would kill them, they were then permitted to go free so the disease would spread to other rabbits before the infected ones died. Our pilot informs us that today rabbits are not as big a problem as they were a few years ago.

Early in the morning we board a motor coach at Dubbo and proceed east along the Great Western Highway toward the Blue Mountains, a part of the Great Dividing Range. At our destination, it is not difficult to see how these mountains got their name — they really appear to be blue. We take a cable car, a cage-like affair with seats, from one cliff to another over the trees and enjoy a magnificent view. Near the town of Katoomba we visit Wentworth Falls and Leura Falls.

While taking one of the trails up to the cliffs for a better view of the Blue Mountains, we notice many interesting trees that do not grow in the United States. The eucalyptus

A sheep ranger brings his flock to water at a conservation tank.

87

trees, which have been known to grow over two hundred feet tall, are different because they shed their bark and not their leaves. Another interesting tree is the baobab which has a trunk shaped like a bottle, and always has water stored in it for the thirsty traveler, even during droughts. Still another, so unique that it has been shown on an Australian postage stamp, is the grass tree, with its clump of grass-like leaves and beautiful clusters of yellow, red and purple blossoms.

As the bus continues on its way to Sydney, capital of New South Wales, we read about how Australia was settled by Europeans. In the year the Constitution of the United States became the law of the land, eleven ships sailed from Great Britain under the command of Captain Arthur Phillip of the Royal Navy. They carried about a thousand passengers, bound for the other side of the world to settle a new land. Eight months later, after a voyage of sixteen thousand miles, they put in at Botany Bay in southeast Australia. It was not a good spot for a permanent settlement so they moved on along the coast, finally stopping at the site of what is now Australia's largest city, Sydney. In later years, this journey was shortened considerably by the construction of two canals, the Suez and the Panama.

Actually, the American Revolution had a great deal to do with the first settlement of Australia. Before 1776, Great Britain had oftentimes sent some of its prisoners to its American colonies. But after the colonies had declared their independence, the British had to find some other place to send convicts from their overcrowded jails. Nearly half of the first group to land on the new continent were prisoners — men who were on the wrong side in politics, or had got into debt, or committed minor crimes which we would possibly not consider crimes today. All told, in the first fifty years of the settlement of Australia, almost half of the people that arrived there were so-called "criminals" shipped from England. Of course, some free settlers joined them,

The baobab or bottle tree is a native of Australia.

88

and looking out the bus window, we can see how the birthplace of Australia has grown.

The tall and modern business center of Sydney contrasts with the wide and rapidly growing area of its suburbs and big factory areas. Later we get another good view of the city from atop the pylon of the Harbor Bridge. A pylon is the tall structure at either side of a bridge, marking the entrance. The observation platform on this pylon is at the same height as a ten-story building. From here, binoculars and telescopes, which are made available to us, make it possible to observe surroundings many miles distant. Out in Sydney harbor there are many freighters, ocean liners, ferryboats and sailboats. In the opposite direction, it is possible to see the Great Dividing Range and many other beautiful sights. As an aid to selective viewing, the observation platform has a huge wall map which helps to identify places of interest. Descriptions of sights that may be viewed are printed in English, Italian and German.

Still later, walking about the streets, we notice that the people of Australia are very much like Americans. They speak English, wear similar clothes, often read the same

In April, 1770, Captain Cook sailed his ship Endeavour into Botany Bay and named the land New South Wales.

A view of Sydney, capital of New South Wales. The bridge spanning the harbor leads to the northern suburbs.

books, and eat the same kind of food. The majority of Australians are almost entirely of European origin and mostly of British descent, although since World War II many new Australians have come from Hungary, Italy, Germany, and Greece, among other countries. There are quite a few Americans living in this country, too.

Our tour of the city continues by taking a tram, Australia's word for streetcar, to nearby Bondi Beach. Sydney's ocean beaches are alive with action. Beyond the breakers we see an amazing assortment of water craft — surf boards, surf boats, canoes and inflated rubber rafts. Many of the surfers depend only upon their own buoyance to keep them afloat. They go in for "body shooting," a technique of riding the breakers unaided by any supporting devices. This calls for precise timing and balance.

Of all water sports, surfing is the favorite among Sydney's young people. At first, few ventured much farther into the water than the fringe of the first waves. But in due time people became very bold, and took up surfing with great enthusiasm. Lives were often in danger because of recklessness. In 1907, the Surf Life-Saving Association of New South Wales was formed, and by 1910, surf bathing and surf board riding (surfing) became popular and safe Australian sports.

The sport of surfboard riding was introduced to Australia from the Hawaiian Islands.

The start of the surf carnival on Manly Beach, one of Sydney's many beaches. Competing teams of surf life savers present themselves to the judges and the spectators.

Melbourne, capital of Victoria, is situated on the Yarra River.

Sydney, more than any other Australian city, loves a parade. The most famous and typical of these is the surf carnival, a manly exhibition of ocean life-saving methods that had their birth on Sydney's ocean front. Highly trained life-savers march with soldierly precision behind colorful club banners and demonstrate with reel and surf boat the water-rescue methods that have made them world-famous. Unlike the paid lifeguards in America, Australian life-savers give their services voluntarily, or even pay for the privilege of risking their lives, as well as devoting hundreds of hours to training and practice. It is not uncommon on a Sunday when there is a sudden wind change or a bad tide, for life-savers to save a hundred people from the water, at great danger to themselves. If a member should fail in his duties, he is expelled from the Life-Saving Association.

On the way to Kingsford Smith Airport in Sydney, our taxi passes factories that are manufacturing washing machines, radios, and many other household items. In parts of Australia there are also many farm-machinery factories, textile mills, food-processing plants, sugar refineries, chemical plants and steel mills. At the airport we board an airliner for Melbourne, the capital city of Victoria.

Victoria is the smallest of the mainland states of Australia, yet it has an area nearly as large as the states of Pennsylvania and New York put together. Upon our arrival in Melbourne, a bus takes us through tree-lined streets and past tall office buildings, modern stores, and miles of homes with trim lawns and gardens. Melbourne is a city active in sports. In fact, Australians are so sports-minded that they declare a public holiday for a horse race: the Melbourne Cup.

We visit the Melbourne Cricket Ground. The English game of cricket is played with a bat shaped like a paddle and with a ball about the size of a baseball. Cricket is somewhat similar to baseball and is played in spring and summer. The Australians play baseball, too, and have some good teams.

In the fall, Australians play their national game called Australian Rules Football, which is a rough, tough and exciting sport. It has elements of football, English Rugby and European soccer. Australians are also fine swimmers,

Australia's beautifully plumaged lyrebird.

The platypus, an Australian egg-laying mammal, at right, and, right above, a platypus breaking out of its egg.

distance runners, and tennis players. When the Davis Cup (the prize awarded to the country with the world's best tennis team) is played in Australia, the event often takes place at Kooyong Stadium in Melbourne.

Before leaving Melbourne, we take a bus to Healesville Sanctuary. Here in a natural setting, it is possible to observe some of Australia's rare native animals. Actually, the animals of Australia are particularly interesting because many of them belong to ages past. This country is sometimes called "the land of living fossils" because Australia contains groups of animals whose relatives have long disappeared from other parts of the world. For example, almost half the various species of native Australian mammals are marsupials — a name given to animals that carry their young in a pouch until they are old enough to take care of themselves. The only marsupial family remaining on the North American continent is that of the opossum.

Australia's best-known marsupial is the kangaroo, which has come to be recognized as the national animal. Kangaroos live almost wholly on plants. Their hind legs are very large in proportion to their forelegs and they have elongated tails. Although the great length of the hind limbs compared with the forelegs makes the kangaroo appear awkward when grazing, the awkwardness disappears as soon as the animal lifts itself erect and begins to hop. The kangaroo can move at thirty miles an hour, with leaps of over twenty feet, and can clear eight-foot fences with ease. A baby kangaroo lives in its mother's pouch most of the time until it is old enough to take care of itself.

Another interesting Australian marsupial is the koala, a rather plump little animal about two feet long when fully grown, with a thick woolly fur, gray on top and yellow-white below. It has a leathery nose, large rounded ears, and pouchy cheeks. (Teddy bears in the stores back home are often made to look like koalas.) The koala is a very good tree-climber, though slow and clumsy on the ground.

The young kangaroo, looking out of its mother's pouch, was only about an inch long when it was born.

93

The baby koala's home is the mother's pouch for about eight months. After that it is generally carried on the mother's back until about twelve months old.

Australia has another strange mammal, the platypus. This animal is the only egg-laying mammal in the world. Actually, when the first stuffed specimens of the duck-billed platypus were received in England in 1799, many naturalists regarded them as fakes. They could not believe that a mammal about the size of a cat could possess a duck-like bill, a furred body, a flattened tail like a beaver, and four webbed feet with claws. Furthermore, it was to be learned later that this remarkable creature laid eggs which resembled those of reptiles. We know that these animals are real because we see them swimming in the water at the Healesville Wild Life Sanctuary.

We also see many other strange animals, including the dingo, or warrigal, Australia's native dog. It differs from our dogs in several ways: it does not bark, it has a different

An emu, the flightless bird of Australia, "shows off" with her three young.

walk, and its ears are always erect. Dingoes are about the size of a sheep dog and they are usually creamy to reddish-yellow in color. The wild native dog is one of the few carnivorous, or meat-eating, animals found in Australia.

The only unpleasant animals in Australia are snakes and crocodiles. The crocodiles live in the northern rivers and swamps and do not often trouble man. But the snakes are numerous and two out of three are venomous, or poisonous. We also observe many strange lizards that can only be found in Australia. There are tailless lizards that bark like a dog, blunt lizards that use their heads like clubs, and legless lizards that look like snakes.

In addition to the animals and reptiles, the Sanctuary contains almost all of the seven hundred species of native birds found in Australia, ranging from the giant emu (one of the large birds of the world and one that cannot fly but does run very fast) to the three-inch long weebill. Their calls vary from the beautiful song of the lyrebird (whose long tail feathers look like the musical instrument we call a lyre) to the mournful wail of the stone-curlew, and the loud, hearty laugh and chuckle of the kookaburra. Some birds are black, some white, and a surprising number are black-and-white. Many of them, such as the parrots, king-fishers, finches, and fairy wrens, are colored with great brilliance. Many of the birds also have remarkable habits. The brolgas join together in graceful dances; the butcher-birds store their food on twigs to be eaten at their leisure; the bowerbirds collect odd items to decorate their nests; and the tawny frogmouths sit so still and look so like a piece of bark or wood that we can pass close by without noticing them. We are having so much fun at the Sanctuary that it is difficult to leave! But we must catch the night express train to Adelaide.

The capital city of the state of South Australia, Adelaide, is often called "the City of Gardens." It is not hard to see how the city received this nickname. There are many gardens

A young koala risks a peek at the photographer from behind its protective mother. The koala lives its entire life in trees and ventures to earth only when moving from one tree to another.

95

Winthrop Hall, part of the campus of the University of Western Australia in Perth.

everywhere. Adelaide has many fine offices and stores. Grapes, olives, oranges, vegetables and almonds are grown on the farms near the city.

If time were available, we could take a boat from Adelaide to Hobart, the capital of Tasmania, and visit what is said to be one of the most mountainous islands in the world. But rather than go there, we board an airplane for Perth, the City of Light. Perth earned this title during Astronaut John Glenn's space flight. On that night, the city's inhabitants turned every electric-light switch on to let the American spaceman know that their prayers rode with him. "Thank everybody for turning them on," Glenn requested from more than one hundred miles above the earth during his first revolution around our planet.

As we fly along, we notice that the green of the fields and forest now seem to be turning brown. Our stewardess tells us that most of the flight to Perth is across the great, dry Nullarbor Plain which is part of the Great Victoria Desert. This desert and the Great Sandy Desert cover almost half of the continent. In some places in this desert region, no rain falls sometimes for two years. There are some lakes and rivers (many of which flow to the center of the continent) that can be found in the desert area, but they have water in them only after a rain. Only a few people and a few animals live in these wastelands of Australia. Though the airplane is the most popular means of transportation here, some people ride camels from place to place. But since gold, zinc, lead, silver, uranium, iron, copper, coal and several other kinds of ores are present in the desert region, small mining towns or camps have been built. Below us several of these camps can be seen, and our stewardess says that many of the houses are built underground so that the inhabitants can escape the heat of the sun. In all these mining towns, getting water is a problem. Actually, the lack of water in this region is one of the reasons why Australia is not more thickly populated.

96

Although our plans call for a stay of only a few hours in the capital city of Western Australia, we are immediately impressed by its beauty. The broad waters of the Swan River which extend nearly two miles in width from the very edges of its streets, the tree-covered hillside, parks, and the bright walls and red roofs of some of the buildings, give this new city a great deal of old-world charm. And Perth could be considered a new city because, while it was founded in 1829, it did not grow until gold was discovered in nearby Kalgoorlie and Coolgardie in 1892. Stories of gold chunks the size of one's fist that could be picked up from the ground brought many people to the area. Perth grew from a little town on the Swan River to a city. Kalgoorlie mines are still producing gold.

There are many karri trees growing all about Perth. These trees are similar to the redwoods in California. They grow over two hundred feet high and up to ten feet in diameter at the base. Karri wood is noted for strength and durability, and is used in building houses, wharves and bridges. In this region of Western Australia, more wildflower species can be found than anywhere in the world. We take many photographs of brilliant red, yellow and blue flowers.

Boarding a jet airliner for Calcutta, India, we say ta-ta (the Australian expression for "good-by") to Australia and to the friendly people of this island continent.

Adelaide, capital of South Australia, is a planned city, laid out in streets crossing one another at right angles.

INDIA

The world's second most populous nation (after China) and a leading country in Asia, about ⅓ of the size of the U.S.A. **Area** • 1,138,814 sq. m. (without Kashmir). **Population** • 449,381,-000. **Language** • State language is Hindi (spoken by about 50% of the population), second language in colleges is English. (There are 14 main languages, 12 originating from Sanskrit.) Urdu is the principal Moslem language (spoken by about 10%). **Government** • India is a democratic republic under a constitution modeled after that of the U.S. and a self-governing member (British) Commonwealth of Nations. **Monetary Unit** • Rupee (= about 0.21 U.S. $). **Chief Cities** • Bombay, Calcutta, Madras, Hyderabad, Ahmedabad, Delhi (all over one million people), and New Delhi (capital). **Religion** • the majority (about 85%) Hindu, Moslem (about 9.9%), Christian (about 2.3%), Sikh (1.7%), the balance other religions. **Mountains** • the Himalayas, a mountain chain with the highest mountain on earth, Mt. Everest (29,002 ft.) in the Kingdom of Nepal, and with peaks in India in Mt. Nanda Devi (25,645 ft.) and Kamet (25,447 ft.). **Rivers** • Indus, Ganges and Brahmaputra are important ones.

A typical market place in the interior of India.

CHAPTER 5

The Land of the Indians

As our airplane wings its way across the Indian Ocean, we can hardly wait to reach the land of the Indians — not the land of American Indians, but the home of the people of India. Early explorers, such as Columbus and Magellan, also wanted to reach India because of spices and the wealth that was supposed to be there. Many ships and gallant seamen perished in quest of a northwest passage from the Atlantic to the Pacific Oceans. When Christopher Columbus found himself on an unknown shore after sailing westward, he somehow (perhaps by wishful thinking) came to the conclusion that he had reached India. That is why the descendants of the ancient inhabitants of North America are called "Indians" to this day. In short, the American Indians received their name because of Christopher Columbus' mistake in supposing that he had reached India when actually he had discovered America.

Studying our atlas as the plane heads toward the mainland of Asia — our journey has already taken us to two island countries in the Eastern Hemisphere — we note many significant facts. For example, Asia has the highest mountain on earth. The lowest spot is the Dead Sea, between Jordan and Israel. Asia also has many vast desert regions. Some of the oldest and youngest, some of the largest and smallest countries are in Asia. China has the largest population of any country in Asia and is also the second largest country in area. It is also very old, and is often referred to as one of the "cradles of civilization." Israel is one of the youngest and smallest nations.

We are greatly impressed by the size of Asia. It is approximately five times the size of the United States and four times the size of Europe. An extreme part of Asia is only a few miles from North America on the Bering Strait near Alaska, and at the Sinai Peninsula it is joined to Africa. But between Europe and Asia, it is difficult to say where one continent stops and the other begins. For this reason, the land mass of these two continents is often combined as one and called Eurasia.

The Asian mainland does not quite reach the equator, but it goes far north to the Arctic Circle. Thus, Asia has some of the hottest and also the coldest regions in the world. We cross the equator again on the way to India, but since we are already "members of the court of Jupiter Rex," we do not get another certificate.

Looking more closely at our atlas, we find that India is much like a triangle, slicing into the Indian Ocean and dividing the waters into the Bay of Bengal on the east and the Arabian Sea on the west. This land, called the Indian Peninsula, is screened off from the rest of Asia by the highest and greatest mountain range in the world, the Himalayas. These mountains were given the name "Himalaya," meaning "home of snow," because the snow never melts on the high peaks of this range. Along this high northern border, India's neighbors are Nepal, Sikkim, Bhutan and Tibet. West Pakistan borders it on the northwest, Burma and East Pakistan on the northeast. At India's southern tip, the island country of Ceylon lies to the southeast across the

A view of the towering Himalaya Mountains with Mount Everest in the distance.

This is the fabled Khyber Pass, route of the invaders of India. Tamerlane, Baber, Alexander the Great and the Moguls used the historic pass to bring their huge armies into India, bent on conquest. Today the route of the caravans through the jagged valleys is a well-paved road.

Palk Strait and the Gulf of Mannar. India is about one-third the size of the United States, but there are over twice as many people living in this Asian country as there are in our country. Indeed, it has the second largest population of the world. China is the only country that is more heavily populated.

The map of India indicates three separate and well-defined regions. They are the Himalayan ranges and their foothills; the broad, fertile river plains; and the plateau in the peninsula proper. In the Himalayas the lower slopes and hills are mainly in grazing lands or forest. Some of the lands are terraced for farming, while some of the lower valleys are covered with fields of wheat. This region, as a whole, has lower temperatures and fewer people than the other two parts of India.

Most of the peninsula of southern India is a low, uneven plateau. Around the edges of the plateau on the west, north, and east are low mountain ranges. On the west and east coasts between the sea and these mountains are narrow strips of coastal plains. This land is very fertile and many Indian people live here. Part of the plateau is dry and thinly populated. Part is covered with thick jungle.

101

Southern India has its paper industry. This is a bamboo yard of a paper mill on the outskirts of Mysore City.

Rice is an important product for India. The grain is studied, developed and improved in experimental paddies throughout the country.

Between the Himalayas and the plateau is the flat, fertile Indian plain, considered to be one of the largest continuous areas of farmland in the world. So much food is grown here that the area is sometimes called "the breadbasket of India." The plain region, through which flows the Ganges and Brahmaputra Rivers, is the most densely populated part of this country.

Studying the atlas still further, we find that India's north-south span is wide. Its northern boundary is about as far north as the state of North Carolina, while its southern boundary extends as far south as the northern extremities of South America. The climate tends to be rather warm throughout the entire country, except in the high mountains of the Himalayas. These mountains block the cold winter winds that would otherwise bring in cold from the northern heart of Asia. South of the mountains, some areas of the large plain region get light frost, but elsewhere the weather is warm or hot the year round. In summer, 110-degree temperatures are common.

102

Plowing by means of oxen in India is an age-old tradition which gives way reluctantly to more modern farming methods.

Our stewardess, who has been in India many times, tells us that most of India has three, rather than four, seasons. Instead of summer, fall, winter and spring, the Indians have a hot season that begins in March and lasts through May. Then there is a rainy season from June until October, followed by a cool season. We are told that the weather in India depends on the direction of a seasonal wind called a monsoon. During the cool season, the monsoon blows from the northeast across India. These are mostly dry winds. But when the winds swing to the southwest and blow across the ocean toward land, India has a rainy season. It is these monsoon rains that are quite important to the farmers of India. If these rains do not come soon enough, the crops cannot grow properly. At the present time, not many of the farmers can get enough water from wells or rivers to irrigate if the monsoons do not bring rain in June. The government of India is spending great sums of money in an attempt to make better use of the rain brought by monsoon and the water from the melting snow in the Himalayas. Dams and irrigation systems are being built in several parts of the country. One of the largest dams in the world, Bhakra Dam, is now in operation, and will help the farmers solve many of their water problems.

As our plane comes in for its landing at Dumdum Airport, Calcutta, we see that the city is located on the east bank of the Hooghly River, the westernmost branch of the Ganges, about eighty miles upstream from the Bay of Bengal. Ships of many nations are tied up at the ten-mile-long dock area. We are informed that the chief exports from here are jute and jute goods, cotton, tea, coffee, rubber and raw hemp; the chief imports are petroleum, rice, machinery and various raw materials.

Taking a taxicab from the airport, we pass through a beautiful section of the city. A large park called the Maidan stretches along the city's southern river bank. Attractive drives, botanical gardens, and sports fields are found here in the park. To the east of the Maidan is Calcutta's finest residential district. As well as having modern residential and business sections, Calcutta has one of the world's largest slums. Many families have only one room to live in. The streets in the old section are crowded with people and animals, not like the wide streets of the new part of Calcutta.

As we ride to our hotel, we are impressed by the clothing worn by the people of Calcutta. Many city men have adopted Western attire, but some continue to dress in traditional Indian clothing. The native costume worn by many of the men is the dhoti, a strip of white cloth wrapped around the hips, drawn between the legs, and tucked in the waistband at the back. A few wear a loose pajama-like garment, the salvar, with a flowing shirt known as the kurta. Various styles of turbans are worn, since this head-dress is good to keep off the heat of the sun.

Most of the women and girls wear a flowing garment called a "sari." It is made from a strip of cloth five to nine yards in length and a yard wide. One end of the cloth is

Where East and West meet: A snake charmer performs for travelers at Calcutta's airport.

tucked into the petticoat waistband, then the sari is wound around the hips gracefully with small pleats in the front. The other end of the cloth is permitted to fall over the shoulder or is thrown over the head like a scarf. A choli, or bodice, may be worn underneath. To complete their dress, girls and women seem to like plenty of bracelets, anklets, and other jewelry. A dot of red powder, or a tiny disk of colored metal called a kumkum, often decorates a woman's forehead.

At our hotel, we meet a United States Peace Corps worker named Harry Robbins. He tells us that he is in Calcutta only to obtain supplies and that he is a farming instructor assigned to a small village in the Ganges Valley. "If you do not mind riding in a truck, I will be very happy to show how farm people in India live," he says, and then adds, "I shall be leaving early tomorrow morning."

We accept his invitation, and in turn, invite him to have dinner with us. We ask Mr. Robbins to suggest a typical Indian dinner. He orders dinner and in due time, the waiter brings each one of us a large brass plate. Rice and a chapatty, somewhat like a baked pancake of wheat flour, are in the middle of the plate. In little bowls are various kinds of curries and sauces. We mix the rice with the curries and dip pieces of chapatty in them. While we eat this food with forks and spoons, Mr. Robbins tells us that Indians, when at home, eat all solid foods with their hands. When the curries are finished, sweets and fruits are served. We finish the meal with a pan supari. This is a special green leaf which is flavored with certain nuts and spices. As we chew it slowly, we experience a pleasant taste sensation. One thing that must be said for Indian food is that most of it is certainly spicy and "hot."

While walking back to the hotel after dinner, we mention to Mr. Robbins that we are surprised that so many Indians speak English. He explains that many people in the cities of India prefer to talk to each other in our language because they come from parts of India as different as Kashmir and Bengal and have no common Indian language. Indians speak about fifteen major languages and dialects. Almost one-third of the people speak Hindustani, a combination of two languages, Urdu and Hindi. The government recently has declared Hindi the official language, but many people of the larger cities still prefer English. Mr. Robbins continues, "In one form or another, the word 'India' has been used by many generations of Europeans and Americans to describe this vast and wonderful country, but in none of the many native languages spoken here is there a single word which means exactly what 'India' means to us." We notice that Indians seldom greet each other by shaking hands. They say "hello" by joining their own hands at chest level, as in prayer.

Mr. Robbins says that religious differences of the people

(Above) The old section of Calcutta. (Below) The Victoria Memorial Building in the modern part of the city.

Indian family at breakfast. Staple sustenance consists of rice and goat's milk.

is a major problem in India. The chief religions are Hinduism, Islam, Christianity, Buddhism and Jainism. Out of every 100 persons in India, 86 are Hindus, 10 Moslems, 1 Christian, and the remaining 3 per cent are Sikh, Jain, Buddhist or Parsee. One important factor in the slowness of India's growth into a great country is that Hinduism believes in a caste system. A member of one caste cannot move into a higher caste, enter an occupation reserved for other castes, or marry outside his own caste. The Hindus do not believe that education or wealth can change a man, once he belongs to a certain state of society. Some people are born in low castes, some in high. Lower than all classes, and outside the Hindu caste system are the "untouchables." We are told by Mr. Robbins that the caste system is gradually becoming less strict. Today in India the untouchables have rights they never had before. These include the right to vote at elections and to attend schools.

As we ride out of the city in the truck, Mr. Robbins points to the hills west of Calcutta and says, "Up there the Indians are discovering much iron ore, limestone, coal, manganese, aluminum, chromite and gypsum. The iron and steel plants in this area are the largest in all Asia. Factories turn out locomotives, railway equipment, farm machinery, electrical equipment, automobiles and trucks, and cement. Although the country is lacking in some raw materials, India may in time become one of the most important manufacturing countries in the world."

Continuing up the Ganges Valley, we pass many flat fields of a rather tall plant with long, coarse, shiny fibers. Mr. Robbins tells us that it is jute and that after the fibers are processed, they are woven into a rough cloth called burlap, or made into rope or twine. We have seen burlap bags containing potatoes and onions in our grocery store at home. There are many other uses for burlap because it is cheap and strong. Calcutta has often been called the jute capital of the world.

108

The Hirakud River Dam is one of the many irrigation projects to which the United States has contributed technical knowledge and earth-moving equipment.

As we pass through the countryside, the dirt road gets rougher and more uneven. Several times we think that our truck will fail to ride over the deep ruts made by oxen-driven carts. On the way, we pass several farming villages. The houses are small and are made of dried mud bricks. Because of heavy rains in this area, the straw roofs of the houses are steeply sloped so that water can run off. The houses are very close together and the dirt streets are narrow so as not to waste good farm land. Most of the villages appear to be unkempt.

In these villages families eat in front of their houses. We understand that the house is used only for sleeping and protection against the rain. There is little or no furniture inside. Everyone, except the youngest children, works in a farm village. The boys go to the fields with their fathers to do the various tasks that must be done. If the family owns any cows and goats, the boys take care of them, too. Girls help their mothers prepare meals, bring water from the well, clean the house and make clothing. During planting and harvest time, the entire family works all day in the fields. The tools with which the farmers work are somewhat crude.

The turban, wound in many ways, is the traditional Indian headdress.

109

Little modern machinery is seen anywhere on the farms that we pass.

"The Ganges Valley has the best farm land in India," Mr. Robbins states. He explains that the farmers in this region raise rice to eat, and sugar cane, cotton and peanuts — called groundnuts in India — to sell. Farther up the valley, where they do not get so much rain as we do here, they raise grains such as wheat and oats. In the southern part of India, the farmers grow rice, sugar cane, tobacco, cotton, jowar, gram and bajra. Jowar and bajra are grain-bearing sorghums somewhat like broom corn that grows in our Midwest. Gram is a pea such as we use in split-pea soup. Coffee and tea are grown on the southern highlands. In northwestern India where there is not much rain, the farmers raise corn and wheat, but for the village people in India, rice is the most important food. Hindus and other Indian people do not eat meat because they believe it is wrong to kill an animal for food.

Finally we arrive at the village where Mr. Robbins teaches. Unlike the other villages, this one has a school, a health clinic, and the roads are in good condition. This community also looks clean, and we see some modern farm equipment in use. Mr. Robbins introduces us to his associates: two school teachers, one an Indian and the other American, a nurse, and three farming instructors.

"When we came to this village a year and a half ago," Mr. Robbins says, "it was like the others we passed on the

Above: Ghats line the banks of the sacred Ganges River. Pilgrims from all over India come to these places, descend the steps of the landings, and "wash their sins away" in the waters of "Mother Ganges." Right: The hour of prayer has come for the Moslems.

Malaria and pest-control are still a problem in India. At left, children in a village school are shown the mosquito and told how it spreads disease; below, a plague-control team in Calcutta inoculates people with anti-plague vaccine; and, bottom, constant rechecking in villages of malaria victims who have recovered, has helped.

way here. But with the help of the Indian and United States governments, and the local people themselves, we were able to teach the villagers new methods of farming and living. We teach the farmers how to grow better crops by using better seed, irrigation, fertilizer and modern farm equipment which the Indian government is making available to them."

We ask Miss Faye Eaton, the American teacher, "How are the children of India as students? Do they learn as easily as Americans of their own age?"

"They are as intelligent as any children in other parts of the world," answers Miss Eaton, "except, of course, they do not have the advantages and books available to boys and girls in the United States. They are very good students and are very eager to learn. But we do not teach children only. The adults as well as the children of this village are taught to read and write, and our nurse, Miss Newton, is showing the mothers how to take better care of their babies, improve their family's diet, and keep their homes and village more sanitary."

As Mr. Robbins takes us to a nearby railroad stop so that we can board a train for Agra, he says, "By living almost like the villagers, we can understand their problems and can try to find solutions for them. But the best thing about the

111

whole Peace Corps project is that the people want our assistance and they want to learn to help themselves. The people of our village will teach neighboring villagers what they learned. In this way, eventually, all the people of India will benefit."

Boarding the train, we thank Mr. Robbins for his kindness in showing us the fine work the Peace Corps is doing in the farm villages of India. We sleep aboard the train and the next morning arrive at Agra, home of the Taj Mahal, considered the most beautiful building in India. Standing in the beautiful gardens of the Taj Mahal, we try to find adequate words to describe this graceful, domed, white marble building with four minaret towers at its corners. It is not hard to understand why it is ranked as one of the great wonders of the world. Our guide explains, "The Taj Mahal is so tremendous and yet so graceful, that it is often called a poem in stone. All kinds of people have tried to describe it, but without much success, so do not feel too bad if you cannot find words for this splendid structure.

"The Taj Mahal was built as a tomb by Shah Jahan for his favorite wife, Mumtaz-i-Mahal," our guide continues. "He was so heartbroken at her death that he vowed to build her the most beautiful tomb in the world. It is said to have taken 20,000 men twenty-two years to complete the Taj. Each stone was set by hand, each decoration carefully worked by the greatest artists and craftsmen of the day."

Palace of the Winds in Jaipur.

The Jagannath Temple in Puri in the state of Orissa.

Inside the Taj, we examine the chamber that holds the tombs of both the Shah and his wife, a gorgeous room made of twelve different kinds of valuable stones, including jade, carnelian and lapis lazuli. There are marble screens and carvings like stone lace, and mosaic inlays in many colors and design.

After leaving the Taj Mahal, we drive by automobile to see the palace of the same Shah Jahan, called the Pearl Mosque. Exploring the palace fortress, we discover a tremendous stronghold with walls seventy feet high and a mile and a half around, with octagonal (eight-sided) towers placed along its length. Within the walls is a confusing network of gateways, courtyards and entrance halls. While visiting the rooms within the palace, we see the one where Shah Jahan, when an old man, was kept prisoner by his own sons. It is said that the old Shah spent his time gazing at the Taj Mahal from his prison window here in the palace.

Our guide suggests that we visit the ruins of Fatehpur Sikri — a capital city built by Akbar, the greatest of the Moslem emperors. Not being content with Agra as his capital, he decided to build a new one about twenty-three miles

113

away. Akbar named this new capital Fatehpur Sikri, or the City of Victory — in commemoration of his many conquests. We enter the palace through Buland Darwaza, which our guide says is one of the most beautiful entrances to a palace anywhere in the world. Once inside, we visit the Diwan-i-Khas, or hall of private audience, where Akbar discussed problems of his country with his friends. We see the famous Pachisi Court, on whose large red and white sandstone squares he played chess with lovely slave-girls as pieces. In the courtyard, we stare up at the lofty tower Akbar erected over the grave of his favorite elephant. This seems to be a splendid capital city for anyone, but our guide tells us that it was used for only fourteen years. One day Akbar and his court suddenly left Fatehpur Sikri and returned to Agra. No one knows the exact reason for this strange decision, but it has been thought that it could have been the lack of an adequate water supply.

After returning to Agra, we visit the shops of the village craftsmen. In this machine age, Agra, like so many Indian cities and villages, is preserving some of its traditional handicrafts — carving in marble and stone, silk fabrics, embroidery, carpet-weaving and leather work. The village craftsmen also make shoes, bricks, pottery, jewelry and make the wooden bullock carts that are so common all over India. In these shops, craftsmen of every description work at skills that have been handed down from father to son in

Parliament House in New Delhi.

the true Oriental fashion. In particular, inlaying in stone is an industry for which Agra is justly renowned. The art is of such precision that even a microscope fails to reveal a joint in a rose composed of sixty petals. These village craftsmen still do most of the manufacturing of small items in India.

Later in the evening, when the moon is shining brightly, we revisit the Taj Mahal. At night the gardens of the Taj look like a fairyland with shadowy trees inky black against the white marble. The shimmering garden pool reflects what seems like a half dozen moons. The great building rising mysteriously before us is like something in a lovely dream, or like a palace on a cloud. There are several other people here tonight, but no one is inclined to speak. Each of us stands quietly, absorbing the glorious scene so as to never forget the Taj Mahal.

In the morning, a train takes us to Delhi. After leaving the train at the station, a taxi drives us to our hotel and then we start our tour of Delhi. Actually, there are really two Delhis—the old city of the Moguls (Moslem emperors) and the new city started by the British in 1911. The latter is about five miles from the old city and is called New Delhi. This new city is the capital of India.

Before the fifteenth century, India was ruled at different times by the Moslems and various other kingdoms, but after Vasco da Gama, a Portuguese explorer, discovered an all-water route to the East, European nations became interested in trade with India. In the eighteenth century Great Britain became the major power in India and for nearly two centuries most of the country was under British rule. On January 26, 1950, the country officially became the Republic of India, a free and independent nation; but it is a member of the Commonwealth of Nations, like Australia. The Indian constitution is modeled after the United States system of state and federal government.

India has a president, prime minister and a parliament. Since our hotel is in New Delhi, we first visit the beautiful

The Tower of Victory in Chittor is one of the many typical structures of Indian architecture.

115

Parliament House, the President's home, and the various other government buildings. After riding through the beautiful India Gate, which is a memorial to Indian soldiers killed in World War I, we visit Delhi, the old Mogul capital. Here is located the famous Red Fort which dominates the city, a symbol of Mogul glory, Lakshmi Naraya Temple and many of the old buildings that date back to the fifteenth and sixteenth centuries.

Outside one of the old buildings, we stop to watch a snake charmer "charm" two five-foot cobras. Though the snakes seem to sway back and forth to the music of the flute player, our guide tells us that it is not the music, but the motion of the hands and the flute that makes the cobras move as they do. They are just trying to keep in line for a strike. But the charmer performs without danger because he has removed the reptiles' poison glands. He keeps the snakes alive by feeding them milk and goat meat.

In the evening we go to a folk-dance festival in one of New Delhi's many theaters. Most Indian dancing is deeply religious in content. For example, Bharata Natyam, the most famous of India's classical dances, is a skillful and highly stylized expression of faith in which gestures and footwork play very important roles. It takes ten years of apprenticeship for a Bharata Natyam dancer to call herself accomplished. But the dancing we like best is the Kathakali. Danced in rich and fanciful headdresses and elaborate facial make-up, Kathakali takes its themes from the great epic stories of the Hindus — the Ramayana and the Mahabharata — and portrays them in the elaborate language of hand gesture and minute facial expression. It is a highly developed art of pantomime, requiring no stage sets or scenery.

In the morning we take a train south to Bombay. After several hours of riding, the train stops at the Indian city of Amber. Since the train is going to stay here for two hours, the conductor suggests that we visit the Palace. To get there,

Two Indian dancers in a typical "Kathakali" pose.

116

we pay a small fee and ride one of the Maharajah's elephants to Amber Palace. Our guide tells us that Charles Dickens, the famous English author, once wrote about the elephant's wrinkled skin that he "employed the worst tailor in the world." But nobody can say that about the Maharajah's elephant we are riding. The large animal is robed in cloth of gold and velvet, wearing anklets and even earrings three feet long, which dangle shimmering in the hot sunlight. On its back is the gilded seat of the howdah. This is where we sit, while the driver (called a mahout) sits on the animal's neck, just in back of the enormous head, prodding the elephant to make it take the right direction to the Palace. These elephants, captured in the southern Indian jungles, are tamed and trained to do many kinds of work.

From atop the giant elephant our approach to the Palace makes us feel as if we are part of a fairy tale. The Amber Palace was begun by Raja Man Singh early in the seventeenth century and was completed over fifty years later. The entrance to the great courtyard on the lower terrace of the palace is through an imposing arched gateway.

117

This picture of a banyan tree demonstrates how the branches grow their own supports.

The royal palace above it is approached by a long flight of steps through a double gateway, called singh-pol, which opens into the court containing the Diwan-i-'Am, or hall of public audience. Behind the singh-pol is the Temple of Kali, which has silver-plated doors and is faced with delicate marble work of great beauty. Open on three sides, the Diwan-i-'Am has gray marble and sandstone pillars supporting a vaulted roof. The pillars are surmounted by finely carved elephants. The fresco paintings which once embellished it are said to have been so beautiful that they aroused the jealousy of the Maharajah because they were more handsome than he, and so the artist had them covered with plaster. As we look back at the palace, reflected in the lake below, it looks like a magic castle in fairyland.

The train we reboard makes another stop near the little village of Bundi. Many shikar or big-game hunts start out from here. We consider ourselves fortunate at this point that we need not walk through the jungle because man-eating tigers, leopards, cheetahs, and wild boars abound in this region. There are many dangerous snakes, too, including the hooded cobra, the krait and the viper. As the train moves through the jungle, plenty of monkeys and colorful parrots are in view, but no big animals. We also notice one of the strangest trees in the whole world — the banyan tree. This giant tree covers more than an acre of ground. As the branches grow, they let down supports that then take root.

We finally arrive at Churchgate Railway Station, Bombay. Leaving the station by taxi, we drive along Marine Drive with its modern apartment houses and hotels on one side and the beautiful Bombay harbor on the other. It is hard to believe that this beautiful, modern city, with one of the finest natural harbors in the world, was only a small Portuguese fishing village some three hundred years ago. As a matter of fact, Portugal thought so little of the village and territory around it that they gave it to their princess as part of her dowry when she married King Charles II of

118

England. King Charles in turn sold the village to the East India Company as a trading post. Today this trading post has grown into one of the greatest cities of the world.

After stopping at our hotel, we take the taxi to Bombay's most fashionable residential neighborhood, Malabar Hill, where the homes and apartments of Bombay's wealthiest people may be seen. From the hill's highest point, we discover that the city itself is on an island. Many bridges connect it to the mainland. Looking out, in the distance, we notice many smoking chimneys. Some of the largest textile mills in the world are located in Bombay, as well as factories that manufacture paper, carpets, fertilizer, chemicals and refine sugar and oil. Both Bombay and Calcutta, India's two largest cities, are very important manufacturing centers in Asia. Bombay is also the headquarters of India's motion-picture industry.

Atop Malabar Hill, we see the beautiful Hanging Gardens and the Pherozshah Mehta Gardens. From the hill, we take a taxi to Crawford Market, the city's major shopping center. The main section is a covered market where vegetables, fruit, fish, meat, poultry, flowers and other items are for sale. The market is in the center of a whole network of lanes where one can buy almost anything from a canary to an elephant. Unfortunately, the latter cannot be accommodated in the jet plane we are taking tomorrow for Israel, the next stop on our trip around the world.

Bori Bunder, the heart of Bombay.

CHAPTER

New Countries from Ancient People

How can a country be both old and new? During the next portion of our journey around the world — a visit to Greece and Israel — perhaps we will be able to find the answer to this question.

Upon leaving Bombay Airport, our plane flies over the Arabian Sea and then over the lands of the Middle East. Europeans once called all of Asia the East. Later, when they "discovered" China and Japan, these countries became known as the Far East and Asian countries adjacent to Europe were called the Near East or Middle East.

Nature has provided the Middle East with varied scenery — bleak, snow-capped mountains and vast deserts where the daytime heat is so intense that houses of brick or stone stay warm all through the cold nights. Over half of the Middle East region is desert. There are tropical areas where date palms grow in lush groves, as well as occasional forests, fertile coastal plains, barren wastes and sparkling seacoasts. The climate along the Mediterranean coast is generally mild and pleasant, but much of the Middle East is uncomfort-

120

ably hot during the long summer season and cold in winter. Snowfall is not uncommon in the mountainous areas in winter, the season when most of the rain falls. Usually, the days are hot and the nights are cold.

Between the mountains in the north and the deserts in the south is a narrow green strip known as the "fertile crescent." It starts with the coast of Israel, Lebanon and Syria, then bends eastward and southward through the Tigris and Euphrates Valleys of Iraq to the Persian Gulf. This is potentially the most productive agricultural area in the Middle East.

The history of the region we are now flying over is a story of invasion and conquest — of the rise and fall of civilizations and empires. Persians, Egyptians, Greeks, Romans, Arabs, Mongols and Turks have swept back and forth across this land bridge connecting Europe, Asia and Africa. Today there are at least two reasons why the Middle East commands the attention of the world — its important location at the crossroads of three continents and its immense supply of oil. Not only does this region supply three-fourths of Europe's and most of the Far East's petroleum needs, but it also contains about two-thirds of the world's estimated oil supply for future years.

Ruins of this old Portuguese fort depict one of many traces of invasion and conquest in the Middle East.

ISRAEL

Small, Middle Eastern country, occupying the greater part of Biblical Palestine. **Area** • 8,000 sq. m. **Population** • 2,376,000. **Languages** • Hebrew and Arabic. **Government** • Parliamentary democracy. **Monetary Unit** • Israeli pound (= 0.33 U.S. $). **Chief Cities** • Tel Aviv, Haifa, Jerusalem (capital). **Religion** • about 88% Jewish, 7½% Moslem, 2½% Christian. **Mountains** • Jebel Jarmaq (3,963 ft.) is the highest; others include Mts. Carmel and Tabor. **Rivers** • Jordan. **Lakes** • the Dead Sea, a salt lake, lies 1,292 feet below sea level.

A view of Jerusalem, with the Scottish church on Mount Zion at the left in the background.

As our airplane nears Israel, we consult the atlas once again and see that the country is shaped something like an Indian arrowhead. About the size of New Jersey in area, Israel is located squarely on the eastern end of the Mediterranean, bordered by the lands of Egypt, Jordan, Syria and Lebanon. Small as the country is, its land varies from mountains and hills in the northern end and central parts to the Negev Desert in the south. Its 130-mile Mediterranean coast is a fertile plain.

Israel's most important river, the Jordan, flows from north to south and empties into the Dead Sea, which lies at the lower part of the earth's surface and has no outlet. The water can escape only through seepage and evaporation, which results in such an accumulation of salts and minerals that nothing can live in it — hence the name "Dead Sea." One of Israel's new developments is in evidence along the shore of the Dead Sea. Chemical deposits used in a great variety of industries are taken from the waters by evaporation.

This once-deserted region is becoming a modern industrial area. Copper, manganese and gypsum are mined in Israel. Petroleum has also been found in recent years in this country.

Israel's Mediterranean coastline gives it a climate similar to Florida and southern California. The summer season, from April to October, is warm and virtually rainless. Winter, from November to March, is cooler and sunny periods alternate with spells of rain. But during this period, warmer temperatures can still be found in Tiberias on the Sea of Galilee, some seven hundred feet below sea level, at Sodom on the Dead Sea, and at Eilat on the Gulf of Aqaba. Temperatures in these spots go above 120 degrees in the summer.

Israel, known before 1948 as Palestine and in Biblical times as Canaan, Judah, or the Promised Land, has been

The Beersheba-Sodom road, a new link between two cities having ancient names.

the birthplace of two religions, Judaism and Christianity, and also the location of many Moslem places of worship. History in the Land of Israel stretches all the way back to the days of the cave dwellers. The Israelite tribes united into one kingdom, but after the death of King Solomon in the tenth century, B.C., the country split in two. Later, the country's important location between the continents of Europe, Africa, and Asia turned it into a battleground. It has been invaded and conquered many times throughout the ages. During these centuries, however, the people of Israel kept alive the hope of again living peacefully in the land of their choice. The World Zionist Organization started in 1897, and in the 1920's a large number of people began to return to what they considered their homeland. But it was not until May 14, 1948 that the Jewish State of Israel was proclaimed an independent country.

Most of the people of Israel follow the religion of Judaism. No business is transacted in this country on the Sabbath, the Jewish day of rest, which is in effect from sundown on Friday until sundown Saturday. Normal activities are resumed on Saturday night and continue until the next Sabbath. The official languages of the country are Hebrew,

124

Above, left: Jaffa in the foreground, Tel Aviv in the background. Above, right: Dizengoff Circle, one of the newer centers in Tel Aviv.

the language of the Bible, and Arabic, but with families coming in from every part of the world, each speaking their own language, these languages are new to many arrivals. Other languages include English, French, Spanish, German, Russian, Polish, Hungarian, Rumanian and Yiddish. Hebrew, however, is the language generally used in schools; also for newspapers, books, and in business.

After arriving at Lod Airport, we take a sherut to Tel Aviv — a taxi is known as a sherut in Israel. Twenty-five minutes later, we enter Israel's largest city and the country's business, industrial and publishing center. Factories that produce glass items, chemicals, textiles, cut diamonds, medicines, fertilizers, cement, and electrical and electronic equipment are to be seen on our approach to the city. In Tel Aviv, itself, there are the headquarters of insurance companies, banks, export and import, housing and building companies.

In 1909, Tel Aviv, one of the world's newest cities, was founded as a division of the old city of Jaffa, one of the world's oldest. According to a Biblical story, it was from Jaffa that Jonah boarded a ship bound for the city of Tarshish. A great storm lashed the small vessel. The frightened sailors thought the storm was due to some evil person

125

on board. They cast lots to discover the person. The lot fell upon Jonah, and he was thrown into the raging sea. As Jonah sank into the waves, he was swallowed by a whale sent by God to save him. At the end of three days and nights, Jonah was cast forth upon dry land.

A little over fifty years ago, the site of present Tel Aviv was only empty sand dunes. Driving down Hakovshim Street, white concrete apartment houses are seen on both sides of the street. Each apartment seems to have a balcony. Farther along the street we find sidewalk cafes with bright-colored umbrellas over the tables. It is not difficult to see why Tel Aviv is often called the "city of restaurants," since there are many establishments that cater to almost every food taste. With so many nationalities living here, it is possible to find German, Viennese, French, Russian, or Polish cooking as readily as traditional Arabic and Palestinian foods. Our taxi driver tells us that Israel is like a European nation, in spite of the fact that it is located in the Middle East. The Jews from central and eastern Europe who helped to establish present-day Israel have had great influence on its culture and the way of life. Israel thinks of itself as a Mediterranean rather than a Middle Eastern nation, but it wants to live at peace with Middle Eastern neighbors.

General view of Haifa Bay.

Later, we visit the "old quarter," or the older part of Jaffa, where many of the young Israeli artists and writers live. Stopping at the colorful Pish Pesh market, we find Yemenite and Israeli handicraft items. This old section of Tel Aviv, although being replaced with modern buildings, makes us feel that we are back in the market place of Bombay.

Walking about the streets of Tel Aviv, there is much evidence that the people of this city love the theater and good music. We see the beautiful National Theater, where plays of Shakespeare, Tolstoy, Shaw, O'Neill, Ibsen, and other famous writers are translated into Hebrew and performed before capacity audiences. Israeli playwrights are also encouraged, and even puppet shows are appreciated. American movies are popular. In the evening we visit the beautiful Frederic Mann Auditorium and enjoy a magnificent concert given by the Israel Philharmonic Orchestra.

In the morning we take a motor bus to Jerusalem, forty miles east of Tel Aviv. Driving along, we are surprised to find such a good farming region. The country's success in farming is remarkable, considering the dry climate, poor soil and the agricultural inexperience of many of the farmers. Although some foods are imported, many of the basic foods are plentiful — milk and milk products, livestock and poultry, eggs, fruits, vegetables and cereals. Citrus fruits are the most important crop and the biggest farm export product. Through scientific methods, a hardy type of beef cattle is being produced in growing numbers. Israel's dairy herds produce more milk per cow than any others in the world except in the Netherlands.

A number of the farms we see are privately owned, like those in the United States, but there are many cooperative farm communities, or kibbutzim, in Israel. Our bus stops at one of them, a kibbutz called Kiryath Anavim, which means the hill of vines. As we look about, we see beautiful orchards and vineyards, a large herd of cows, and thousands of

For two hundred years the Crusaders defended their positions in the Holy Land against the Moslems. They built stone castles and fortifications on every strategic point in what is today Israel. The picture shows the Crusader's Wall in Acre.

127

King David's tomb in Mount Zion, Jerusalem.

A view of the living quarters of modern Jerusalem.

chickens. There are many buildings which we understand are dormitories, a school, a communal dining hall, a nursery and a medical dispensary.

A boy comes up to the bus and says "shalom," which means "peace," but it is an all-purpose greeting. "What is your name?" he asks us.

After we tell him our names, he tells us that his name is David Aviad, and that he came to Israel from Europe eight years ago. He is now fourteen years old. David says that he is learning English in school and would like to practice it by answering any questions we may have.

We ask, "What is a kibbutz?"

David replies, "It is a farm community where everybody works together. In a kibbutz, no one owns the land, the tools, the building, or the crops. Everyone works for the community as best he can and then all share alike. All the profit made by our farm settlement goes towards its improvement."

"Do you go to school?" we ask.

"Yes," says David, "I go six mornings a week. I learn about farming in addition to Hebrew, English, mathematics, science and history. In the afternoons I work in the orchard,

128

or feed the chickens and geese. After I am through work, I go for a swim in our swimming pool, or play games with the boys."

David also informs us that committees are elected by the adults of the kibbutz. It is the duty of these committees to assign the tasks each member of the community must do. Some work in the barns, others in the fields, orchards and vineyards. A few lead the sheep to pasture. Some must work on administrative duties connected with buying for the whole community, the storing of food, and the care of the children, the aged, and the sick.

David continues, "Since all kibbutz parents have full-time jobs, children live in separate dormitories. My little sister stays in a communal nursery where nurses and older women look after all of the children. Everyone eats in a big dining hall. On the Sabbath, families are together for the entire day. We like it here at Kiryath Anavim."

Our bus driver tells us that he is ready to continue the journey to Jerusalem. We say "shalom" to David and board the bus again. Driving along, we can see first-hand that Israel is a most progressive country. Vast irrigation and reclamation projects have greatly increased the productivity of the land. Farming is now possible in the northern Negev, a former desert. Arable land there will be increased as new settlements spring up where wasteland existed before. Our bus driver explains that Israel plans to build five new cities in this area during the next ten years. The first and northern-most of these will rise on the site of Arad, an ancient

Agricultural experimental station in the Negev Desert at Beer Orah.

The intricate irrigation systems of Israel have transformed desert regions into plains of corn, grain and alfalfa in a comparatively short time. At left, the most modern harvesting methods are employed in the Negev.

129

Canaanite kingdom in the Judean foothills west of the Dead Sea. Reforestation on a huge scale is changing the appearance of the countryside and providing the lumber urgently needed for building. Trees are highly valued in Israel. Former barren hillsides and valleys are being planted with young pine, cyprus, and eucalyptus trees. Many of these trees are in memory of soldiers who died for Israel.

Jerusalem, where over three thousand years ago King David united the ancient tribes of Israel, is again the seat of government of the Jewish nation. This makes it the oldest of the world's capital cities. Jerusalem is also a Holy City for three of the world's major religions. There King Solomon built the First Jewish Temple, with a great rock as a foundation for the altar. From this same rock, Moslems believe that Mohammed went up to Heaven on a winged horse. Jesus Christ taught and died in Jerusalem.

The tombs and towers of ancient fortifications give modern Tiberias, a winter resort on the Sea of Galilee, a contrasting appearance.

Classroom in the Children's Village of Kibbutz Glickson.

The happy flower-girl symbolizes eternal youth and beauty of the Plain of Sharon, vaunted by Solomon's "Song of Songs."

Looking down from one of the high hills that seems to protect Jerusalem, we discover that there are really two cities — the old walled city and the new city covering a much larger area outside the wall. Most of Jerusalem's ancient religious shrines are within the walled old city held by the Jordanian Arabs. New Jerusalem has broad avenues, gardens, hotels, stores, cafes, modern apartments, office buildings and beautiful synagogues that are places of worship for those of the Jewish faith. There are also about fifty factories, new school buildings, swimming pools and government headquarters, including the Parliament Building. The Republic of Israel has a parliament called the Knesset. The Knesset elects the President, while members of the Knesset are elected by the people. The government is presided over by the President and directed by the Prime Minister who is appointed from the strongest party in the Knesset.

In the afternoon we visit Jerusalem's famous Biblical zoo, which contains all of the animals, trees and flowers mentioned in the Old Testament. Signs in both Hebrew and English give the appropriate Biblical quotation. For instance, above the crocodile pit, the following verse is

A new immigrant from Yemen.
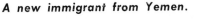

Jordanian policeman checking the papers of pilgrims at Mandelbaum Gate.

found: "The great dragon (crocodile) that lieth in the midst of his rivers — Ezekiel 29:3." The lion's Biblical quotation is found in the Book of Proverbs: "A lion which is the greatest of the beasts of the Earth and who draws not back before any other."

In the morning we head toward old Jerusalem and the Mandelbaum Gate, the only place where tourists can cross between Israel and Jordan. Here we visit some of the shrines associated with Christ's death, such as the Garden of Gethsemane and the Church of the Holy Sepulcher, built over Calvary, where Jesus was crucified. Actually, Jordan was the scene of many other Biblical events. From Jebal Neba (Mount Pisgah) Moses is said to have viewed the Promised Land. Joshua, who led the Israelites into the Promised Land, captured one of the world's most ancient walled cities, Jericho, then a Canaanite stronghold. Jericho may have existed as early as the fourteenth century B. C. Bethlehem is also in the Jordanian portion of the Holy Land.

From Jerusalem we drive through Jordan. As we travel through the small country (it is approximately the size of Indiana), it seems apparent that farming is the principal occupation of the Jordanians. The most important crops are grains, fruits and vegetables. In other sections of

Church of the Nativity in Bethlehem, Jordan.

Jordan, nomadic, or wandering, herdsmen make a living by grazing sheep, camels, goats and fine Arabian horses in the areas where there is enough rainfall to grow some grass. There are no important natural resources, aside from the mineral deposits of the Dead Sea, and a few industrial plants. Today, as they did in ancient times, people still operate olive oil presses and flour mills by hand. Rugs and carpets are woven on hand looms. Motor power is rare, but not as rare as it was ten years ago.

Unfortunately, we do not have time to tour Jordan's largest city, Amman, since the airplane that is taking us to Greece is ready to leave. Once airborne, we look at the atlas and discover that our next destination is on the continent of Europe. The name "Europe" comes from a word meaning "sunset," while "Asia" comes from a word meaning "sunrise." It is not hard to deduce why the ancient Greeks used these names. To them the sun rose from the lands we now call Asia and set over those of Europe.

Studying the map closely, we discover why Europe is often called "a peninsula of peninsulas." It is actually a large peninsula connected to the mainland of Asia, and it is also composed of many smaller peninsulas. We are now bound for one of them at the southernmost tip of Europe.

133

GREECE

Occupying southernmost part of the Balkan peninsula, as well as many islands in the Ionian and Aegean seas. **Area** • 51,182 sq. m., of which 9,854 are islands — Crete, Rhodes, Chios, Samos, and Lesbos being the most important. **Population** • 8,451,000. **Language** • Greek, Turkish. **Government** • Constitutional monarchy. **Monetary Unit** • Drachma (= 0.03 U.S. $). **Chief Cities** • Athens (capital) and its port, Piraeus, comprise over one million people; Salonika; Candia and Canea on the island of Crete. **Religion** • majority Greek Orthodox (official church), about 2% Moslem. **Mountains** • Mt. Olympus (9,570 ft.) is the highest; Parnassus Mountains rise to 8,062 feet and Taygetus Mountains reach 7,895 feet. **Rivers** • none are commercially navigable, Vardar is among the largest.

The Acropolis, towering over modern Athens.

A section of modern Athens, seen from the Acropolis, with Mount Lykabettos in the distance.

Our map reveals that Greece is surrounded on three sides by seas — the Ionian to the west, the Aegean to the east, and the Mediterranean to the south. On the north lie Albania, Yugoslavia and Bulgaria. To the northeast and east is Turkey. Indented by gulfs and inlets, the coastline of Greece is one of the longest of any country in Europe, longer than the coastlines of Spain and Portugal put together. Including its adjacent islands, it has an area about the size of the state of Alabama, and a population slightly larger than that of New York City. For nearly four hundred years this small peninsula was the center of ancient art, literature and science.

Greece can be divided into four major geographic regions. In the north are the provinces (states) of Epirus, Macedonia and Thrace. Central Greece includes Thessaly and Attica. The Peloponnesus peninsula on the south is separated from the rest of the mainland by the Corinth Canal. To the southeast are the islands of the Aegean Sea. We have been assured that no matter where we are in Greece, we can see mountains. The main range, the Pindus, runs down the center of the peninsula from north to south and continues through the Peloponnesus below the Gulf of Corinth. Macedonia and Crete also have mountains. As a matter of fact, most of the islands are rocky and mountainous, too. Greece's highest mountain is Mount Olympus, legendary home of the gods of early Greece.

Our stewardess tells us that the ancient Greeks worshipped many gods. Zeus was the king of the gods and some other main gods and goddesses were: Apollo, god of the sun; Athena, goddess of wisdom and war; Eros, god of love; Nike, goddess of victory; Poseidon, god of the sea; and Ares, god of war. When the thunder rolled and the lightning flashed, the Greeks concluded that the gods were angry or that they were having a quarrel.

The Greeks had many stories — called myths — about these gods. For instance, a Greek myth credits a battle between Zeus and several giants for the formation of the islands of the Aegean Sea. The giants threw huge rocks, piling up the mountains of Greece, as they tried to knock Zeus from the sky. Many stray rocks splashed into the sea to form the islands.

In spite of their belief in many gods, the early Greeks were greatly interested in man and his place in the world. Their inquiries into such matters were the beginning of modern science and philosophy — in fact, our word "philosophy" is from the Greek, meaning "love of wisdom." Greeks such as Socrates, Plato and Aristotle advanced ideas that have influenced thought down through the ages. Pythagoras, one of the early Greek philosophers, stated that the world was round — over two thousand years before Magellan proved it. About 450 B. C., Leucippus developed the idea that everything was composed of tiny particles, which he called atoms. Hippocrates, who became known as the "Father of Medicine," separated the practice of medicine from magic and superstition and set it on its way to becoming a science.

In the centuries that followed Greece's golden age (fifth century B. C.) the Greeks came first under the rule of Alexander the Great and then of the Romans. In the year A. D. 330, Roman Emperor Constantine moved his capital from Rome to Byzantium (once a Greek city), and renamed it Constantinople — now the Turkish city of Istanbul. After about a thousand years as part of the Byzantine Empire, Greece was conquered by the Turks in the 1400's.

The Greeks finally won independence for a small part of their country after an eight-year struggle against the Turks in the early nineteenth century. Not until the early twentieth century, however, did they completely liberate the whole nation.

As we approach Ellinikon Airport, our stewardess points

An amphora, a Greek vase from the sixth century B.C., its form and paint well-preserved.

136

The ruins of the Erechtheum on the Acropolis.

The caryatids, supporting the south portico of the Erechtheum, represent the servants of the gods watching over Athens.

out the Plains of Marathon, scene of a great Greek victory over the invading Persians more than two thousand years ago. She tells us that it gives its name to the long-distance race run in today's Olympic Games. A runner by the name of Pheidippides brought news of the victory to Athens and then dropped dead, his noble heart overstrained. From Marathon to Athens is a distance of 26 miles, 385 yards and this is the distance that an Olympic marathon runner must cover today.

The Olympic Games began in Greece back in 776 B. C. These games took place every four years at Olympia, in front of the Temple of Zeus. The contest included throwing a spear, throwing a discus, running, jumping and wrestling. A simple olive-branch wreath was given the winner of each event and acquiring it was considered a great honor for a young Greek athlete. The modern-day Olympic Games were started again in 1896 at the Panathenean Stadium, and since then they have continued at four-year intervals in various countries, attracting athletes from all over the world. Traditionally, a runner brings a flame (by lighted torch) from the site of the ancient games to the host nation. The Olympic flame then burns day and night throughout the present-day games. Thus from Olympia, Greece, the light of the ancient athletic spirit still shines in the world.

It takes us only half an hour to go from the airport to our hotel in Athens. During the great period of Greek history in the fifth century B. C., the present capital city of Greece was the center of culture. Here the first government called a democracy was established. "Democracy" is from the Greek word meaning "rule by the people." It consisted of an assembly of all the adult male citizens and a council elected by them. This total participation in government (slaves excepted) was only possible in the small city-states of that time. The New England Town Meeting is the nearest approach to the ancient Greek democracies. In later centuries, when empires and class rule prevailed in Europe, democracy remained an ideal in the minds of men and greatly influenced the rise of modern representative government. Modern Greece, although it has a king, is under the leadership of a prime minister and a parliament, called the Chamber of Deputies.

Our sightseeing tour begins at the Acropolis, the hill on and around which Athens was originally built. This site was selected because it was easy to defend against enemies

The ruins of the temple of Apollo in Delphi, seat of the legendary oracle.

The throne room in the palace of King Minos, which was excavated in Knossós, on the island of Crete.

from a high position. Later, when the need for a fort decreased, the Acropolis was changed to serve as a religious center. Actually, the Acropolis is the most famous landmark of Athens, and one of the best known hills in the entire world. Our guide says, "In 480 B. C. invading Persians fought their way to the top of Acropolis and burned the temples and other buildings there. The Persians were finally driven back and defeated. But the Acropolis was not rebuilt immediately; Athenians wanted the ruins to remind future citizens of the sacrifices made in war. For 30 years the blackened marble ruins remained. Then, in 449 B. C., Pericles, a popular Athenian leader, decided to rebuild the Acropolis. He called the greatest architects and sculptors together to plan and build the most beautiful temples in the world. This they did. After forty years of labor, the architectural masterpieces were finished, and the world had gained a monument to the ageless wisdom and culture of the Greek people."

Most beautiful of the buildings on the Acropolis was the Parthenon, built to honor the goddess Athena. This style of architecture, which the Greeks brought to perfection 2,500 years ago, has been imitated all over Europe and in the United States. Probably the best example of it in America is the Lincoln Memorial in Washington, D. C. Unfortunately, much of the Parthenon has been destroyed during

Almost impossible to reach, the Monastery of Meteora stands high on a lofty mountain.

A Greek girl, wearing the national costume of the island of Crete.

An old Greek wine pitcher in the form of a head, above, and, at right, a pair of silver bracelets from the fifth century B.C.

the many wars fought in Greece, but there is enough of the Parthenon left for us to imagine how beautiful it really must have been.

Visiting the remains of the other buildings, we see the Erechtheum with its unusual porch, or portico. The pillars of the south portico were carved in the form of women in draped attire and called "caryatids." They support the roof of the porch on their heads in the manner of women who carried their water jars to the fountain. The Erechtheum is so named because it was built as a temple for Erechtheus, an early king of Athens in Greek mythology who was responsible for having olive trees on earth.

According to a Greek myth, Erechtheus had to choose between Athena and Poseidon as the city's favorite goddess or god. Poseidon offered a never-failing spring of salt water as his gift. He struck the ground with his trident and salt water gushed from the spot as a symbol of mastery of the sea. But then Athena struck the ground with her spear, and up sprang an olive tree with a fruit that would give food to the king's people. Wise Erechtheus chose Athena and her olives. The city was, of course, named after this goddess. Pointing to a tree growing near the south wall of the Erechtheum, our guide states, "There is the sacred olive tree of Athena — or at any rate, its direct descendant."

Continuing to look about, we pass by the Propylaea, the ancient gateway to the Acropolis through which religious processions always entered in ages past. Beautiful, too, is

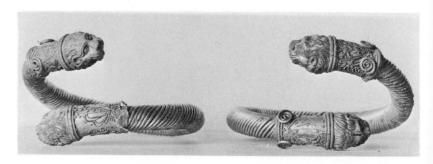

the Temple of the Wingless Victory, whose goddess Nike
had her wings taken from her to prevent her flying away
from Athens. On the southern slope of the Acropolis we
discover the Theater of Dionysus, where Greek tragedies
and comedies were performed before audiences of up to
18,000 people. Because of the large area of the auditorium,
the actors had to wear brightly painted face masks so that
the features could be easily distinguished from a distance.
Also, they often padded their bodies to make them appear
larger and wore platform shoes to add to their height. Many
of our modern drama and stage techniques can be traced
directly to early Greek tragedy and comedy.

Coming down from the Acropolis, our bus passes the
Agora, the market place where the ancient Athenians did
their shopping, talked about the news of the day, and
listened to their poets. Then, as the bus moves slowly
through the narrow, crooked streets of old Athens, we have
the feeling that the city is a grown-up village rather than
Greece's largest city. The houses are of Turkish design and
there are very few windows on the ground floor. The top
floors of these homes jut out over the street. Behind the
houses are yards with gardens and lines of clean laundry

141

Donkey transportation in rural Greece.

Baking of bread by a peasant woman on the island of Poros.

Wandering trader in the "flea market" of Athens.

drying in the sun. The streets are crowded with peddlers and pushcarts filled with things for sale. Other peddlers lead donkeys carrying baskets of fruits and vegetables. As we move along, we witness several agitated discussions between customers and peddlers about the prices of goods. But, of all the streets in old Athens, the one called the "Street of the Dolls" proves most interesting. For over 2,500 years, there were so many shops on this street that made nothing but dolls, toys, and dolls' furniture that it was given this descriptive name.

In the newer parts of Athens, the streets are wide and there are several large public squares. Just off Constitution Square, we find out that the Parliament, military headquarters and various other governmental offices are located in the former Royal Palace. Behind this building lies a shady, pleasant public park that was once part of the palace grounds. The King and Queen of Greece now live in a small palace on the far side of the park.

We hurry back across the park to Constitution Square in order to watch the changing of the guard at the Tomb of the Unknown Warrior. The *evzones,* who are members of the Royal Guard of the King, wear the Greek national costume of a white pleated *fustenella* — a frilly skirt-like tunic or kilt — worn over black tights. This quite attractive uniform also includes: a loose-sleeved white shirt, black embroidered jacket, long white stockings with black tas-selled garters, a scarlet cap with a long cord and tassel, and red shoes with turned-up toes and huge pompons of red, white and blue. In winter, the *evzones* wear a *fustenella* of a deep-blue color rather than the stiff white linen ones they now have on. In some parts of Greece the *fustenella* is still worn as everyday wear, especially by shepherds.

Our guide explains that every Greek province has its own traditional costume. It is handed down from generation to generation, and is worn on festive occasions. In Epirus, in northern Greece, for example, the traditional dress for

women is made of a hand-woven white fabric, with an apron embroidered in red and black wool or silk. This embroidery also appears on the border of a long felt jacket. A short waistcoat embroidered with gold or colored thread is worn beneath the jacket. The men of Epirus wear a black scarf wrapped turban-wise around their head. Until recently — and sometimes even today throughout Epirus, Macedonia, and the islands — peasant women not only made their own fabrics, but prepared the dyes as well.

The next day we start out on an automobile tour of the Greek countryside. After leaving the city, we find little villages of white farm cottages scattered in the valleys between the high mountains. Outside these villages, there are vineyards of grapes, groves of olive and pistachio nut trees, and orchards of oranges, lemons, tangerines and plums. Many of the grapes and plums that are gathered are spread out to dry in the sun and then marketed as raisins and prunes. A small, seedless type of grape is also grown and dried to make currants. Greece grows olives for food as well as for an important export — olive oil. In other sections of Greece farmers raise tobacco, cotton, wheat and rice. As we ride along, only a few cows are seen. Our guide explains the reason for this: "There are not enough

The olive harvest in Greece. Next to raisins, the olive is the most important crop of Greece.

good grazing lands for them. As you can see, little grass grows during the summer, except on the steep mountain slopes." He also tells us that these good grazing spots can only be reached by sure-footed animals like sheep and goats. There are plenty of sheep and goats in the mountains of Greece at this time of the year and they provide meat, milk, cheese, hides and wool.

The country, as a whole, has a climate like parts of southern California; that is, hot dry summers and mild rainy winters. In some northern sections and high in the mountains, however, there are frequent snows and the winters are quite cold. Not much rain falls during the growing season, and since there are no great rivers or irrigation systems in the country, the Greeks draw water from deep wells for their summer crops. This is difficult work, but Greek farm families must work hard to grow enough food for themselves, and then they have little left to sell. Having only a token income, the farmer cannot afford to buy modern farm equipment or use modern farming methods, so he uses oxen and crude plows to till the soil. Farming methods and rural life in Greece have changed little during the past several centuries.

In the morning, we take a short bus ride from Athens to Piraeus, the major seaport in Greece. Looking out into the busy harbor, we see several passenger liners, including the one we shall board. There are also freighters, yachts, ferries, warships, steamers packed with tourists, and various kinds of fishing vessels. We are told that some Greeks turn to the sea to make their living. Many freighters and tankers owned and operated by Greeks move goods to and from port cities around the world.

Greek farmers, as we have seen, are not able to raise enough cattle and other meat-producing animals to feed the people because the land is mountainous and rocky. Fishermen must therefore help with their catches. The fish within Greek waters are generally small in size. Sardines, herring,

144

sturgeon and mackerel are the kind that are usually caught. We also learn that sponge fishing is the basis of an important business for the people of the Aegean Islands. The clear waters furnish the finest silky sponge specimens in the world. But centuries of harvesting have exhausted the once-rich sponge beds, and divers now spread out farther from home, searching for new fertile grounds. Today, Greek divers are following their trade as far away as Egypt and Tunisia.

The ships at Piraeus' docks unload cereal grains, automobiles, chemicals, sugar, machinery, coal, oil, lumber and many raw materials, then leave the harbor with tobacco, raisins, currants, olives, olive oil, marble, textiles, laces, wine and sponges. Piraeus is also a big industrial city with many factories that make goods from farm products, such as textiles from wool and cotton, cigarettes from tobacco, oil from olives, and canned food. Other manufacturing plants make products from minerals, such as cement, glass and fertilizer. But because Greece has little fuel oil and hydroelectricity, and no coal, it must purchase these sources of power from other countries. This means that except for the Piraeus-Athens region and Salonica in the north, there is little industry in Greece.

In our stateroom aboard ship, we realize at last how a country can be both old and new. Both Greece and Israel are among the oldest nations in the world — and among the youngest. Both might be said to have become totally independent and free to rule themselves in the twentieth century. But now we bid Greece "ya-soo" ("good-by") and say "ciao" ("hello") to the golden boot of Italy.

Windmills are landmarks all over the Greek countryside.

Piraeus, a suburb of Athens, and its important harbor.

ITALY

Roughly shaped like a boot, Italy was a closely knit geographical unit before it became a modern nation. **Area** • 116,224 sq. m. **Population** • 50,457,-000. **Language** • Italian. **Government** • Republic. **Monetary Unit** • Lira (= 0.16 U.S. $). **Chief Cities** • Rome (capital), Milan, Naples, Turin, Genoa. **Religion** • about 99% Roman Catholic. **Mountains** • the Alps (highest peak, Gran Paradiso, 13,323 ft.) and the Apennines (9,565 ft. at Monte Corno), as well as the active volcanoes of Vesuvius (3,981 ft.) and Etna (10,075 ft.). **Rivers** • Po, Adige, Arno, Tiber. **Lakes** • Maggiore, Lugano, Como, Garda.

This ancient Greek theater, hewn out of solid rock, is still used today for open-air dramatic performances. It overlooks Taormina on the island of Sicily, and serves as a tangible reminder of the Greek colonies in what is today Italy.

The Golden Boot

While crossing the Ionian Sea from Greece, we look at our atlas and see that Italy is a peninsula, shaped like a huge boot, flaring widely at the top, and cocked in a kicking position. The big island of Sicily is almost in contact with the toe.

The top of the geographical boot is mountainous, with the high and beautiful ranges of the Alps. Sharing the Alps with Italy, west to east, are France, Switzerland, Austria and Yugoslavia. The Alps form a great semicircle. From these mountains extend the lovely narrow mountain lakes of Northern Italy. Rising in this rugged area of Italy, and flowing east into the Adriatic Sea, is Italy's biggest river, the Po. From the mountains in the west extends the great range of the Apennines that run down the center of the boot to its very toe.

The Italian mainland, the two large islands (Sicily and Sardinia), and the many small islands which make up the Republic of Italy, are not much larger in total area than the state of Arizona, but Italy has about one-fourth the population of the United States.

Italy's climate is similar to that of California. It is sunny and warm the year round in the south. Except in the mountains, summers are warm all over Italy. Winter weather ranges from cold in the north, where snow, sleet, chilling rain and fog are common, to mild in central Italy.

Putting the atlas away, we go out on the deck of our ship and find the beautiful harbor of Naples ahead of us. Along the waterfront are warehouses, factories, shipyards, freighters being unloaded and loaded, and several passenger liners. The houses and buildings of the city appear to be climbing the sunny hills that rise above the harbor. Slumbering among the high hills is peaceful-looking Mount Vesuvius. An occasional column of blue-gray smoke nevertheless rises lazily from the volcano — just enough to remind us that fires still burn deep within its volcanic cone. In the past, eruptions of Mount Vesuvius were catastrophic.

"Out there in the bay are the Sirens' Rocks," says Mr. Pastorelli, an Italian merchant whom we met on our ship. "According to an old legend, sailors of the ancient world were lured to their death by the beautiful song of the sirens or mermaids that lived there." He also tells us that the

General view of Naples with Mount Vesuvius overlooking the harbor.

Traces of ancient Greek culture are found in areas of Italy south of Naples. These are the ruins of a Greek temple near Segesta in northwestern Sicily.

Greek hero, Ulysses, when he sailed past, first took the precaution of stuffing his crewmen's ears with wax to prevent them from hearing the songs. To avoid steering the ship to destruction as it sailed past the enchantresses on their rocks, Ulysses himself had been tied to the mast. The story goes that one of the mermaids, Partenope, fell in love with Ulysses and swam after his ship. He escaped her, however, and she died on the shore near Naples.

"While this is only a legend," Mr. Pastorelli continues, "it is a fact that the Greeks landed on this coast and set up several settlements. Among these was Neapolis, the ancient name for Naples. The people who live in Naples today call the city 'Napoli.' "

From the moment we land in Naples we are aware of its noisy life. The air is full of laughter and chatter, bursts of song, and sudden argument. Street vendors crowd the waterfront area, peddling their wares in a loud musical chant. Some of the peddlers have carts drawn by small donkeys; others carry on their heads the things they have to sell. Ice cream, or *gelati,* as the Italians call it, is sold from small pushcarts.

149

After checking into our hotel, we board a sightseeing bus which takes us on a quick tour of Naples. Then the bus travels a road that takes us alongside the beautiful Bay of Naples. The blue water of the bay is dotted with many small fishing boats. Fish is a major source of food for the people of southern Italy. Our guide tells us that we are taking the same route along the coast that the wealthy Romans followed when they traveled from Neapolis to their homes in chariots or litters. This road in those days led to the luxurious country towns of Herculaneum and Pompeii. There are still beautiful villas along the way, with gardens stretching down to the sea.

Then we reach Pompeii. It is a town with many modern stores and hotels. The landscaped park near the entrance to the town gives us no idea of what we shall see beyond the deep stone arch in the wall. It is a startling sensation to walk out upon a dead city, silent and barren under the glaring sun. Sleepy Mount Vesuvius, watching over it, does not look as though it had ever roused itself to spread ruin and death over the plain below. But one day in the year

150

Pompeii's Civil Forum, seen from the south. Mount Vesuvius is in the background.

A. D. 79, there was an earth-shaking explosion, and the top of the long-silent volcano blew off. A cloud of black smoke filled the sky, blotting out the sun, and then a dark rain of cinder and ashes fell to the ground. While some of the residents of Pompeii fled, many stayed behind, thinking that they would be safe inside their homes. But the heavy fall of ashes and deadly volcanic fumes killed them, and several days later, when the sun shone brightly again and harmless smoke drifted up from Mount Vesuvius, Pompeii was no more.

It was forgotten for nearly seventeen centuries. In 1748, a farmer who was digging a well unearthed some small statues and took them to the local authorities. The Italian government became interested and began digging into the ancient ruins. Today, as we walk about the ruins of Pompeii, we see that almost all of the ancient city has been dug out and restored to its original state. Because Pompeii was buried in the midst of its life and was undisturbed for centuries, the uncovered city gives a good picture of the way the Romans lived. Our guide leads us along the narrow

Bread was still in the ancient ovens when archaeologists dug them out of the ashes at the end of the nineteenth century.

151

Peasant from the Po Valley.

stone-paved streets and low brick walls of houses. We see many tiny shops where olive oil, wine, baked goods and many others items were sold. We walk through the ruins of the forum, which was a gathering place for community life — for worship at the temples, commerce and politics. Nearby are the theaters and the area where the gladiators fought. Some of the houses are very beautiful. Then we investigate the public baths where the wealthy young men spent a good part of their time. There are also rooms for the steam baths, the cold baths, the quarters where the massage, oiling and perfuming were done. All of these processes were very important to the luxury-loving Romans.

Later we visit the museum and observe the bronze ornaments worn by women, vases, lamps, pots and pans, and dishes used by the people of Pompeii. There are beds, chairs and other furniture. Even cakes and a half-eaten loaf of bread can be seen, as well as meat ready for cooking, and one unbroken egg. This is assuredly one of the oldest eggs of its kind. All of these things, and many others, we are told were magnificently preserved by the volcanic ashes that killed the residents of Pompeii in A.D. 79.

Back in Naples once again, we stop at a restaurant that serves pizza—the same round pie filled with cheese, sausage, and spices which has become quite popular back in the United States. Our waitress tells us that we will not see pizza in most of the other parts of Italy. She says that pizza originated in Naples, and is still very popular here.

Before going to sleep, we think it might be a good idea to review something of Italy's past. In a guidebook we read that though this nation is comparatively young, the history of the land of Italy is long, dramatic and colorful. During two periods of its history, this country was the leader of the entire western world.

The first of these periods was that of the ancient Roman Empire, before the Christian era, when Rome conquered or dominated all the countries bordering the Mediterranean.

152

The Roman Empire extended well into Britain and northern Europe. But when the Empire became weak, barbarian tribes from the north began taking over. In the year 410, the city of Rome itself was partly destroyed. Thereafter the Empire split into small separate countries.

The second period of greatness came for Italy during the European Renaissance. The word Renaissance was borrowed from the French. It means rebirth, or to be born again. This period in European history spanned the Middle Ages and early modern times. The Italian Renaissance, which was roughly from the late thirteenth or early fourteenth century, to the early sixteenth century, owes its brilliance to the outstanding achievements of explorers, artists and scholars. Wealthy merchants and bankers sponsored voyages of exploration and the arts. Marco Polo's famed travels in the Orient foreshadowed later voyages of discovery. Christopher Columbus discovered the New World for Spain, and Amerigo Vespucci, from whom America's name is derived, crossed the Atlantic several times to explore it. Galileo's memorable exploration of the heavens, however, did not take him out of the country.

The arts flowered as never before, and many of the Renaissance masterpieces are still unsurpassed. Among the great masters were Michelangelo, Leonardo da Vinci and Raphael. The genius of many of these artists found more than one outlet. For example, da Vinci, in addition to painting the *Mona Lisa* and *The Last Supper,* was a brilliant sculptor, musician, inventor and mathematician.

The poems of Dante and Petrarch and the prose of Giovanni Boccaccio are examples of the period's literary masterpieces. Although Italy's pronounced musical talent, especially for dramatic vocal music, found expression in the Renaissance, most of the great composers and musicians came later. Music as we know it started largely in Italy. That is why almost all of the musical terms we use today (forte, fortissimo, piano, pianissimo, and so on) are Italian.

Grape harvest in the Brolio district of Italy.

153

In the second half of the 1500's Italy became a battleground again, with Austria, France and Spain as the principal contenders. Through internal quarrel and foreign invasion it was divided into a number of small, independent states, many under control of foreign countries. Then came a series of revolutions led by such men as Mazzini, Cavour and Garibaldi, with the liberation and unification of Italy as their goal. Liberation was finally achieved in 1870 and Italy, under King Victor Emmanuel II, became a unified nation again. Once more it began to play an important role in world affairs.

Today Italy has no king. The parliament of Italy consists of two chambers: the Chamber of Deputies and Senate. Elected by the people, the Parliament makes the laws for the country. It also elects the President and appoints a Prime Minister, whose job it is to see that the laws are put in force, or carried out.

So much for the history of Italy. We must get some sleep, because tomorrow is likely to be a busy day.

Early the next morning, we leave Naples and drive north toward Italy's largest city, Rome. It is also, historically, probably the most famous city in the world. As the bus travels along a superhighway, we pass hills cultivated with olive trees, grapevines and citrus trees. There are small vegetable farms on terraced lands.

"But the farmers here cannot produce all the food that is needed," says our bus driver. "Too much of the land is mountainous and cannot be used for crops. The farmlands along the Po and its tributaries are the most fertile in all Italy." He continues by informing us that the Po Valley produces most of Italy's sugar beets, corn, alfalfa and hemp, and nearly half of its wheat crop. Here, too, are pastured most of Italy's dairy and beef cattle. In the nineteenth century rice was introduced as an ideal crop for the marshy flooded plains of the lower Po Valley. Now rice has become an important ingredient of Italian cooking.

154

On reaching Rome, we immediately start our tour of the city from the main public square, the Piazza di Venezia. Located in the center of the old section of Rome, streets lead out of the square in all directions. In the square itself there is a beautiful palace that was built about 1450. There is also a huge white marble monument to King Victor Emmanuel II, the first king of modern Italy. Behind the monument a flight of steps leads to the top of Capitoline Hill, one of the seven hills upon which ancient Rome was built. The building in front of us is the old Senatorial Palace, which is now used as Rome's city hall. The other buildings atop Capitoline Hill are museums in which we see many ancient statues and priceless works of art.

From the top of the hill we see the slow-flowing Tiber River which winds its way through the city, dividing it into

Rome, the "Eternal City," is a bustling, modern metropolis, with reminders of a glorious past everywhere. This is an air view of the Via dei Fori Imperiali, the Street of the Imperial Forums, with the modern monument to King Victor Emanuel II (twentieth century) in the foreground and the Colosseum (started in the first century) at the other end.

155

Arch of Septimius Severus on the Forum Romanum.

two parts. On the left, or east, bank can be found the ruins of the ancient Roman Empire, as well as most of modern Rome's government buildings, business offices, major hotels, theaters, restaurants and shops. On the opposite side of the Tiber is where the modern residential sections, many churches, Vatican City, and a very old district called the Trastevere are located. A dozen or more bridges span the river, many of which date back to ancient times, and are true works of art. Throughout the city, the Tiber is restrained by stone walls to prevent it from overflowing its banks.

On the other side of Capitoline Hill are the ruins of the ancient Roman Forum. Originally, the Forum was the town market place, but as Rome grew, new and more beautiful buildings and temples were added. It then became the center of political and religious life of Rome. Today the ruins we see include columns and arches and worn stones of temples, courthouses, memorials, and the palace of the

156

Senators. South of the Forum is the Circus Maximus, the great hippodrome of ancient Rome that could accommodate some 200,000 spectators.

Walking along, we pass Palatine Hill, another of the seven hills of the city. It was near here, according to legend, where the two twin brothers — Romulus and Remus — were abandoned, and where a she-wolf raised them. When Romulus grew up, he took a plow and marked off a square plot around Palatine Hill. This was the boundary of his original city. The legend is most interesting, but the probable facts are that Rome began as a village for sheepherders about 500 B. C.

Our next stop is the Colosseum, opened by Emperor

Via Appia Antiqua, the Old Appian Way, was once travelled by Roman war chariots and is still able to take the rigors of twentieth-century automobile traffic.

157

Titus in A. D. 80. Now it is a majestic ruin. Once it could seat some 50,000 people. The audience sat shaded from the hot sun by cloth awnings. They watched gladiators fight each other to the death, or Christian martyrs and other unfortunates being thrown to the lions. Sometimes the Colosseum was flooded with water. This was done deliberately so that warships manned with sailors and soldiers could fight real battles for the amusement of the people. After Rome fell, the Colosseum became a stronghold for bandits. For some time the building was completely abandoned and served as a lair for wild wolves. However, the ancient walls still stand, having withstood the rigors of time, earthquakes, vandals and wars for nearly nineteen centuries.

Near the Colosseum is the Arch of Constantine, the best-preserved and most elaborate of all the Roman arches. It was built in A. D. 315 to celebrate the victory of the Emperor Constantine over Maxentius. A short walk to the south from the Colosseum leads us to the Baths of Caracalla. They were built about A. D. 212 by Emperor Caracalla, and provided luxurious facilities for approximately 1,600 Roman bathers at a time. In those days, remember, houses did not have bathtubs or showers. Water facilities could only be found at public baths. This structure also had a library and a gymnasium. But it is all in ruins today. Later, we walk by the flat ground of the Campus Martius, called the "Field of Mars," on the left bank of the Tiber where Roman legions drilled. We also view part of the Appian Way, a military road built by the Emperor Appius Claudius in 312 B. C. It runs between rows of cypress trees and is lined with ancient monuments and old Roman tombs. The Appian Way is still used as a motor highway south of Rome.

On the way back to our hotel, we stop at the Pantheon, the only ancient Roman building still in perfect condition. Begun in the year 27 B. C. by Marcus Agrippa to celebrate his victory over Anthony and Cleopatra, it was completely rebuilt by the Emperor Hadrian. It was dedicated in honor

158

of seven planetary gods. The first Christian Roman Emperors abandoned the Pantheon, and the barbarians pillaged it. The Pantheon was saved when a Byzantine emperor presented it to Pope Boniface IV. Thus the Pantheon has been used sporadically as a church for nearly two thousand years. We learn that the language of ancient Rome was Latin, but the official language of Italy today is Italian. Many people speak English, too.

In the evening we walk to the Spanish Steps, probably the most beautiful flight of steps in the world. This monumental staircase, with flowers and palm trees on each side, goes up Pincian Hill from the Piazza di Spagna to the old Church of Trinita dei Monti. At the bottom of the steps is the famous Barcaccia Fountain, in the shape of a boat with a cannon. Near the fountain is the palace of the Spanish ambassador. Also at the foot of the steps are the flower-sellers with their masses of fragrant blooms sheltered under huge bright-colored umbrellas. The view from the top of the steps is one of the most beautiful we have seen so far.

In the morning we take a taxi to Vatican City, a city within a city, an independent country inside a country. In this tiny country that is completely walled off from the rest of Rome, the Pope — head of the Roman Catholic Church — holds complete power.

On the way there, our driver tells us that the Vatican issues its own postage stamps and auto license plates, prints or mints its own money, maintains a radio station that broadcasts all over the world, and operates an international bank. It also has its own groceries, restaurants, garages, drugstores, power plant, and post office. Among the Vatican's industries are a studio for making mosaics, a tapestry workshop, a printing press and a book bindery. It publishes its own newspapers and magazines, and is in direct telephone contact with virtually every major city in the world.

As we enter Vatican City through one of the three gates in the wall, we see two Swiss Guards standing watch. They

The Arch of Constantine in Rome.

The famous Spanish Steps leading to Trinita dei Monti Church.

St. Peter's Basilica in Vatican City, the world's largest church.

are part of the Pope's personal army, which is composed of young men recruited from Switzerland. The first Swiss Guardsmen came to the Vatican in 1506, and the guard has been maintained without a break ever since. The brilliant red, yellow and blue uniform and armor they wear were designed in the sixteenth century by Michelangelo, one of Italy's most famous artists.

Although the Vatican is the world's smallest state, it contains the world's largest church, St. Peter's Basilica. The Basilica occupies the site of a former amphitheater, the Circus of Nero, where thousands of Christians were killed by the Romans. Saint Peter is believed to have been killed here, and buried in a nearby cemetery. Various churches were built on this spot over the centuries, until the present vast Renaissance structure was begun in 1506. Several gifted artists, including Michelangelo and Raphael, helped develop the plans and supervise the building of the basilica, which took more than one hundred years to complete. Inside the church, we find that the enormous interior is very bright, rich with marble, mosaic and religious memorials.

160

Under the high altar, we are told, is Saint Peter's tomb. From its huge dome we can look down on the buildings and gardens of the Vatican City.

The Vatican Palace has over a thousand rooms. The Sistine Chapel and the Picture Gallery are world renowned. The Vatican Museum contains some of the world's greatest art treasures. On our way back to the hotel, we stop at Castel Sant' Angelo. It was built in A. D. 135 as a tomb for Emperor Hadrian and his successors. During the fifth century it was converted into a fortress. Its present name derives from a miraculous event which, according to legend, took place in A. D. 590. It was reported that Pope Gregory the Great, leading a procession to pray for the end of the plague in Rome, saw a vision of the Archangel Michael. The Archangel was seen to be sheathing his sword, and the vision was interpreted as a sign that the plague would end. The bronze statue of the saint on top of the building was erected to commemorate the event. Sometimes the castle was occupied by the Popes when Rome was invaded.

Although Rome is most famous for its historic points of interest, it is also an industrial city. There are factories that make automobile parts, sewing machines, printing machinery, typewriters, textiles, motor scooters and chemical products. Some of the smaller industries produce handicraft items made from wood, metal or leather. We are told that most of the factories are on the outskirts of the city. The Via Veneto is Rome's most important business street. Its half-mile length is lined with offices, shops and outdoor cafes. It ends at the Pincian Gate of the ancient Aurelian Wall which once enclosed the city, and around which much of the newer portions of the city have been built. Automobiles, streetcars, and motor scooters rumble and clang through the archways of the old wall. As we stand on a street corner listening to the wild honking clatter of the various vehicles, we can understand why Rome has often been called "the world's noisiest city."

The Swiss Guards, "soldiers" of the Vatican State.

While walking about, we observe sculptured fountains on every public square and almost every street corner. In some fountains the water gushes out of a basin. In others it spurts slender streams high into the air, while in still others, the water sprays around figures of mermaids and sea gods, around prancing stone horses, or out of the mouths of bronze tortoises. Of all the fountains we see, the Trevi is the one we like best. As most tourists do, we toss a coin in the blue-green water of Trevi Fountain, for an old legend has persisted that anyone who drops a coin into this fountain will return to Rome. We certainly want to return some day.

In the evening we go to the main railway station of Rome, Stazione Termini, a modern building opened in 1950. But because of a Roman building law which requires that all new construction must not destroy any part of an ancient ruin, part of the very old wall built by the Emperor Servius Tullius can be seen in front of the station. From this railway station, a night express train will take us to Venice, often called the Queen of the Adriatic.

Next morning, as the train approaches our destination over a long bridge, or causeway, we get our first glimpse of Venice. It is a strange sight, indeed. The city seems to rise directly from the sea. Its buildings seem to float on the water. There are no automobiles, buses, trucks, street-cars, carriages, or even bicycles to be seen. Canals form the "streets" which connect more than 115 small islands on which the city is built.

At the railroad station, a gondola picks us up to take us to our hotel. A gondola is a long narrow boat with curved ends. A man called a gondolier stands in the stern of the boat. It is his job to row and steer the craft with a single oar. There are many other boats on the canals. Some of the gondolas are bigger than the one we are in, but these are rowed by several men. There are also many motorboats and barges piled high with various produce. The steam-boats, called "vaporettos," are the "water buses" of Venice.

162

At left, the beautiful Cathedral of Florence, and below, the famous Leaning Tower of Pisa.

They carry people from place to place, just as motorbuses do in other cities. In Venice, policemen cruise about in boats to make sure that power craft observe the speed limit and that all boatmen obey the traffic-light signal located at the junction of two important canals. As we wait at one intersection, a Venetian moving van — a barge loaded with furniture — makes its way down a canal from one home to another.

Our gondolier tells us that there are more than 160 canals in Venice. Spanning these canals are some 380 bridges. A few sidewalks serve the city, but these are narrow. Generally, the front steps of the houses go right down to the water's edge. In front of each house is a mooring pole, striped with the family colors, where the family boat is tied up when not in use. Most buildings of Venice are constructed on piles, or poles, driven deep into the mud and the river bed.

After a short rest at our hotel, we start our sightseeing tour of Venice. The gondola travels along the Grand Canal, the city's most important waterway, where many colorful shops and restaurants can be seen. As our gondolier steers his boat with ease through the thickest traffic jams, he tells us that when the barbarians invaded Northern Italy in A. D. 452, people who lived on the mainland fled to the small mud island at the mouth of the Po River. Here they built thatched huts on piles. As time passed, the security of their isolation enabled the Venetians to become prosperous and powerful.

163

They built ships and sent them all over the world in search of trade. In due time, the crude huts were replaced by fine homes and luxurious palaces. By the end of the seventh century, Venice had become an independent country. Its ruler, or doge, became one of the most important men of Europe. The last doge gave up his kingdom in 1797, to make way for the rule of Napoleon. After Napoleon's loss of power, Venice became part of Austria. Toward the end of the nineteenth century, Venice became part of Italy.

The journey down the Grand Canal ends at Venice's only large public square, the Piazza (Plaza) of St. Mark. Here we see the cathedral of St. Mark, one of the most beautiful churches in Italy. It is said that in the year 828, Venetian merchants stole the body of Saint Mark from its resting place in Alexandria, Egypt, and brought it here to Venice. A small church was first built to serve as the Saint's tomb, but then a great cathedral was started in the eleventh century and finished some centuries later. It was a law of the country during this time that any Venetian engaged in trade with the East must bring back some treasure to make St. Mark's Cathedral more beautiful. We see pillars that were taken from temples, gold work from Egypt, rare gems from India, as well as the four Greek bronze horses that stand about the main entrance. These horses came from the City of Constantinople (now called Istanbul) in Turkey.

The square itself is paved in marble. The cafes, or restaurants, that surround the square have hundreds of chairs and tables set out on the broad pavement of the square. While eating lunch at one of these cafes, we notice that thousands of pigeons gather to be fed by the tourists. Being good tourists, we feed the pigeons, too. In the clock tower above the square, two giant metal Moors strike out the hours with a bronze sledge-hammer on a large, bronze bell. They have been doing it ever since 1497.

Another building that we visit while at the plaza is the Palace of the Doges, which in time past has been the scene

Venice's St. Mark's Cathedral with its huge unconnected bell tower. The Palace of the Doge is at the right of the bell tower.

164

Gondolas move along the Grand Canal near one of the many famous bridges of Venice, the Rialto Bridge.

of as much cruelty and mystery as any building in the world. During the six and a half centuries of its existence, it has been burned down twice, but each time it has been rebuilt. The most famous bridge of Venice, the Bridge of Sighs, connects the Palace with the prison across the Grand Canal. Across this bridge convicted criminals passed to the dungeons to which they had been sentenced by the doge.

Early the next morning a motorboat takes us to nearby Murano Island. Here we watch skilled craftsmen making beautiful glass objects. While observing a man "blowing" a vase, our guide tells us that the Venetians were the first glassmakers to produce clear, sparkling glass. The secret of how it was done was carefully guarded. No craftsman who knew the secret was permitted to leave Venice and work elsewhere. The trade of glassmaking was never taught to a non-Venetian. Several centuries ago, however, one of the doges became alarmed at the possible fire hazard to Venice created by the glassmakers. Because the glass had to be heated to an almost liquid state, so that it could be blown or molded into the desired shapes, the great open hearths were dangerous. For this reason the doge ruled that the glassmakers had to move to Murano Island. Venetian glass business has been there ever since. Most of the industries of Venice are located at Porto Marghera, a few miles northwest of the city — on the mainland of Italy. Here there are busy shipyards, oil refineries and chemical plants.

Lake Como, one of Italy's scenic lakes and a vacationer's paradise in Northern Italy.

We spend the rest of the day riding up and down the canals of Venice in vaporettos. Tomorrow we shall fly to Switzerland, the land of William Tell.

CHAPTER 8

The Land of William Tell

The next stop on our journey is at "The Land of William Tell." Our tickets, of course, do not read that way. Rather, they say our next stop is Switzerland. To the Swiss, however, their country is the land of William Tell, because he is the man who helped them win their freedom.

"Have you heard the story of William Tell?" asks the hotel clerk. When we say that we have not, he relates the following story: Early in the fourteenth century, the country that we now know as Switzerland was ruled by the Emperor of Austria. The parts of the Austrian kingdom were ruled by bailiffs or governors, appointed by the Emperor. Some of them ruled honorably and with justice, but many of them oppressed the people and were cruel.

Legends say that the land near Lake Lucerne, in present-day Switzerland, was ruled by a very cruel governor named Gessler. To test the loyalty of his subjects, Gessler placed a hat belonging to the Duke of Austria on top of a pole in the market place of the small village of Altdorf and decreed that all passers-by were to take off their caps and bow before the hat as though it were the Duke himself. Two

SWITZERLAND

The most mountainous country in Europe. **Area** • 15,944 sq. m. **Population** • 5,810,000. **Language** • German, French, Italian, Romansh (a language based on Latin). **Government** • Federal republic. **Monetary Unit** • Franc (= 0.23 U.S. \$). **Chief Cities** • Zurich, Basel, Geneva, Bern (capital). **Religion** • 57% Protestant, 41% Roman Catholic. **Mountains** • the Swiss Alps cover more than half the country; highest peaks are Dufourspitze (15,203 ft.), the Matterhorn (14,690 ft.), Finsteraarhorn (14,026 ft.), and the Jungfrau (13,653 ft.). **Rivers** • the Rhine and the Rhone. **Lakes** • Geneva, Constance, Zurich, Lucerne, Neuchâtel, Lugano, and Maggiore.

guards were placed on either side of the pole to enforce this order.

One day a skilled archer named William Tell came to the village with his son, Walter, and they walked right past the hat, refusing to bow before it. Soldiers took father and son before Gessler. After sentencing both of them to death, Gessler thought of a cruel way of punishing Tell. He said that both he and his son would be permitted to go free if Tell would shoot an apple off Walter's head at a hundred paces. If Tell refused, Gessler added, both he and the boy would die, anyway.

Tell took an arrow from his quiver and slipped it under his belt. Then he took another, and after taking careful aim, fired it from his bow. The arrow split the apple in two. Surprised and displeased with the result of the test of skill, Gessler called Tell to him and asked what the first arrow had been intended for. Tell answered, "Had I killed my son, that arrow was to slay you."

In a rage, Gessler broke his promise of freedom for Tell and commanded his soldiers to put him in prison. A few nights later, Tell escaped from prison and went into the forest. When Gessler and his soldiers tried to recapture him, he shot and killed the cruel governor with an arrow from his bow. The story of William Tell's bravery was soon heard by the people. They joined together and drove the Austrian army out of their country. In Switzerland we shall see many statues erected in honor of William Tell.

Since there is only water about Venice, we must take a plane to Switzerland that can take off from water — a seaplane. Up we go in it, and what a view there is of the city! We can see the canals that we traveled about in our gondolas. As we take our last look at Grand Canal and the many beautiful places along its banks, our pilot heads the seaplane northwest across Italy.

Suddenly our plane begins to climb higher and higher. Far below we begin to see lofty mountains, most of which

At the "Drei Laender Ecke," the "Three Countries Corner" at Basel, the borders of Switzerland, Germany and France come together.

168

are covered with snow. So much of Switzerland is mountainous that this little country, one-third the size of the state of New York, is sometimes called the "roof of Europe." But these high mountains help to protect Switzerland's borders. Since the seventeenth century, the Swiss have been free to rule themselves despite the fact that they are surrounded by powerful nations. Bordered by France on the west, Germany on the north, Austria, Liechtenstein and Italy on the east, and on the south by Italy, Switzerland nevertheless is a natural fortress because of its high mountains.

Measured by latitude, Switzerland should have a climate similar to Quebec, in Canada, but it does not — it has a much milder, gentler climate. In fact, the climate is so pleasant that tropical palm trees and flowers grow on some of the southern slopes of the Swiss mountains. The wide

169

valleys are also very good for farming. Switzerland's mountains contribute to its mild weather by providing protection against winds. The varying elevations between the lowland valleys and the mountains enable a person to swim in a valley lake, yet ski only a few miles away in the mountains.

Many of the large rivers in Europe, like the Rhine, the Rhone, the Ticino, and the Aar, begin in Switzerland. There are many lakes, too. Our pilot lands the seaplane down on one of these beautiful, blue bodies of water. He announces that this is Lake Geneva, and that a small boat will soon come out to our plane. This boat then will take us to a dock in the city of Geneva.

This city has often been called "the peace capital of the world." For many years, people have been coming to this city to discuss world problems and try to find a way for people to live together in peace. Walking down the main avenue, we see the famous Peace Palace, or the Palace of Nations, as it is sometimes called. This building was the

The imposing structure of the Palace of the League of Nations at Geneva.

The oldest spring festival in Switzerland, the Chalanda Marz, held on the first day in March, is one that goes back to Roman times. Today it is mainly a children's day, with community singers going from house to house, accompanied by the sound of cowbells.

A watchmaker at his bench in Geneva.

meeting site of the League of Nations whose place is now taken by the United Nations which meets in New York City. Geneva is also the headquarters of the International Red Cross, established here in 1864. The flag of this organization, with its red cross on a field of white, is the Swiss flag with its colors reversed. This city is also famous all over the world for the watches made here.

For a very long time most of the finest craftsmen in watchmaking have been Swiss. Switzerland produces more watches than any other country. Many Swiss watchmakers work in their own homes, making only a certain part of a watch. Then they send it to a factory which gets other parts from other watchmakers, and the watch is put together to produce a finished product. Because so many of the pieces that go into a watch are quite small, the watchmakers often wear special magnifying glasses to make the parts look bigger than they actually are. But small watches are not the only product made by the watchmakers. Swiss clocks are as interesting as the watches. Many of these clocks are made with beautifully carved cases, and large tower clocks are made for churches and buildings. Some have musical chimes, and Swiss cuckoo clocks delight everyone.

Romantic gorges, foaming rivers, somber forests and sunny pastures are viewed in succession from the swiftly moving electric trains in Switzerland.

After a visit to a watch factory to witness and marvel at the precision work first-hand, we board a railway train and travel east to the heart of the Swiss mountains. The railroad cars are quite different from those in the United States. They are made up of little rooms, or compartments, with two benches facing each other. An aisle runs the length of each car so that passengers may go from one car to another. Also, unlike most of the railroads in the United States which obtain motive power from coal or oil, Swiss trains are run by electricity, because Switzerland has no oil and almost no coal. But the Swiss have made use of their unlimited water power. A great deal of snow falls in the high mountains, and melting snows make mighty streams. The Swiss people have learned to utilize the power of waters rushing down the mountainsides to make electricity. Hydroelectricity, as such power is called, is employed in many ways, in addition to running railroads.

Running railroads through the high mountains is difficult. The Swiss have solved the problems of crossing mountain rivers and deep valleys by building great bridges. When

172

mountains too steep for a train to climb have been encountered, tunnels have been built through them. There are a number of very long railroad tunnels in Switzerland. In fact, the longest railroad tunnel in the world, the Simplon Tunnel, is about twelve and one-half miles long. One end of the tunnel is in Switzerland; the other end is in Italy.

After an interesting ride on the train, we reach a village in a small valley among the high mountains. Here we plan to stop and stay overnight. Looking about the village, we see that most of the houses are grouped around the two important buildings of all Swiss towns: the church and the inn. These houses, or chalets, as they are called, are built of wood, and are two or more stories high. The roofs are very steep, in order to shed summer rain and winter snow, and are securely held down by stones so that strong winter winds will not blow them away. Windows are small and have shutters that help to keep out winter snow and cold. The ground floor, which often is made of stone, is generally used in cold weather as a stable for the cows, sheep and goats. This keeps the animals warm, and the family can tend them without going out into the deep snow. Steps from the stable lead to the floors above, where the family lives. Almost every Swiss home has an outdoor balcony where the family can relax and enjoy the clear mountain air.

Werdenberg, a delightful Old-World town in the Rhine Valley, is dominated by its ancient castle. The houses, as in many Swiss towns, are of wood.

Most of the houses in small Swiss villages are grouped around the church and the inn.

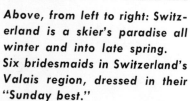

Above, from left to right: Switzerland is a skier's paradise all winter and into late spring.
Six bridesmaids in Switzerland's Valais region, dressed in their "Sunday best."
Near Lugano, Switzerland, women still do their own spinning.

The winters high up in the mountains, unlike those in lower valleys and plateaus, are very long and can be severe, but the people enjoy them. There is always plenty to do. The animals must be fed, cared for, and the cows milked. The men go hunting, whittle out toys and other items, or work in small factories. The women weave cloth and make clothing for the entire family; they also make beautiful laces and do embroidery work. The children help their parents and play games. They must, of course, attend school, for Switzerland has a fine public-school system. They often go to school on skis or sleds in winter.

During the winter, people from all over Europe and many other parts of the world come to the inns or hotels in the larger villages. They, along with the Swiss people, enjoy skiing, ice-skating, tobogganing, and other forms of healthful recreation that Switzerland offers. Because it is summer during our visit, we find only a few men and boys in the village. When the first warm weather comes, most of them take the farm animals to pastures high in the mountains. These high mountain pastures, which are used only during the summer months, are called "alps." It is from them that the entire mountain range got its name, the Alps.

174

When these men leave for the mountains in the spring, the village holds a celebration. Everyone dresses in an old-fashioned costume, and musicians add to the gaiety. The animals wear wreaths of flowers. One of the cows has a milking stool placed between her horns as a sign that she is queen. Practically all of the villagers go a mile up the steep trail with the herdsmen, boys and animals. It will not be until after the summer months that families will again be reunited.

During their stay in the alps, the boys tend the animals while the men make butter and the famous Swiss cheeses. The huts in which they spend the summer are very crude. Furnishings consist of a simple table and bench. An armful of hay is used for bedding. Now and then one of the men carries some cheese down to the village and climbs back up the mountain with supplies.

When the first cold days of autumn come, the men and boys are glad to take the animals back down to their homes in the valley. As when they left in the spring, there is another celebration, with dancing, singing and lively wrestling matches — wrestling is a favorite sport of the Swiss. In addition, the festival usually includes some rousing tunes

A peasant woman in the Fex Valley near St. Moritz, Switzerland, starts work in a pasture dotted with crocuses.

In spring, herds of cattle, led by festively adorned cows, leave the village for higher pastures.

boomed out in an alpenhorn contest. The Swiss alpenhorn is a musical instrument found in no other country. Carved from wood, and fifteen feet long, its clear, mellow notes can be heard for more than six miles as they echo among the mountains. After the celebration is over, the men prepare for winter, while the boys go back to school.

While the men and boys are up in the mountains, the women, girls and young children work, too. They take care of the small farms at home. They raise potatoes and other vegetables for home use, and grain and hay for the farm animals. Because the fields in the villages are small, the greatest amount of work is done by hand rather than with farm machinery.

In the summer, many Swiss people rent rooms to tourists who arrive in their town for a rest or vacation. The mountains, the deep canyons, rushing streams and waterfalls are all scenic attractions. Most tourists enjoy the cool, fresh mountain air. They sail on the lakes, fish in the streams, and visit the various little shops. Mountain-climbing is also popular. Mountaineers act as guides, using an ice-axe to cut notches in the ice that serve as footholds. When necessary, the climbers are tied together with a rope for their

176

A shepherd and his flock, high up in the mountains, with the snow-capped peaks of the Bernina Range in the distance.

safety. Some of the more famous mountain peaks popular with climbers in Switzerland are the Matterhorn, Jungfrau and Monch. Actually, taking care of tourists is one of the leading businesses of the Swiss. It is therefore not strange that Switzerland is often called "the mountain playground of Europe."

After the completion of our stay in the village, we get on board a motor coach. Most of the Swiss roads are hard-surfaced and are well-kept. They are generally built at the lowest places in the mountains, called passes. The driver must go slowly on these roads, since there are many sharp curves. He had to take a very strict test before he was allowed to drive a motor coach on these twisting mountain roads.

While going through one of the passes, the Saint Bernard pass, we stop at the small monastery of St. Bernard. Our Swiss driver calls it a "hospice." This hospice was founded in A. D. 962 by a religious man, St. Bernard of Menthon, after whom the two passes, the Great Saint Bernard and the Little Saint Bernard, are named. Living in the hospice today are monks who provide help and shelter for those caught in mountain storms. While there, we see several

177

large, strong, intelligent dogs. This breed of dog, too, is named after the founder of the hospice, St. Bernard.

Though these dogs are seldom used in rescue work because of newer ways of travel and communication, they are still found at most hospices and monasteries in Switzerland. In the past, these dogs were trained by the monks to rescue and bring help to lost travelers. Many thrilling tales have been told and retold about life-saving rescues brought about by St. Bernard dogs.

As we rest in the hospice, one of the monks tells us the story of Barry — one of the best-loved dogs that ever roamed the Alps. The monk begins by saying that Barry was born in the early 1800's and even as a puppy, showed unusual intelligence and strength. He was always the first dog to reach a lost traveler and always seemed to know how to bring him back to the hospice. One time, it has been said, Barry found a small girl who had strayed from her parents and who had become lost in a bad snowstorm. Keeping her warm by laying as close to her as possible and licking her face with his soft tongue, he somehow made her understand that she should climb upon his back and hold on to his fur, whereupon Barry very carefully carried the young girl safely back to the warmth and shelter of the hospice.

The monk continues, "After better than ten years of faithful service, during which time about forty persons were saved by him, Barry was permitted to retire. He rested and dozed by the hospice's fireplace. The younger dogs could now make the rescues for which he was so famous. However, one winter night, about three years after his retirement, a terrible blizzard raged. When all the other dogs could not find a foot traveler who had been reported missing, Barry was put back into active duty. He quickly picked up the scent of the missing man and went to rescue him. But mistaking the big dog for a wolf, the nearly frozen man grabbed his knife and stabbed his would-be rescuer. Although badly wounded, Barry crawled back to the hospice. He brought the

178

Dairying is an important industry in Switzerland. The pictures on this page all have to do with making cheese during the summer months. Left, from top to bottom: (1) Preparing kindling for the cold nights. (2) Distribution of cheese made in alpine dairy huts during the summer season. (3) "Dairy people" on their way home from high alpine pastures.
Above: "Salting the cheese" is an important task in the picturesque dairy huts of the Bernese Oberland.

Travel in the Swiss mountains is sometimes hazardous, and in the past, specially trained St. Bernard dogs often came to the rescue of wayfarers who were lost or in distress.

SAINT BERNARD

monks to the lost traveler, and then quietly died. Faithful to the very end, Barry finished the job that he had set out to do." Patting one of the big dogs on the head, the monk adds, "We can all take a lesson in faithfulness from these brave dogs of St. Bernard."

As we continue our motor-coach journey north, we leave the high mountains and enter the Swiss plateau. On this lower land, it is easy for farmers to use modern machinery. For this reason, the farms are much larger than those in the mountains. Sugar beets, oats, rye, wheat and potatoes are grown here. There are also many pear, peach and apple orchards, and grape vineyards.

Many of the larger villages and cities of Switzerland are in this part of the country. Bern, the capital of Switzerland, is located near the center of these lowlands, and like other Swiss cities, it is very colorful in the summer, with

180

gay flowers blooming in boxes outside every window. Most of the houses have balconies that face other balconies across the narrow streets. Our sightseeing walk leads us to the impressive Parliament Building, where the Federal Assembly meets and where the country's laws are enacted. The Federal Assembly is made up of two chambers: the National Council, which is like our House of Representatives, and the Council of States, which corresponds to our Senate. The people of each canton, or state, elect the members of the Federal Assembly. The Federal Assembly, in turn, elects a president to make sure that the laws are enforced.

After a short visit to the Parliament Building, we walk along Marktgasse, or Market Street, looking in the many shop windows. Ahead is the remarkable clock tower, called "Zytglogge." When the minute hand reaches twelve, a rooster crows and a parade of carved bears begins around the base of the clock. Next a knight at the top of the tower strikes a huge silver bell with a hammer to tell the correct hour, while a clown below shakes his fist at the knight. The whole show is over in only a few minutes. However, if we should miss any part of it, we could come back in another hour. The clock has been following the same routine since 1530.

A girl from Bern wears her colorful traditional hat.

On the other side of the bridge that crosses the Aare River we observe a group of people standing around an iron fence. They are looking down at the bears of Bern in their pit in the ground. Three brown bears reach up to us, begging for food. We buy carrots and fruit at the special booth nearby and toss them to the bears. We are not allowed to feed them candy or sugar.

A nearby policeman tells us that the name Bern is derived from the German word *bären*, meaning bears. "When Count Berthold founded the town in the year 1191," the policeman continues, "he invited his guests and the entire court to a great hunt. 'I will name our new town after the first animal that I kill today.' he proclaimed. The first

Bern, Switzerland's capital, with the medieval marksman's fountain in the foreground and the clock tower in the distance.

The alpenhorn, a typical Swiss "musical" instrument, is blown outdoors and requires special skill and "lung-power."

animal was a bear. And so the town was called Beartown, or Bern. This animal became the symbol of the people here, and ever since 1441, bears have been kept in this pit."

Like the policeman, the rest of the Swiss people are very friendly. Many of them speak, read and write as many as four languages. We are surprised at the number of languages spoken by the people in such a small country. When we were in western Switzerland, almost everyone spoke French. In southern Switzerland, the majority of people spoke Italian. Where we are now — in central Switzerland and to the north — almost everyone speaks German. If we had visited the eastern part of the country, we may have heard still another language spoken. It is called Romansh, and is a very old language which is spoken only in this part of the world. Fortunately for us, almost everyone in Switzerland who is in business speaks English. This is because many of the tourists are Englishmen or Americans.

A train takes us from Bern to one of the great railway centers of Europe, the city of Basel. Located on the Rhine River, it is one of the oldest commercial centers of Europe. The Rhine River is important to the Swiss people because it is connected with the other European rivers by canals so that the things made in Swiss factories, such as scientific instruments, machinery, chemical products, textiles and chocolate, can be sent by boat to France, Germany and even to the sea. As we have seen, Switzerland has no seashore, no seaports, and thus no navy!

While walking about Basel, we learn that it is one of the oldest Swiss cities, and except for Zurich, it is the largest. The history of Basel goes back to A. D. 374, when the Romans built a fort here and called it "Basilia." Many of the shops and business offices are located in fine old buildings, and some firms display their name and product on very handsome signs. In the afternoon we visit the art gallery, the museum, and the University of Basel, which was founded thirty-three years before America was discovered (1459).

182

Boarding a river steamer for the trip down the Rhine, we end our stay in Switzerland. While wishing to stay longer in this wonderful country, we remember that it has been said that the Rhine is a most beautiful river to travel. It is also one of the busiest rivers in the world. As we learned earlier, it has its source among the Swiss Alps. After it leaves Switzerland, the Rhine serves as a boundary between France and Germany for 150 miles. Next it flows through Germany for about 450 miles, and finally past the Netherlands to the North Sea. Our trip down the Rhine River will end at Rotterdam, the second largest city and the greatest seaport of the Netherlands.

Vistas along the river Limmat in Zurich.

A flag-tosser displays his special skill during a parade. Flag-tossing is comparable to baton-tossing as practiced by an American drum major or majorette.

GERMANY

Central European country, divided after World War II into German Federal Republic (West Germany) and German Democratic Republic (East Germany). **Area** • Total land area: 136,462,000 sq. m. **Population** • West Germany: 56,947,000; East Germany: 17,102,-000. **Language** • German. **Government** • West Germany is a federal republic. **Monetary Unit** • West Germany: Deutsche Mark (= 0.25 U.S. $). **Chief Cities** • Berlin, largest city in Germany, is divided into East and West zones and is capital of East Germany; Hamburg, Munich, Cologne, Essen, Düsseldorf, Bonn (capital of West Germany). Major cities in the East are Leipzig and Dresden. **Religion** • Protestant (mostly Lutheran), Roman Catholic. **Rivers** • Rhine, Danube, Weser, Elbe, Oder. **Mountains** • highest elevation is in the Bavarian Alps (Zugspitze, 9,719 ft.); other important ranges are the Algäu Alps, the Swabian Mountains, and the Harz Mountains. **Lakes** • Lake Constance (borders on Austria and Switzerland).

Typical landscape of the Rhineland-Palatinate in Germany.

CHAPTER 9

From the High Land to the Low Land

GERMANY

Our trip down the Rhine River will take us from the highest country in Europe, Switzerland, to the lowest country, the Netherlands. We have seen mountainous land and fairly level land, but now we shall visit a country where some of the land is below the level of the sea.

After leaving Basel, the first stop of our river steamer is at Mainz, an important city since the days of the Romans when they built a fort here, at the junction of the Main and Rhine Rivers. Mainz is more renowned, however, as the place where printing was invented. Inasmuch as our stay here is only for an hour, we seek out the Gutenberg Museum without delay. On the site of this museum stood the shop of Johann Gutenberg who, about 1450, invented a practical method of printing from movable type with a printing press. With it, the same letters could be used over again and rearranged so that different words could be

185

One of the many medieval ruined castles along the Rhine. This picture was taken near Mainz, where the river Main flows into the Rhine River.

spelled. This made it possible to print books cheaply and rapidly. (Before the printing press was used, monks had to copy writings by hand.) Thus, books were made available to more people, and many historians consider that Gutenberg's invention had the greatest single influence in the spread of knowledge.

When we return to the steamer, Mr. Buchholz, a passenger, tells us that if we were to go up the Main River a short distance we would arrive at Frankfurt, a city of many banks and businesses, and a center of rail and air transportation. To most Americans, Frankfurt is a city of special interest. In most German cities, open-air stands sell sausages and wursts, and each city claims that their own sausages and wursts are best. But some experts who really claim to "know their sausages" state that Frankfurt makes the best in the world. In any case, it is from Frankfurt that America first got the sausage called the frankfurter.

As we continue our steamer journey down the Rhine, we see several large castles on the steep cliffs that tower high above the water. In days gone by, the princes of smaller states who lived along the banks levied toll on Rhine River

Eel fishermen on the Rhine with the legendary Lorelei Rock in the background.

traffic. They built their castles and fortresses on the cliffs and not only plundered the countryside, but completely controlled river commerce. Thus did they become known as "robber barons." In one castle near Bingen, there remains intact a dungeon into which stubborn barge captains were lowered by rope — there being no stairs — and kept prisoner until they agreed to pay the toll. The Rhine did not become toll-free until 1868.

"The most famous of all Rhine River legends is connected with that spot," says Mr. Buchholz as he points to a huge rock that projects out of the water. "It is called Lorelei Rock, because it was there that a beautiful maiden named Lorelei would sit, combing her long golden hair with a golden comb and singing delightful songs. She herself was so lovely and her voice was so sweet that sailors were fascinated and forgot to steer their boats while they looked and listened to her. As a result, their river craft were smashed to pieces on the huge rock.

"It is not hard to guess how a legend like this can get started," Mr. Buchholz goes on. "See how the river narrows suddenly and curves sharply just where the Lorelei Rock

The Eschenheimer Tower in Frankfurt is one of the original watchtowers in the old city walls which was left standing in the middle of the modern city.

187

juts out of the water? Since this is a difficult part of the Rhine to navigate, there is little doubt that many shipwrecks occurred here, which must have led to the beginning of the legend."

As our journey continues, we see many grape vineyards, birthplace of the famous Rhine wines. There are also fields of oats, rye, hops, wheat, rye, sugar beets and tobacco. Frequently, the sloping land is terraced. In addition to giving the farmer more land to use, these terraces keep the rain water from running off quickly into the river.

We are surprised at the near-absence of farmhouses as we know them in the United States. Instead of living on their farms, those who cultivate the soil live in hundreds of tiny villages clustered over the landscape. They walk to the fields in the morning and return home at night. Barns are also a rarity in Germany. Usually hogs, sheep, cows, horses and fowl are kept, with fertilizers and feed, in various rooms or parts of the farmers' homes in the villages. With the possible exception of England, this land is the most highly industrialized in Europe. However, farming methods are not very modern, because the small size of the typical German farm renders tractors and other up-to-date equipment somewhat impractical. For this reason many German farmers confine themselves to methods and equipment used by their forefathers, moving on foot and pulling heavy loads in small carts. It is not unusual to observe women — and even the children, when not in school — working in the fields beside

A vineyard near Erbach in the Rhine Valley.

Hundreds of tiny villages are clustered over the landscape.

The City Hall in Rhens is one of many late Gothic buildings on the Middle Rhine.

the men. And for reasons of economy, cows are often used in place of horses as draft or pulling animals. Even though the German farmers carefully cultivate every bit of usable land, they are still not able to produce enough food for all the people. Germany buys, or imports, some of its food from other countries, and pays for it with products made in its factories and plants.

Later, when the steamer approaches a sharp turn in the river, Mr. Buchholz points to an opening between two huge rocks. He says, "That is Dragon Cave, where Siegfried, the brave German knight of old, killed a dragon. According to the legend, Siegfried, while journeying from his home in Xanten to Worms, stopped near here to visit an old friend, King Childerich. But the old king was deeply worried. His beautiful daughter, Gunhild, had been carried away from the king's castle by a rejected lover, Duke Hunold, and was a captive in a cave guarded by a horrible dragon. King Childerich offered his throne as a reward to anyone who would release Gunhild. Thirty brave knights had already paid with their lives as a result of venturing on this dangerous undertaking. But scarcely had Siegfried heard the

Hamburg, one of Germany's major cities and a major seaport of Europe.

Girl wearing costume typical of Northern Germany.

story from his old friend than he declared himself ready to do battle with the monster. Early the next morning he set out on the fateful expedition. One stroke of the hero's famous sword, Balmug, laid the dragon dead. He released Gunhild and brought her back to the castle. Later, he captured Duke Hunold and brought him before King Childerich for punishment. Then Siegfried continued on his journey to Worms." As we look at Dragon's Cave, or Drachenloch, as the Germans call it, we can well imagine Siegfried fighting the dragon.

"There are many old Rhine legends," Mr. Buchholz says. "For instance, over there are the Seven Mountains that you may have read about in the story of 'Snow White and the Seven Dwarfs.'" He explains that it was among those mountains that Snow White hid from the wicked queen who wanted to kill her, and where the seven dwarfs rescued her. Many of the Rhineland legends owe their existence to the Grimm brothers — Jakob and Wilhelm — who collected many of these tales. They traveled through the German countryside in their time, searching out and listening

190

eagerly to the various legends and folk stories. One of their books, *Grimm's Fairy Tales,* contained such old favorites as "Rumpelstiltskin," "Hansel and Gretel," "Little Red Riding Hood," "The Frog Prince" and "Cinderella." Most of these stories were told at German firesides long before the Grimm brothers put them down on paper.

We consult the globe of the world which is in the river boat's lounge. Studying it carefully, we find that Hamburg, in northern Germany, is almost due east of Hudson Bay in Canada. Munich, in southern Germany, is at about the same latitude as Quebec. This should indicate a fairly cold climate, but the mildness which Europe in general takes from the sea, warmed by the Gulf Stream, extends also to Germany. It is seldom very hot in Germany, but it is also seldom very cold.

Germany is divided into three geographic areas that vary distinctly in general characteristics. Northern Germany, part of the Great European Plain, does not have particularly rich, or fertile, soil; its large forests alternate with fields, marshes, and small shallow lakes. Central Germany is hilly

City Hall at Munich, capital of Bavaria in southern Germany, at left, and Bavarian peasants in their national costumes.

191

and fertile, particularly in the Rhine Valley. Southern Germany is mountainous. The Bavarian Plateau, which covers most of the region, increases in elevation westward to the Schwarzwald or Black Forest mountain ranges, and stretches southward to the Bavarian Alps.

We note from our map that Germany is bordered on the north by the North Sea, Denmark and the Baltic Sea. On the west the country borders on the Netherlands, Belgium, Luxembourg and France. Switzerland and Austria are on the south, and to the east are Poland and Czechoslovakia.

Although this country was once a united nation, and although the people have a common heritage and speak the same language, there are two separate Germanys in Europe today — West Germany and East Germany. The correct name for West Germany is the Federal Republic of Germany. East Germany's correct name is the German Democratic Republic.

Our next stop is Bonn, the capital city of the Federal Republic. We learn that the Federal Republic is made up of ten states, called Lander. The people of each state elect men to represent them in the National Parliament — the Bundesrat corresponds to the Senate of the United States and the

Girls in native costume of the Black Forest region, above, and a couple from the Western Algäu, at right.

Bundestag is similar to the House of Representatives. The prime minister, or chancellor, as he is called in Germany, is elected by the parliament. We visit the new modern Parliament Building and watch the members of the Bundestag debating a proposed law.

From the Parliament Building we visit a vine-covered house at Bonngasse 10. In this little house, one of the world's most famous musical composers, Ludwig van Beethoven, was born on December 16, 1770. We are surprised to learn that some of his greatest symphonies were written when he was completely deaf. He could not himself hear the beautiful music his mind had created. After he conducted the first performance of his famous *Ninth Symphony,* the audience applauded wildly. But Beethoven did not realize how well his work was appreciated until he turned around and saw the people applauding. Later we visit the new modern Beethoven Hall, one of the best concert halls in Europe. The German people take a serious interest in music and, in addition to Beethoven, have developed some of the greatest composers the world has ever known — Bach, Mendelssohn, Brahms, Wagner, Schuman, Weber, and Handel.

North of Bonn the Rhine Valley widens out and the hills

Market day in front of the City Hall in Bonn, capital of West Germany.

Berlin, the divided city and former capital of Germany before World War II. The war-scarred Brandenburg Gate is now a border checkpoint for traffic. A sign reads: "Attention! You are now leaving West Berlin." On the other side is Communist-dominated East Berlin.

193

gradually disappear. Soon the cities are much closer together. A short time after our vessel leaves Bonn, the towers of the Cologne Cathedral, one of the most beautiful churches in the world, appear on the horizon. This famous structure was begun in the year 1248 — and it was not completely finished until 1880. Located almost on the river bank, its twin 515-feet spires tower over the low buildings of the city. During World War II, about nine-tenths of Cologne was destroyed by bombing raids, including almost all of the old medieval buildings. But almost as if by a miracle, the cathedral escaped with only minor damage.

Mr. Buchholz, our fellow-passenger aboard the steamer, tells us that Cologne originally belonged to the Ubii, a Teutonic tribe. In A.D. 50, it became a Roman colony. Its original name was Colonia Agrippina — Colonia for colony, and Agrippina after the wife of the Roman emperor, Claudius. Later, the name was shortened to Colonia, eventually modernized to Köln, and Anglicized to Cologne. During the thirteenth to sixteenth centuries it became one of the major trade centers in western Europe. Today, Cologne is Germany's third biggest city, a center of trade and industry for the lower Rhine Valley. There are many items manufactured in Cologne. Perhaps its best known product is the toilet water called "eau de Cologne."

Our boat does not stop at Cologne, but later it puts in at Düsseldorf, the chief city of the Rhine-Ruhr Valley industrial area. Though it bustles with industry, it is in no sense an ugly manufacturing city. It is also the home of large banking firms and the head offices of large industrial corporations. Düsseldorf, because of its Academy of Painting, has been for a long time one of the important centers of art in Germany. At Düsseldorf we say "Auf wiedersehen und danke" ("Good-by and thank you") to Mr. Buchholz.

Under way again, we notice that a group of young vacationers have come aboard our river steamer with their bicycles. They are going to the Netherlands with us. The

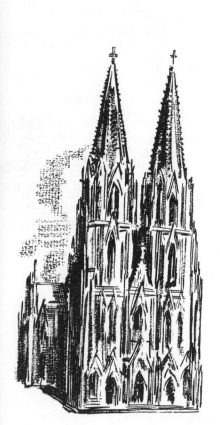

The cathedral of Cologne.

194

A typical sight in the Rhine-Ruhr Valley.

ship's steward tells us that the most popular means of transportation in the Netherlands is the bicycle. It is both easy and pleasant to bicycle through this flat land. For this reason cyclists from all parts of Europe come to the Netherlands. The vacationers invite us to join their group, if we can rent bicycles in Rotterdam.

After leaving Düsseldorf, the smoking chimneys of factories and towers of oil refineries seem to increase in number. There are also more working boats on the river — barges loaded with iron ore, coal, coke, timber and other raw materials for the great factories of the Rhine-Ruhr Valley. This region is Germany's most important industrial area, as well as being one of the greatest in Europe. Because of the huge deposits of high-quality coal in the Valley, it is the center of Germany's steel industry. The iron ore is imported from nearby France and Luxembourg, as well as from Spain and Sweden. In addition, the coal supplies power to run machines. Mills and factories in this area produce iron and steel products, textiles, fertilizers, dyes, medicines and chemicals. Passing where the Ruhr River meets the Rhine, we see the city of Duisburg, the largest river port in Europe.

195

THE NETHERLANDS

Northwestern European country, popularly known as Holland. **Area** • 13,025 sq. m. **Population** • 11,967,000. **Language** • Dutch. **Government** • Constitutional monarchy. **Monetary Unit** • Guilder (= 0.27½ U.S. $). **Chief Cities** • Amsterdam (capital), Rotterdam, The Hague (official seat of government). **Religion** • about evenly divided between Protestant (mostly Dutch Reformed) and Roman Catholic. **Mountains** • none, average height of the land is only 37 feet above sea level; almost 40% of the land surface has been reclaimed from the sea and is protected by a system of dikes. **Rivers** • almost 5,000 miles of rivers and man-made canals; the Rhine and the Meuse are the major rivers.

The Netherlands is "windmill country."

Continuing down the Rhine, our river steamer leaves Germany and enters the Netherlands, frequently called "Holland." But it should be remembered that there are eleven provinces in the Netherlands, which are like individual states in the United States. Two of the most important provinces are North Holland and South Holland. Thus, when the whole country is referred to as "Holland," it is the same as speaking of the entire United States as "Texas" or "Illinois." The Netherlands is only about one-third the size of the state of New York. Incidentally, it was the Dutch people from the Netherlands who first settled New York City in 1624.

Somewhat to our surprise, we learn that most of the young people in the party of cyclists speak English. The majority of the group are Germans, but there are several young Dutch people who were in Germany visiting friends and relations. One of the girls, whose name is Grietje van Helden, speaks English very well. She offers to be our guide and interpreter while in the Netherlands.

Sailing farther downstream, we ask Grietje to tell us something about her homeland — perhaps, as a start, about the fields we are passing. She replies, "Those fields are below sea level, as is about one-fourth of my country. Just remember that Holland means 'hollow land,' while the Netherlands means 'low lands.' Both names describe my country well."

To keep sea water from flooding the countryside, a system of dikes has been constructed. A dike is a high bank of earth, concrete, rocks, or sand — in effect, a low, long dam which holds the water back. In the United States, dikes are called "levees," and they are used to keep rivers from overflowing their banks.

Cruising along, we are charmed by the picturesque windmills. To the Dutch they are also vitally important sources of power for water pumps used in the centuries-old battle against the sea. The provinces of Holland were once a marshy region separated from the North Sea by a chain of

Bicycles are an important means of transportation in Holland. Bicycle paths run alongside most highways.

sand dunes and crisscrossed by large rivers. A few inhabitants lived on the sand dunes and in the eastern, hillier part of the country. The rest of the land was in constant danger of being flooded and ruined.

The determined Dutch first built dikes during the tenth century to guard against these floods. Windmill-driven pumps controlled water levels. Even today many of the country's windmills are still performing that job, as well as grinding wheat. Now modern pumping stations powered by steam or electricity are rapidly taking over the work previously done by the old windmills. However, Grietje assures us that the windmills will be saved so that tourists like us can continue to admire them. In several provinces it is against the law to destroy these ancient machines and many are being commemorated as national monuments.

Grietje says, "Maybe some of you have heard the story of Jan and the dike." For those who answered no, the story she tells us goes something like this: One day, a young boy by the name of Jan was walking along a road which was next to a very important dike. Suddenly he noticed a trickle of water coming out of the dike. As he watched, the little hole seemed to be getting bigger. Jan knew that this slight opening could widen until the water would break through the dike, flood the countryside and eventually destroy many homes. Jan shouted for help, but since no houses were near, no help came. The hole was getting bigger all the time. There was nothing nearby to stop up the hole. Thinking for a minute, Jan then thrust his arm into the hole as far as it would go. Hours went by, and Jan kept his arm in the hole, hoping someone would come by. He was about to give up in exhaustion when he heard voices and saw lights. His mother had sent out a search party for him. Some of the men relieved him of his brave job. Others soon repaired the dike. Jan had saved the lives of many people.

"Whether this story is true or just a legend," Grietje continues with a glow of pride, "it shows the determination we all have in fighting against the danger of flooding."

198

The Dutch have done more than protect their lands from floods. They are reclaiming land that once lay under the sea. After building a series of dikes, the salt water of the ocean is pumped out. Fresh water from the canals is then permitted to cleanse the land. This washing operation continues until all the salt has been removed from the soil. The water itself is finally pumped out and the land can then be used as pastures or for agriculture. This property reclaimed from the sea, and protected by dikes, is called "polder" land by the Dutch.

One large polder project was the creation of farmland in draining the IJsselmeer, formerly called the Zuider Zee, once a shallow inlet of the North Sea. The Dutch built a twenty-mile dam, called the Grand Dike, across the seaward neck of the Zee to form Lake IJssel — the largest artificial lake in the country. This Zee project alone increased the country's agricultural land by about 10 per cent. Grietje jokingly says, "God created heaven and earth — however, we Dutch created the Netherlands."

The royal cortege at the opening of a session of Parliament in the Hague.

Finally, we reach Rotterdam, largest port in Europe, and second largest in the world, after New York City. One side of Rotterdam is connected to the North Sea by the fifteen-mile New Waterway Channel, and on the other side by means of the Rhine and Meuse Rivers.

After making arrangements to meet our cyclist friends in the morning, we take a taxi to our hotel. We notice immediately that Rotterdam is a new city. The old one, with its houses and buildings that dated back to the fifteenth and sixteenth century, was almost completely destroyed by Nazi bombs during World War II. Large areas have been rebuilt and the new buildings are modern in design. There is one place that was not destroyed by the bombing which we wish to visit. This is Delftshaven, which is now part of Rotterdam's harbor. It was from Delftshaven that the English Pilgrim settlers of Massachusetts who had first gone to the lowlands in pursuit of religious freedom, set sail for what was to be the historic *Mayflower* voyage in 1620.

In the morning we rent bicycles and join our friends just outside the city limits of Rotterdam. Then we all head north to the Hague. We ride along special bicycle paths that have been built beside the highway. This makes cycling a great deal safer. It is easy to ride a bicycle in this part of the Netherlands because there are no hills. However, in the Limburg region, there are some hills that rise as high as 300 feet.

After several rest periods, we reach The Hague, or Den Haag, as the Dutch call the city. So far on our trip, the capital of the country has also been the seat, or headquarters, of the national government. In the Netherlands, however, Amsterdam is the capital, while The Hague is the seat of government. We learn that the Netherlands is a "constitutional monarchy." This means it has a king or queen who inherits the crown from generation to generation. But this country also has a constitution that puts certain limits on the ruler's power. The Parliament, or States-General as it is called, makes the laws and runs the government. The

200

Parliament is elected by the people, and should any eligible Dutch citizen fail to vote (all those over the age of 23 may vote), that person is subject to a fine. The people vote secretly in a closed booth.

The Hague was originally a forest where Count Willem II built a hunting lodge in 1248. Thus the city can pride itself on having a history of over seven centuries. In the heart of the town is the medieval Inner Court, around which the principal government buildings are located. The most beautiful building in this Inner Court is the Hall of Knights, or Ridderzaal. This structure was built around 1280 and was intended as a banquet hall for the knights. Today the Ridderzaal is the scene every year of the colorful and impressive opening of the combined Chambers of the States-General by the Queen. Grietje gleefully reminds us that since 1890, queens only have ruled the Netherlands, inasmuch as no sons were born to the royal family during those years.

The Royal palace is only a short walk from the Inner Court of the government buildings. Since it is not open to the public, however, only a glimpse of it may be seen from the nearby gardens. Grietje tells us that the royal family has another palace in Amsterdam. Later, we go to the Peace Palace, a beautiful building in which representatives from the United Nations meet to settle disputes among nations. The American millionaire, Andrew Carnegie, donated money to construct this building. The beautiful decorations were gifts of many nations. Among the things seen are rare woods from Brazil, vases from China, silver from Spain, and carpets from Turkey.

Before leaving The Hague, we decide to go to Madurodam, a miniature city where the towers reach no higher than our eye-level. This "baby" city is built so that everything in it is one twenty-fifth of life size. But everything within it is unbelievably real and shows a typical Dutch city in action. We hardly know what deserves our admiration most in the Madurodam: the choral-singing church; the small Amster-

Air view of the Peace Palace in The Hague.

201

Children in the town of Staphorst wear the same type of dress and wooden shoes ("klompen") as those worn for hundreds of years in this district.

dam street organ; Queen's Golden Coach; the busy ships, trains and jet airplanes; or the tiny illuminated news-screen flashing the latest headlines from the outside life-sized world. At night the lights of this miniature town go on one by one.

Madurodam was named for George Maduro, a Dutch patriot executed by the Germans during World War II. It was constructed in honor of all Dutch heroes who gave their lives in that savage war. As we are about to leave Madurodam, a group of blind children arrive. Soon, in this miniature city, their all-seeing hands may trace out the shapes of roofs, towers, docks and cars. It is in this way that many find out for the first time the reality of a canal, bridge, railway station, windmill or castle.

Continuing northward, many fine black-and-white cows are observed feeding on the thick grass which grows on the polder. The Netherlands is a dairy country and produces butter, cheese, condensed milk and chocolate products, all of which need milk to make. Many of these products are exported to other countries. Farmers in other parts of the Netherlands raise rye, oats, wheat, potatoes, sugar beets, berries, fruits and vegetables. Because of the Gulf Stream, the climate here is quite excellent for dairy farming.

While out in the polder tending the cows, we notice that many of the Dutch farmers wear wooden shoes. These shoes, often called *klompen,* serve a very good purpose in a country of heavy rains, muddy roads and soggy polder. Under such conditions back home, we would put on our rubbers or boots; but these cost more than wooden shoes in the Netherlands. Of course, the farmers do not enter their houses in their muddy shoes. They leave them on the stoop by the front door, and go inside in their stockings. When the entire family is at home — as, for example, at mealtimes — the size of the family may be determined by the pairs of *klompen* on the stoop. However, people living in cities and towns wear the same type of shoes as we do, and so do the farmers when their fields are not wet.

202

In the wintertime, the cows are kept in a barn next to the farmhouse. Some farmers in this country have built their homes so that one side is for family use and the other side is used as a barn. As with everything else in the Netherlands, these barns are scrupulously clean. To point out the cleanliness of the Dutch, Grietje informs us that the coal mines in the Limburg region are kept spotlessly clean — some of them are even painted white.

Several hours later, our cycling group stops at a farm that has a sign in front of it which reads: YOUTH HOSTEL. "All our friends are members of the Youth Hostel Association," Grietje tells us. A hostel is a place where food and overnight lodging is available at low cost. The Association encourages inexpensive travel as a means of exercise and recreation. Members may bicycle, ride horseback, canoe, or hike from one hostel to another, but automobile travel is not permitted. The Association uses the word "Youth" in its title, but there are many adult members.

Even though we are not members of the Association, Mr. deGroot, owner of the farm, invites us to stay with the group. Mr. and Mrs. deGroot are called hostel parents. It is their duty to supervise members of the Association who stay at their farm.

After we eat, Grietje explains more about the Youth Hostel Association. "Youth hostels," she says, "were first started in Germany by a schoolteacher in 1910. The founder's idea was to encourage people to spend more of their time outdoors. His plan became so popular that it spread to most of the countries in Europe, and to the British Isles. Today, hostels are found in most parts of the United States, Canada and South America, as well as in Europe."

Grietje is glad to know that we intend to join the Youth Hostel Association when we return to our own country. Before going to sleep, we talk about the countries already visited, about school, and many other things. But since we are all tired from our long bicycling trip, everyone is happy to go to bed early.

The next morning the bike trip continues north toward Haarlem, the City of Flowers. Soon we pass through fields of hyacinths, narcissuses, jonquils, lilies and tulips. The sandy polder soil in this region has been turned into a living carpet of flowers. The tulip is generally regarded as the symbol of the Netherlands, but this flower, which originated in Persia, was first brought here several centuries ago. They all grow from bulbs. These bulbs are exported to all parts of the world.

The nearby city of Aalsmeer is one of the leading centers in the world for cut flowers and flowering plants. Before dawn, the year around, flowers and plants from Netherlands hothouses and fields are rushed by trucks from Aalsmeer to Schiphol, the country's large airport, loaded into airplanes and flown to other countries. In the United States many beautiful flowers seen in florists' shops could have come from here just the day before.

One of the things most appreciated about our tour of the world is the chance to eat different types of food and cooking. Every country visited has some food specialty. Now we have an opportunity to eat some of the world-famous Dutch cheeses. The city of Alkmaar, the great cheese center

This is one of many canals in Amsterdam.

of the Netherlands, is our next stop. Looking about the market place, we see thousands of golden-yellow balls of cheese. Porters carry the cheese on stretchers from the farmer's wagons or barges to the weigh house. After it is weighed, the cheese is brought to the market place. When the cheese is sold, porters load it aboard other barges and it is taken to warehouses. From there, it will be shipped to places all over the world.

The second night's hostel stop is near the old fishing village of Volendam. After eating and making arrangements for sleeping, we ride into the village and discover that the people here dress in the costumes seen in picture books. That is, the women of Volendam wear pretty lace bonnets, or attractive pointed caps. Their dresses are of many beautiful colors and their skirts are very full. An apron, a necklace of bright coral and wooden shoes complete their costume. Young girls dress in the same fashion.

Volendam girl.

While the men's costume is not quite so colorful, it is very quaint and interesting. Men wear baggy trousers, held up by wide belts, often also with big silver buttons. Outside of their loose-fitting blouses, they wear double-breasted coats, which frequently are red-striped. Round lambskin caps, woolen socks and wooden shoes complete their apparel. Boys dress very much like the men of the village, who are often seen along the waterfront, squatting on their haunches, smoking their long pipes or chewing tobacco.

Riding toward Amsterdam, we notice that there is a great network of rivers and canals in the Netherlands. Virtually every town can be reached by water. Passenger boats take people from one place to another. Nearly half of the Netherlands' freight is moved across the country by water routes. The rest is carried by trucks and railways. The canals serve still another purpose. In winter, ice-skating becomes the favorite pastime, as well as a means of transportation. Children skate to and from school, while entire Dutch families skim over the frozen canals to church or market.

Reaching Amsterdam, we say good-by to our new friends and promise to write them about the rest of our trip around the world. The Netherlands' largest city reminds us of Venice, because canals divide the city into many islands connected by bridges. Amsterdam has no fewer than fifty canals and about four hundred bridges, so it can be readily understood why the city is best viewed by boat.

Our boat ties up alongside a diamond-cutting factory. Here we observe how rough diamonds, which are dug from mines in Africa, are cut and polished so that these valuable stones can sparkle beautifully. Machines may be utilized to do some of the polishing, but most of the work in the diamond-cutting factory is done by hand. The cutting operation must be done very carefully, since one mistake could cost thousands of dollars.

As a "water-taxi" takes us through the old part of the city, we notice that the narrow brick houses with their red tile roofs are only a couple of stories high. In the newer sections, the modern apartments and office buildings are seldom more than four or five stories. There are no skyscrapers, due to the simple fact that the ground is too soft to support tall buildings. Most buildings in Amsterdam, as well as many other Dutch cities, must rest on wooden piles. Our guide tells us that the Royal Palace, now in view, is built on 13,659 wooden piles to prevent it from sinking into the sandy mud.

Our cruise of the city continues by several old churches that date back to the fifteenth century, and then to the Cryers' Tower. What accounts for the tower's name? Tradition says that, as early as the sixteenth century, sailors' wives came to this tower to cry and wave a farewell to their husbands when they left for other parts of the world. This was also the point of departure of Henry Hudson's voyage for New Amsterdam, now New York City. He left from here in his ship, the *Half Moon,* on April 4, 1609. Later, we visit Amsterdam's famous art museum, the Rijksmuseum, and

206

This air view of the center of Amsterdam shows the typical architecture of Dutch houses.

see paintings by such great Dutch artists as Rembrandt, Vermeer, Van Gogh, Jan Steen, and Frans Hals.

Amsterdam is about eighteen miles from the North Sea and is connected with it by the North Sea Canal. Tomorrow we shall board a passenger ship that will take us through the canal and then on to Scandinavia.

NORWAY

Narrow, mountainous strip on the Western Scandinavian peninsula. **Area** • 125,182 sq. m. **Population** • 3,667,000. **Language** • Norwegian. **Government** • Constitutional monarchy. **Monetary Unit** • Krone (= 0.14 U.S. $). **Chief Cities** • Oslo (capital), Bergen, Trondheim — all seaports. **Religion** • Protestant (the Lutheran Church is the official church). **Mountains** • Mt. Galdhöpiggen (8,097 ft.) and Mt. Glittertind (8,048 ft.) are the highest. **Rivers** • Norway's coastline is cut by many fiords; the Glåma is the longest and most important river. **Lakes** • Mjösa, Femund.

Picturesque Norway at its best: Geirangerfiord, with a farmyard, foreground, and Mount Saathorn, 5835 feet high, in the distance.

CHAPTER 10

On To Scandinavia

NORWAY

Leaving the Netherlands, our travel takes us to a region that at one time was thought to be an island. The early Romans used the word "Scandia" to refer to a large "island" believed to be north of the Baltic Sea. However, Scandinavia today is generally considered to be the combined countries of Norway, Sweden and Denmark. In some instances, Finland and Iceland are also understood to belong to the family of Scandinavian nations.

A long time ago the people of Norway, Sweden and Denmark were considered Northmen or Vikings. Although these three Scandinavian countries are closely linked by common boundaries, they are not now a political unit. They were united as states, under one crown, in 1397 by Denmark's Queen Margaret. This union lasted until 1523 when Sweden became an independent country again. Norway and Denmark remained united until 1814 when Norway became a part of Sweden, a tie which lasted until 1905.

209

The customs of the Scandinavian countries are similar, but the languages of Norway, Sweden and Denmark are different enough so that books must be translated from one language to another. Yet, while the languages are distinct and separate, they are still so much alike that a person from one of these countries can usually understand his friends from the others. English is a language taught to all children in elementary or grade school.

The first Scandinavian country visited by us is Norway. It, along with Sweden, makes up the Scandinavian peninsula. Norway, with an area about the same as that of the state of New Mexico, is long and narrow, wider at each end than it is in the center. At one place in Norway, it is only four miles from the sea to the eastern border. Also, we observe that nearly one-third of this mountainous country lies north of the Arctic Circle. The northernmost point, near Nordkapp (North Cape) lies as far north as Point Barrow, Alaska. Lindesnes, at the southern end, is on about the same latitude as Juneau. Nordkapp to Lindesnes is almost half the distance between Washington, D. C. and San Francisco.

Norway is the northernmost country in Europe, but it is not so cold as its northern situation suggests. The warm currents of the Gulf Stream raise the temperature considerably above the average for the latitude. We are told, for instance, that the coast climate is fairly temperate, and rarely is a harbor blocked by ice, even in the far north. Inland, conditions in winter are very much more severe. Mountain roads are blocked by snow and the lakes freeze. The summer is generally warm everywhere, with temperatures occasionally as high as anywhere in Western Europe. For farming, fishing, shipping, the favorable climate is most important to a country so far north. It enables Norwegians to live and work, even in the northern parts of their country.

Looking at the Norwegian coastline, we notice that it is broken by many narrow, twisting bays or channels called "fiords." With steep hills or cliffs on each side, these fiords

Bride and groom from Hornindal in the costume of the region.

Oslo, the capital of Norway, a major European year-round port, is a modern city in design and architecture.

This is one of the many Spitsbergen Islands, or Svalbard, as the archipelago is called in Norwegian. All of the islands are in the Arctic Ocean, but few of them have a permanent ice cap, as the Gulf Stream provides sufficient warmth.

are really deep, steep-sided valleys made by rivers and glaciers many centuries ago. The ice melted and ocean water covered the bottom of the valley. The water in most fiords is so deep that large ships can sail into them.

In studying the map even more carefully, it is noted that a great many islands exist along the coast of Norway. Even so, not all of the islands along the shoreline of this country could be shown on the map, because there are some 150,000 of them. On some of the islands there are farms and villages, while others are just great barren rocks. The coastline is jagged and indented by many fiords. Because of the zigzagging shores, it is calculated that if the country's coastline were stretched out, that line would be long enough to extend about one-fourth of the way around the earth.

We sight the Norwegian coast, and our ship sails up the broad approach to Oslo Fiord, passing little villages and towns of gay wooden houses. Then the waterway narrows until it is only a few hundred yards across, with steep cliffs on each side. Here the fortress of Oscarsborg keeps guard over Oslo with its heavy guns. Finally, the fiord broadens out again between hills and the beautiful harbor of Oslo is before us.

Preparing to leave our steamer ship, we look about the harbor of Norway's chief seaport and notice that vessels of all kinds are anchored in the harbor or tied up at the docks. Our steward points to some white ships off to our right and says that they are whaling vessels that go to the Antarctic each fall. The biggest ship among them, he tells us, is a whaling "factory-ship." Its outward appearance is similar to a large freighter, but it does not do the actual hunting of the whales. It employs the smaller vessels we see about it to do the harpooning and the killing. Once a whale is dead, it is inflated with compressed air and towed back to the factory ship, where it is hauled on deck through a giant opening in the stern (back) of the vessel. The whale is then cut up, the meat refrigerated and the blubber, or fat, rendered into oil. Norway produces more whale oil than any other country in the world. This oil is used for making soap, medicine, margarine, and lubricants for fine machinery.

Oslo forms a half-circle around the harbor. With its white houses, red-tiled roofs, and forested hills in the background, Norway's capital and largest city has a very pleasing setting. It is not necessary for us to summon a taxi inasmuch as our hotel, as well as most of the important buildings, is near the docks. The Oslo City Hall is also right across the street from one of the main wharves.

The outside of the City Hall seems rather uninteresting. However, once we enter the courtyard, it is quite different. Here is found a vast hall with a black and gray marble floor and enormously high walls. There are huge paintings, or murals, in bright colors that depict scenes from Norwegian history and the everyday life of the people. Fishing, timber-felling, sawmills, trading, farming, shipbuilding, exploration — a panoramic story of Norway from its earliest time is displayed on these walls.

After leaving City Hall, we stroll along Karl Johans Gate,

A whaling station in one of the Norwegian fiords.

The "Gokstad boat," one of the early Viking longboats, as it was found, the place where it was found, and a reconstruction of it.

Oslo's main street. Along this tree-lined avenue are many of the city's important buildings. The National Theater, the University, the Oslo Cathedral, and the Stortinget, or Parliament Building, all can be found on this street. Norway has a constitutional monarchy with a king, but the people elect a *Storting,* or Parliament, to make the laws. The street ends in front of the Royal Palace.

While walking through the beautiful Royal Gardens, we catch sight of a slim towering structure to the west. The garden guard informs us that the structure is the Holmenkollen Ski Jump, where Norway's most important winter sports events take place. He tells us that people have traveled on skis in Norway for over two thousand years, but only in the last one hundred years has it become a popular sport. Norwegian skiers generally rank very high in international sports contests.

From the Royal Gardens, our journey continues by bus to Bygdoy, a suburb of Oslo. At Bygdoy are found ships that made Norwegian history. First we see three Viking longships. These ships, low and long with curving bow (front) and stern (back), were built to weather the roughest seas. One of the vessels, called the Oseberg ship, is about seventy feet in length, built of oak wood throughout. It has places

The harbor of Hammerfest, northernmost city in Europe, in Finmark County, North Norway. It is the home port of Arctic sealing and whaling fleets.

for thirty-two oars, sixteen on a side, and wooden shields along the sides of the vessel protected the oarsmen against wind and water spray.

Our guide explains, "The longship carried a single sail much wider at the foot than at the top, and it was decorated in brilliant colors or embroidered in gold." He also tells us that the figurehead at the bow was that of a fierce dragon which the Vikings believed would frighten enemies and sea serpents. The dragon head was detachable and it was forbidden by Viking law to exhibit it when a ship neared the shores of home (to avoid scaring their own people). At night, the crew spread a tent over the deck and slept in leather bags. Since they could not cook at sea, they ate dried meat, dried bread, nuts, and meal mixed with fat. They washed the food down with water.

These three ships indicate that the Northmen were fearless and hardy sailors. History tells us that they made many raids on Britain, and even sailed into the Mediterranean Sea in similar ships. One Northman, Leif Ericson, while on his way to raid Greenland in the tenth century, was blown off course by easterly winds and carried across the Atlantic to some spot on the American coast, possibly in the Canadian province today called Nova Scotia. He stayed there for a whole winter to repair his ship and to gather food before making the trip back across the ocean. Other Vikings in their quest for adventure, trade and wealth may have even sailed as far south in the Western Hemisphere as the land that is now the United States.

Milking goats in the Norwegian mountains. The goat is an important animal in the roster of Norwegian livestock.

In another part of the museum, our interest is caught by the polar exploration ship, the *Fram*. This vessel traveled farther north and south than any other surface vessel in the world. "I must say surface vessel," explains our guide, "because the United States submarines *Nautilus* and *Skate* both went directly under the North Pole in 1958. But we Norwegians are proud of the *Fram,* and of Fridtjof Nansen and Roald Amundsen who sailed it.

"In the summer of 1893, Nansen and a brave crew of thirteen men left Oslo aboard the *Fram* for the North Pole," he continues. "When the *Fram* became frozen into an ice floe, Nansen and one companion decided to explore farther north on skis, and with dog sleds carrying kayaks." A kayak is a kind of canoe made by stretching sealskins over a wooden frame with a pointed bow and stern. It seems that while the two men never quite reached the North Pole, Nansen, his entire crew, and the *Fram* returned to Norway in 1896. Admiral Peary, an American, in 1909 became the first man to reach the North Pole, but Roald Amundsen was the first to reach the South Pole in 1911. The *Fram* was used by Amundsen on his expedition.

In another building in the museum, our attention is drawn to the famous balsawood raft, *Kon-Tiki,* on which Thor Heyerdahl and his crew of five made their daring 5,000-mile trip from South America to the Polynesian Islands of

The face of this grand old man of Finmark mirrors his constant association with the elements.

215

the South Pacific in 1947. The expedition was undertaken to prove that it was practically possible for the prehistoric civilized people of South America to settle Polynesia, a theory which had been denied as impracticable by some scientists. Inspecting the raft, we look at odd bits of rope that were used to tie the logs together, stare into the shack the men used for sleeping quarters while drifting along, and see the poles used for warding off the sharks that came near from time to time.

Early the next morning, we leave Oslo by means of a motorcoach. On the outskirts of the city, there are mills and factories that produce ships, lumber, paper, wood pulp, matches and woolen goods. While there is very little coal or oil in Norway, water power is abundant, and this source is used to make electricity for lighting homes, and for heating and cooking, as well as for turning the wheels of transportation and industry.

After leaving Oslo and its suburbs, the road passes through a country of rolling hills and well-tilled fields. The big barns for grain and the many cattle in the fields indicate that this is a good dairying and cattle raising country. The principal farming crops are hay, wheat, oats, barley, rye, corn and potatoes. Most of the farms are small, under twenty-five acres, since relatively little land can be cultivated in Norway. Only five per cent, or one-twentieth of the land, is suitable for agriculture.

The farmer was probably born on his own farm, as were his father and grandfather before him. Most of the farms have many buildings. Near the farmer's house there are barns for the cows and horses, henhouses for the chickens, sheds for the tools and wagons, and storehouses for grain and hay. The farmer's house, itself, is usually two-story and is built of wood with a stone foundation. The lower part serves as a fairly cool cellar to keep butter, milk and cheese, and the family lives upstairs. The home is built tightly to keep out the cold winter winds, but the roof looks rather

Skiing in Norway is not merely a sport, but a means of transportation.

216

strange. Many of the roofs of the houses, as well as the other farm buildings, are often covered with sod — containing grass or roots of grass — to help keep water out. It seems odd to see grass growing on the roof of a house.

Near the house are big stacks of wood which are generally used to heat the farmhouses. Most homes in Norway have electricity, but tractors and modern farm machinery are used with difficulty because the Norwegian valleys are so steep.

Journeying west, our bus seems to have trouble climbing some of the hills. These hills soon change into mountains, sometimes partly bare and then covered with trees. There seem to be few people living in this area, but the scenery is beautiful. Our driver points out that according to an old Norwegian legend this is the land of the trolls. The trolls are misshapen and stunted creatures who especially like to carry off pretty young girls to their homes beneath the mountain.

"You may catch sight of one peering out of the mountain side," the bus driver says. "According to the folk tale, the troll tries to hide. His wild hair and beard are only dead grass, his crooked nose is a knob of rock, and his twisted mouth an irregular crack in the rock surface. But we need not worry! In daylight a troll is powerless. He is only dangerous after dark, and by then, our bus will be in Bergen."

Bergen, Norway's second largest city in size and importance, is built around a fiord. Looking out of a window from our hotel room, we see the city backed by seven high mountains which rise almost from the water's edge. We decide to take a cable car to the top of one of the mountains. From here, the whole city of Bergen spreads out before us like a map. In the center, the buildings are fairly modern and the streets are wide. In the old part of the city, however, narrow cobblestone streets and old wooden buildings are common. There are also many houses that seem to cling tightly to the slopes of the mountains.

Lapps in wedding "peski" — a jacket made of white reindeer fur.

Looking out toward the harbor, we see hundreds of fishing boats. Norwegian fishermen catch more fish each year than the fishermen of any other European country and Bergen is the most important fishing center in Norway. As we continue to look about, it starts to rain. Running back to the cable car, we recall hearing while on the bus that Bergen is the rainiest city in all Europe. Once on board, the conductor jokingly tells us, "It rains 360 days a year here in Bergen, and the other five days are cloudy."

Early the next morning an airplane takes us high along Norway's rugged coastline to Arctic adventures. During the flight, the airplane's loudspeaker announces, "This is your captain, Knut Bergheim, and I wish to inform you that we are passing over the Arctic Circle." The stewardess gives us a certificate to that effect.

A car takes us from Barudfoss Airport to Tromso, the so-called "capital of the Arctic." Some of this land north of the Arctic Circle is rich with iron ore. Most of the desolate land up here is the home of the Lapps. Lapland, or the land of the Lapps, has no fixed boundaries. These people wander across the northern regions of Norway, Sweden, Finland and Russia.

This was certainly news to us. Many of us had heard about the Lapps — distant relatives of the Eskimos — but somehow it did not occur to us that the Lapps today were living their ancient way of life. A large proportion of the Lapps are still nomadic, following their herds of tame reindeer on annual migrations to the higher plateaus. Some of the herds number thousands of animals and represent considerable wealth to their owners.

Reindeer meat is the chief item of the Lapp's diet. It is supplemented by a rich cheese made from the deer's milk. The Lapps live in tents and wear clothes made of reindeer skin. When they want to go someplace in a hurry, they hitch a sled to a reindeer. In short, reindeer provide the Lapps with food, clothing, shelter and transportation.

218

The Lapps are generally not over five feet tall. They wear colorful costumes in which blue, red, and yellow predominate, a riot of colors as exotic as the midnight sun itself. Actually, one of the wonders of our journey beyond the Arctic Circle is the magic of the midnight sun, shining for seven summer weeks. This fascinates us greatly. It is the same old sun, but it is just that it happens to be shining at midnight. Influenced by this trick of nature, even the birds stay awake. We are tempted to follow their example. Daylight around the clock somehow makes us feel extra happy; sleep does not seem necessary, or very little is needed. The sun approaches the horizon, then quickly rises again. Sunset merges into sunrise, and the land north of the Circle is lighted at all times with sunlight.

In the winter, however, the sun does not rise up here at all. The communities in this region then use electric light both day and night. The people who live in Tromso the year around find it hard to stay awake during the dark winter days. And similarly, it is hard to go to sleep during the bright summer nights.

SWEDEN

The largest of the Scandinavian countries. **Area** • 173,423 sq. m. **Population** • 7,604,000. **Language** • Swedish. **Government** • Parliamentary democracy, with the King serving as head of state. **Monetary Unit** • Krona (= 0.19 U.S. $). **Chief Cities** • Stockholm (capital), Goteborg, Malmo. **Religion** • Lutheran Protestant (state church). **Mountains** • highest is Kebnekaise in Lapland (6,965 ft.). **Rivers** • Göta. **Lakes** • Vänern, Vättern, and Hjälmaren are the largest of Sweden's many lakes.

View of Sweden's capital, Stockholm, "the City on the Water."

The airplane that is taking us to Stockholm, Sweden, stops at the city of Kiruna. This city is reported to have the largest area of any city in the world — two large hills are within its limits. In Kiruna, too, is found one of the world's richest iron ore deposits. Visitors are allowed to descend below the ground surface to watch the mining operation in progress, and may also see the ore being refined in the steel mill at Lulea to the south. Like Norway, Sweden cannot be considered a major steel producing nation. Swedish steel, however, is used for special tasks in many tools and devices such as rock drills and springs for watches. Unfortunately, our plane is stopping only to pick up other passengers, and we cannot visit Kiruna and Lulea.

Flying over northern and central Sweden, it is immediately realized that the giant forests below us must be most important to the people of this country. But it was not until about a century ago that Sweden began to use the lumber from their huge forests. Large quantities of timber were sold to the countries of western Europe whose forests had been cut long before. These countries now look primarily to the forest land of Sweden and Norway to provide the lumber they need to build factories and houses. Lumber and wood products are therefore Sweden's leading export. They account for about one-third of the country's total income from exports.

Our stewardess tells us that the trees are generally cut during the winter months. Then the logs can be easily dragged down to the frozen rivers by sleds drawn by tractors or horses. The logs are piled up on the river ice. When spring comes and the ice melts, the rushing waters carry the logs to the mouths of the rivers. In mills and factories at the river's mouth, the logs are turned into lumber, furniture, skis, matches, wood pulp and other wood products. As with the swiftly rushing rivers of Norway, the Swedish ones are used to produce electric power for the mills, factories and homes.

Before landing at Stockholm's Arlanda Airport, we look at a map of Sweden. In both shape and size, Sweden resembles California. It is one of the largest countries of Europe, yet its population is less than that of New York City.

While most of its land is hills and highlands, Sweden is not a mountainous country like Norway. Actually, the Kjölen Mountains that run north and south along the border dividing the two Scandinavian peninsula countries are Sweden's only major mountain range. From these heights the land gradually slopes eastward to the Gulf of Bothnia and the Baltic Sea. A good portion of the southern part of the country is composed of lowlands. While it lies in approximately the same latitudes as neighboring Norway, Sweden's winters are a great deal more severe. This is due to the fact that it does not benefit as much from the warming influence of the Gulf Stream. Snow lies on the ground many months in the winter. Ice blocks the Gulf of Bothnia harbors for about two months in the south and six months in the north.

As our airplane approaches Stockholm, we can see why the Swedish capital is often called "the City on the Water," or "the Venice of the North." It is almost entirely surrounded by water. Built on a string of islands where Lake Malaren joins the Baltic Sea, Sweden's largest city is more than seven hundred years old. Bridges have been built between islands and to the mainland, and people go to and fro in automobiles, on bicycles, in buses, on foot and in trolley cars, never pausing to think about a time, early in the city's history, when the only way to get from one place to another was by boat.

One of the first things we want to see in Stockholm, after checking into the hotel, is the Royal Palace. It is located on the island where Birger Jarl, the founder of the city, built his great castle. Jarl's original castle burned down, but the palace was started on the same site in 1697. As we stroll about, it is not difficult to understand why a structure so beautiful took almost eighty years to build. By the way, it

The fourteenth-century wall at Visby, Swedish port on the Baltic Sea, is a popular tourist attraction.

222

is the only place in the world with royalty in residence which visitors may enter. So we keep craning our necks hoping to see a member of the royal family, but no luck!

Since ancient times, Sweden has always had a monarch. But, as in Norway, Sweden is a constitutional monarchy. The actual leader of the government is the prime minister. His power depends on a favorable majority in the parliament. Since the members of that body are elected by the people, it is public opinion that rules the country. The parliament, known as the *Riksdag,* is one of the world's oldest legislatures, dating from the fifteenth century.

Leaving the Royal Palace, we walk through the older parts of Stockholm, which the Swedes refer to as "Old Town." Here the streets are so narrow that the buildings on either side of the street seem to touch each other. At the end of one of these streets, an open-air market is discovered. Wandering about the stalls, we observe several large water-filled glass tanks in which fish are swimming. From these tanks Swedish housewives select and buy their fish.

From Old Town our tour continues north across a bridge in the business section of the city. Here the streets are wide and buildings are modern. Ahead of us are five tall skyscrapers in a row. One thing that impresses us about Stockholm, whether we are in the old or new section, is the cleanliness of the city. In this respect, it is reminiscent of our earlier visit to the Netherlands.

Later in the day, a modern electric streetcar takes us to Skansen, Stockholm's famous zoo and museum. This zoo contains the wild animals — polar bears, reindeer, seals, moose, elk, bears, hares and others that can be found in Sweden. The most interesting part to us, however, is the exhibition of old houses and churches from various parts of Sweden. Many of these old structures were built in the eighteenth century. On a special stage, we witness exhibitions of Swedish native, or folk, dances. The guide tells us that each section of the country has its own type of native

Timber is one of Sweden's most important natural resources.

223

costume. Expensively embroidered women's costumes are often handed down from mother to daughter. The dancing, accompanied by the sound of country fiddles and accordions, goes on until late at night.

While in Stockholm, we decide to go to a restaurant and try "smorgasbord," as the Swedes call their buffet supper. A variety of foods is set on a big table. First we taste the fish dishes — the smoked eel, salmon, and pickled herring. Next, we have a little of each of the cold meats and several salads. Then we come back for the hot sausage, baked beans, meat balls and vegetables. The supper is finished with Swedish cheese and crackers.

From Stockholm, a water expedition to the Isle of Gotland awaits us. An old legend says that this island used to come to the surface of the sea only at night. With the dawn it disappeared again beneath the waves. But then a bold man named Thjelvar landed on the island during the night and with fire frightened away the trolls that "ducked" the island every day to keep people from settling on it. The trolls never came back to the Isle of Gotland and people did settle on it.

Arriving at the city of Visby on the Isle, we pass through one of the narrow gates which leads us inside the ancient walled city of northern Europe. The centuries have bypassed Visby, and we seem to be back in the time of knights and merchants who made the city famous in the Middle Ages. In

Swedish folk dancers in native costume.

those days the Isle of Gotland was a free and independent country which made its own laws and money.

Wandering about through the crooked streets takes us past old houses and church ruins. An old man sitting on a nearby bench says, "According to an old legend, St. Nicholas' large circular window, which faced west, had two brilliant gemstones so large and bright that when the sun shone on them, they acted as a lighthouse to guide sailors safely back to Gotland." He further explains that one day Valdemar, the King of Denmark, removed the gems from the window and placed them on a ship headed for his own country. The boat never made it to Denmark. It was wrecked during a storm not far from the island. The old story goes on to say that the rose-colored stones seen through the clear water on the bottom of the Baltic Sea are pieces of the huge gemstones.

Back on the mainland again, we board a boat for a trip on the Göta Canal. This canal links Stockholm on the east coast with Göteborg, Sweden's second largest city, on the west coast. The canal is more than a century old, and runs right across the country for 347 miles, actually combining many rivers, lakes and canals. Castles and churches along the way interest us greatly. The real thrill of the canal trip is the feeling of sailing right through the middle of the countryside with tree branches close at hand, stretching out to touch the ship's smokestack. There are also cows grazing only a few feet away.

At a stopover point on the Göta Canal, we get off the boat and travel by bus as far south as we can get in Sweden, to the province of Skane. This province is generally known for its farmland; the gently rolling fields remind us of our own Midwest. Skane was once a part of Denmark. The straits separating Sweden and Denmark are so narrow here that Kronborg Castle in Helsingor (Elsinore) can be seen without difficulty. Helsingborg is Sweden's main gateway to central Europe; the ferry from here goes to Denmark.

Summer in Sweden's Dalarna highlands, an ideal vacation spot.

225

DENMARK

In Southern Scandinavia, occupying Jutland peninsula as well as the Baltic islands. **Area** • 16,576 sq. m. **Population** • 4,654,000 (excluding possessions of Faeroe Islands and Greenland). **Language** • Danish. **Government** • Constitutional monarchy. **Monetary Unit** • Krone (= 0.14½ U.S. $).

Chief Cities • Copenhagen (capital), with over a quarter of the country's population; Aarhus; and Odense. **Religion** • Lutheran Protestant (state church). **Mountains** • highest elevation is Mollehof (561 ft.). **Rivers** • none of major importance.

Main Square in front of Town Hall (highest spire) in Copenhagen, Denmark's capital city.

Once across on the ferry, we visit Kronborg Fortress, Denmark's most famous castle. Accompanying us as we walk about the castle, our guide informs us, "In the past, Kronborg was a fortress that guarded the entrance to the Baltic Sea. All ships that came from the North Sea into the Baltic had to pass this point of land, and every ship that went by here had to pay money to Denmark.

"Up there," the guide continues, pointing to the top of one of the towers, "guards were stationed who watched all the ships to see that every one stopped and paid for the privilege of going past this point. Of course, about a hundred and ten years ago Denmark stopped asking for this payment. Many ships that are going to the Baltic Sea now go through the Kiel Canal in Germany instead of going all the way around Denmark."

After leaving the castle and while driving along, we glance at the map which shows us that the land of the Danes consists of the long mainland peninsula of Jutland, two large islands, Zealand and Fyn, and some five hundred smaller islands which dot the entrance to the Baltic Sea. For centuries Denmark has been called "the Key to the Baltic Sea." This country is only about half the size of the state of Maine. However, it is generally warmer in the winter and cooler in the summer than the northeastern section of the United States. The Gulf Stream prevents weather that is unbearably cold.

Denmark is a farming country. There are no mining districts, no big forests, and no huge industrial areas. However, Denmark has gained a reputation as the country of scientific farming. Although it is a small country with a not-very-rich soil, it is one of the world's largest exporters of meat and meat products, and of butter, eggs and cheese.

Approaching Copenhagen, we understand why this city is often called a "City of Beautiful Spires and Towers." The entire skyline is a series of spires, steeples and towers. Each city block seems to have a beautiful spire and each has its own interesting design. It would be quite difficult for us to choose the most beautiful one. Later, we shall climb up into one of the spires that is open to the public for a better view of the city we are now entering.

Copenhagen grew from a twelfth-century fishing village and its name in Danish means "merchant's haven." In 1443 it became the capital city of Denmark. Copenhagen is now the country's largest city and the major center of manufacturing. Fine chinaware, textiles, glass items, furniture, chemicals, bicycles, silver items and ships are built and manufactured here. Since Denmark has few raw materials, they must be imported from other countries. This means that Copenhagen is an important seaport. Ships flying the flags of many nations can be seen in the harbor area bringing products into Copenhagen and taking away items that carry the label, "Made in Denmark."

The business life of Copenhagen is located in a section called Stroget. Here are many of the city's stores, office buildings, museums, theaters and hotels. The streets in this part of the city are wide, bright and colorful, with open-air flower markets and beautiful gardens. Red brick buildings, copper roofs, and the red-and-white Danish flag flying everywhere also add to the beauty of the city.

Our tour of Copenhagen starts at Amalienborg Square. Here can be found one of the city's four royal palaces. While walking about the square, we hear band music and see people scurrying out of shops. Looking up a nearby street, it is possible to see executives, stenographers, and messenger boys leaning out the windows of office buildings. The crowd in the square is getting bigger, too. What is drawing the people? It is the Royal Guard on its way to take over the watch at Amalienborg Palace.

First, several burly policemen come marching along, getting cars and bicycles out of the way so there is room for

One of Copenhagen's main business sections: the bicycle is as important as the automobile in America.

the parade to pass by — and, incidentally, also to keep the public moving in front of the band, for there is quite a crowd leading the way for the Royal Guards. Then the thirty-six guardsmen, in their colorful uniforms and bearskin hats, march along, preceded by a 31-piece band, six drummers, and three fifers. While we watch, these soldiers take the place of guardsmen who were walking in front of the Royal Palace. After the colorful pageantry of the changing of the guard, the band gives a concert.

Walking along, we pass Christiansborg Palace, which is now a home for government offices and the *Folketing*, the Danish Parliament. Like Norway and Sweden, Denmark has a king, but his power is limited by a constitution. The *Folketing* makes the laws. Farther along the bank of the canal, across from Christiansborg Palace, fishermen's wives sell their husbands' daily catch. Like the Norwegians, the Danes consider fish an important food source.

Sitting on a rock out in the harbor is the beautiful statue of Langelinie, the "Little Mermaid" from Hans Christian Andersen's beloved fairy tale. We notice flowers by the statue and are told that Danish sailors have a custom of

Shipbuilding, above left, is one of Denmark's major industries. Above right, the "Little Mermaid" statute, inspired by Hans Christian Andersen's famous tale, looks out over Copenhagen's harbor.

bringing flowers to the "Little Mermaid" before they leave Copenhagen, believing that it will safeguard their voyage.

One of the broadest streets in the city is H. C. Andersen's Boulevard. This, of course, is named after Hans Christian Andersen, the most famous Danish author. He was born on the island of Fyn and left for Copenhagen as a fourteen-year-old boy. Although he lived in great poverty for many years, he made a success in writing plays and adult novels, but he is chiefly remembered for his fairy tales, which are like no others that have ever been written before or since. People everywhere remember them for the wise things they say about life, for the wit and fun in them, for the love they show, as well as the adventures they describe. Some of Andersen's best-remembered stories are "The Elfin Mount," "The Tinderbox," "The Princess and the Pea," and "Little Ida's Flowers."

In the evening we go to the Raadhuspladsen, which is known as the Town Hall Square. The main structure is, naturally, the City Hall. Just to the right is the famous Jens Olsen's World Clock. This clock contains about 15,000 parts and indicates all sorts of things. It tells, for example, local Copenhagen time, the time anywhere in the world, the time of the rising and setting of the sun and major stars, the eclipses of the sun and moon, and the revolutions of the planets. However, it is not because of the City Hall or the World Clock that we are in the square. It is because tonight is Midsummer's Eve.

According to an old custom, bonfires are lit this night in all Danish cities and towns so that witches can fly out of the fire and ride their brooms to the Harz Mountains in Germany. It is in these mountains that all the witches of the world are supposed to gather on Midsummer's Eve. After the big bonfire in the Town Hall Square has been lighted, a concert is given on the Danish musical instrument called the "lur." These old Viking horns are extremely difficult to play and only a few Danes are able to squeeze the weird and sorrowful tones out of the ancient instruments. Midsummer's Eve in Copenhagen is a night we will long remember.

The next day a bus takes us to the Tivoli, Copenhagen's world-famous amusement park. When the Tivoli started in 1843, the gardens were laid out beyond the city's old walls. Today it lies in the heart of the city, surrounded by towering buildings. The Tivoli offers entertainment of all kinds. There are such rides as a merry-go-round, a roller coaster, and a giant Ferris wheel. There is also a ballet performance on the big open stage. While walking about the park, we hear some children shout, "Here come the Tivoli Guards!"

Fredericksborg Castle is only twenty miles north of Copenhagen.

People press forward to find as suitable a place as possible along the route which the guards will follow. Grownups and children alike come running from every corner of the garden to watch the Tivoli Guards as they march their way along the paths of the park. We see them, then, and to our surprise, they are young boys, dressed exactly like the Royal Guard, and they have their own band leading them. The Tivoli Guards are a carefully selected group of boys under fourteen years of age who are trained to play band instruments and march like the real Royal Guard. It certainly must be an honor to be a member of the Tivoli Guards.

Tomorrow morning we leave Copenhagen and travel by air westward to the British Isles.

Tonder, an old town in South Jutland, near the border of Denmark and Germany.

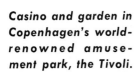

Casino and garden in Copenhagen's world-renowned amusement park, the Tivoli.

ENGLAND

The largest and most important part of the Island of Great Britain (which also includes Scotland and Wales). **Area** • 50,873 sq. m. **Population** • 44,117,000. **Language** • English. **Government** • Parliamentary democracy; the Monarchy has no political power, although it acts as the official head of the United Kingdom of Great Britain and Northern Ireland and the British Commonwealth of Nations. **Monetary Unit** • Pound (= 2.80 U.S. $). **Chief Cities** • London (capital and, with over 8 million people, the second largest city in the world); Birmingham, Liverpool, Manchester, South Shields, Sheffield, Leeds. **Religion** • majority Protestant (Church of England is the established church, though all major Protestant denominations are present), Roman Catholic, Jewish. **Mountains** • Scafell Pike (3,120 ft.) in the Pennine chain is the highest. **Rivers** • Thames, Trent, Ouse, Tyne, Mersey. **Lakes** • Windermere, Ambleside, Ullswater.

The Trooping of the Color ceremony during the annual military parade in London near Buckingham Palace. Her Majesty, Queen Elizabeth II (in center back), takes the salute.

11

They Talk Our Language, But...

"There is England over there," our stewardess says, pointing out the coastline of the British Isles to us. As our plane descends in preparation for its landing, the Thames River comes into view. Smoke from hundreds of factory smokestacks appears to spread back from the river. Then, from our plane's window, we see the actual sights that we have seen on postcards and in newspapers, magazines and books — Big Ben, London Tower, Westminster Abbey, Buckingham Palace.

A glance at the atlas shows us that England is a small country, smaller than North Carolina or Iowa. The whole of the United Kingdom — England, Scotland, Northern Ireland, and Wales combined — is hardly bigger than Minnesota. The island of Great Britain includes England, Scotland and Wales. North Ireland, while a part of the United Kingdom, is not on the island of Great Britain. It covers about one-sixth of the island of Ireland. The rest of this island is the Republic of Ireland, sometimes called by its Irish name, Eire. The islands of Great Britain and Ireland,

233

Big Ben's Clock Tower and the Houses of Parliament in London.

The Coronation of Queen Elizabeth II in Westminster Abbey.

plus several smaller ones such as Man, Zetland, Orkney and Skye, are also called the British Isles.

While not even large when compared with the world's other big islands, Britain is generally considered to be about the most important one on earth, historically and politically. Judged by latitude, the British Isles should be a happy home for Eskimos. London is farther north than Newfoundland, and Northern Scotland is about level with Hudson Bay. But the same Gulf Stream that warms the Netherlands and the Scandinavian countries also provides a mild moist climate. Many people have the false impression that the country's climate is an excessively rainy one. Actually, London, the capital of the United Kingdom, has less rainfall during a year than do many regions of the United States; but it comes in very frequent drizzles. Most people get used to it eventually.

A careful study of the map reveals that few parts of England are farther than seventy-five miles from the sea. The British coast line is also enormously broken, with hundreds of fine harbors. They, combined with the fact that the British are excellent sailors, have helped make Britain the most important seafaring country in the world.

After our airplane lands at London's Heathrow Airport, fourteen miles west of the city, a taxi takes us to our hotel. Driving along, our cabbie, as the English call their taxi drivers, tells us that there are really three Londons. First there is the City of London, the original one-square-mile site of the Roman capital of "Londinium." The second is the county of London which includes the city of London and twenty-eight other metropolitan boroughs, or districts, and covers 117 square miles. The county of London is surrounded by outer districts, all of which also belong to London. This vast area, known as Greater London, covers 693 square miles. It has been often said that Chicago and New York City grow upward, while London spreads out.

Our driver tells us that this was not always the case. When

234

the Romans surrounded the original city with a high stone wall, this marked the city limits for almost fifteen centuries. London's population grew and buildings increased during this time, but the city did not spread outside the walls. Actually, Queen Elizabeth I in the late 1500's enacted a law which forbade the construction of any houses or buildings within three miles of the wall. But this was all changed when the great fire of 1666 completely destroyed London. When it was rebuilt, London spread out beyond the old walls and the largest city of Europe has not stopped spreading since.

A short while later our taxi enters a part of London known as the West End. There are many fine apartment houses and hotels here. In fact, our hotel is located near Piccadilly Circus in this section of London. In England, where several streets come together, the conflux is called either a square or a circus. They may be any shape. Looking at Piccadilly Circus, we see that it is almost a circle. This place derives its name from the pickadil, or ornamental collar, worn by smart young men-about-London in the seventeenth century. Piccadilly Circus is the heart of London's theatrical and restaurant district.

After checking into our hotel room, we board a bright red, two-level or double-deck, bus in front of our hotel for

Fleet Street, the heart of London's newspaper district.

a sightseeing tour of the city of London. Our bus stops for a few minutes at Trafalgar Square to permit us to see the monument to Lord Nelson, one of Britain's greatest naval commanders. In 1805, at the Battle of Trafalgar, he defeated the French and Spanish fleets. This victory by the British navy destroyed Napoleon's hopes of sending an invading army from France across the English Channel. The National Gallery, which contains one of the world's finest collections of paintings, stands on one side of the square. Several old men are kneeling on the sidewalk outside the gallery. They are sketching pictures in colored chalk on the pavement to earn a few pennies. Also near the square is the lovely old church of St. Martin's-in-the-Fields, the fields having long since vanished.

The main street joining the West End of London with the City is the Strand. As our bus follows the Strand into Fleet Street, we enter the City at a point called Temple Bar. Our tour guide says, "Ordinary people can go in and out of the City as they please, but the Queen traditionally must ask permission of the Lord Mayor of London to enter the City." He explains that her coach or car is stopped here at Temple Bar where the Lord Mayor and other City officials ceremoniously hand her a large "key to the City." Temple Bar was once actually a stout wooden bar, or gate, placed across the width of the street to keep the king and his followers out of the city of London, but the last barrier, or bar, was removed in 1778. Giving a "key to the City" to a distinguished visitor is done as gesture of honor and hospitality in many cities of the United States.

As our bus continues up Fleet Street to Ludgate Hill, the beautiful St. Paul's Cathedral appears in sight. This cathedral has the unique distinction among all the great churches of the world of having been completely designed by one man — the great architectural genius, Sir Christopher Wren. Looking at the dome carefully, we notice that it seems very much like the dome of the Capitol Building

Trafalgar Square, London, with the Nelson memorial statue.

Aerial view of London looking west along the Thames River from the Tower Bridge (foreground). A section of the Tower and Tower gardens can be seen in the bottom right-hand corner. The second bridge from the bottom is London Bridge.

Messengers of the Bank of England (in high hats), before the windowless facade of the state-owned bank.

in Washington, D. C. The guide says, in reply to our inquiry, that the dome of the Capitol was copied from that of St. Paul's. The Cathedral is the burial place of many of Britain's military heroes.

A few minutes later, our bus stops in front of the Bank of England, popularly known as the "Old Lady of Threadneedle Street." The original bank was located on Threadneedle Street in the early eighteenth century and derived its popular name from the sad story of the sister of an old trusted bank clerk who was hanged for forging a banknote. The bank building itself is low, massive, and a windowless structure. This bank is owned by the British government and is the heart of the English banking system. Its messengers and clerks are known by their pink coats and scarlet waistcoats.

Everywhere in the city are street names that seem rather strange and amusing. In the vicinity of St. Paul's, for instance, there is Amen Court, Ave Maria Lane, Creed Lane and Sermon Lane. In the Cheapside area, a region which was formerly a market, the names of the streets have preserved the memory of the commodities which used to be sold there, such as Bread Street, Honey Lane, Milk Street, Ironmonger Lane. Fish were sold on Friday Street.

Just east of the city on the Thames River stands the grim Tower of London. One of the oldest of London's historic buildings, it was built as a fortress to guard the city by William the Conqueror. Much of the history of England could be written from the records of this ancient fortress. Originally, it was built just inside the city's walls so that William the Conqueror's soldiers could keep a watchful eye upon the inhabitants of the city at all times. It also served to protect the city from enemy ships that could conceivably sneak up the Thames River. Later the Tower was used as a political prison, a jail where people who oppose or have different opinions than those of the ruler, or rulers, are kept as prisoners. Such famous prisoners as Queen Anne Boleyn, Lady Jane Grey, and the second Earl of Essex were beheaded here. Here, too, the boy King Edward V and his little brother, the Duke of York, were kidnapped and murdered by their evil uncle, who then became King Richard III. Queen Elizabeth I, when still a princess, was held for several weeks as a prisoner here. In this tower, too, Sir Walter Raleigh, one of the leaders in the founding of the first English settlements in North America, wrote a book on his travels about the world.

While visiting the Tower, we see one of the world's most famous collection of gems — the British Crown Jewels.

A courageous "Beefeater." This yeoman wears gloves as protection against the claws and sharp beak of "Charlie," one of the Tower's ravens.

The Tower of London, on the left bank of the Thames. To the left in the foreground is the Traitors' Gate.

They are kept in a safe made of glass and steel, under glittering bright lights. Among the gems that can be viewed are such priceless objects as the Imperial State Crown with 2,700 diamonds and 277 pearls, the Black Prince Ruby which is almost as large as a hen's egg, and the Royal Sceptre. The Crown Jewels are only removed from the Tower on such occasions as a coronation of a king or queen. The guardians of the jewels and other attendants seen in the Tower are commonly known as "Beefeaters," or "Yeomen of the Guard." They wear scarlet doublets and knee breeches, a quaint costume that dates back over five hundred years. These yeomen are retired soldiers, and they live with their families in modern apartments on the upper floors of the Tower.

The coachman of the Lord Mayor of London wears the traditional uniform when the carriage is used on official occasions.

Looking out of the Tower, we notice both the Tower Bridge and London Bridge. The latter brings to mind the old nursery rhyme, "London Bridge is falling down . . ." Our guide tells us that the bridge in the rhyme was built by the Normans shortly after their conquest of London. For nearly six hundred years this narrow, swaying bridge was the only roadway across the Thames. In the 1830's it was in danger of collapse, so it was decided to tear it down and to replace it with a new London Bridge. Today, there are fifteen bridges across the Thames in and around London.

Between Tower Bridge and London Bridge, there are wharves along the riverfront. Tower Bridge is a drawbridge. It opens to let quite large ships into this section of the river. The docks and warehouses begin below Tower Bridge and extend for miles downriver. They help make London one of the great ports of the world. Thousands of ships travel up and down the Thames each year and flags of many nations fly from the vessels tied up at the docks. Men are very busy unloading and loading cargo. Much of the cargo that enters the port of London is food and raw materials for the factories of England. The products manufactured in England, such as textiles, machinery, chemicals, plastics,

Beautiful Balmoral Castle in Scotland.

A guard, dutifully motionless, outside Buckingham Palace, London.

glassware and precision instruments, are exported to many parts of the world. Other busy ports in England are Liverpool on the west coast and Southampton on the south.

Talking to Englishmen on the bus and in the street, we notice that they speak the "British" English. At first it is difficult to understand them. The British accent is different from that used in most parts of the United States. Thus, their words and manner of speech sound strange to us. But it must be remembered that even in the various areas of the United States ways of speaking also differ widely.

The British use many words in ways that are different from our use of the same words. For example, they call a radio set a *wireless.* Also, a druggist is a *chemist;* a policeman is a *bobby;* a hardware dealer is an *ironmonger;* a candy store is a *sweet shop;* and a movie theater is a *cinema.* They call potato chips *crisps;* a biscuit a *scone;* a fruit pie a *tart;* a pair of rubbers a pair of *galoshes;* a cookie a *biscuit;* oatmeal *porridge;* a sugar bowl a *sugar-basin;* a baby carriage a *perambulator;* and an elevator a *lift.* When an Englishman wishes to mail a letter, he says, "post a letter." While they talk our language, we find that they use many words in a different manner, but we are not too worried about these slight discrepancies.

Our second day's tour starts with a visit to Buckingham Palace, the royal family's London home. The royal family has three other official residences: Windsor Castle, upriver on the Thames, and Balmoral Castle and Holyrood Palace in Scotland. Our guide tells us that the royal family is in residence at the moment because the royal flag may be seen flying. The palace is not open to tourists, but tourists are allowed to go through the Royal Mews, with its royal horses, harnesses and carriages.

Our guide tells us to hurry so that the changing of the guard may be seen. We discover a crowd standing in front of Buckingham Palace waiting to see this ancient and colorful ceremony that goes back to the Middle Ages. Today's guardsmen wear red jackets, dark blue trousers and tall, shaggy bearskin hats, called "busbies." They march stiffly back and forth across the palace courtyard to the beat of drums and the slow cadence of a military band. Banners flap in the breeze. Then a mounted troop of Horse Guards — with their breastplates and helmets glistening, and plumes flying in the wind — trots into the courtyard. Each man sits his horse impressively straight and stiff. Finally the guardsmen who have been on duty march off, leaving their places to a new group of guardsmen.

From Buckingham Palace, our bus takes us to Westminster Abbey, the most hallowed shrine in Britain. Since William the Conqueror, all of England's kings or queens have been crowned here — except two (Edward V and Edward VIII). The Coronation Chair is used by the monarch when he is crowned. Underneath the chair is a large flat stone. We ask our guide why a stone is under the Coronation Chair. He tells us that before Scotland and England were united, the Scottish people crowned their ruler while he was seated on a large stone, called "the Stone of Scone." When the two countries joined together as one, the Stone of Scone was placed under the English Coronation Chair so that the king or queen could sit on both seats while he or she was crowned royal ruler of both countries. In the Abbey are the burial places of many of England's most famous people.

The Coronation Chair with the Stone of Scone (white arrow pointing to the stone).

Across the street from the Abbey is the Houses of Parliament Building with a lofty clock tower that houses "Big Ben." This 13½-ton bell chimes out clearly on the hours, while smaller bells in the tower ring the quarter hours. Big Ben takes its name from Sir Benjamin Hall who had the bell built. The name is also commonly applied to the tower clock, which has four faces — one on each side of the tower. The tower at the other end of the Parliament is called Victoria Tower. When Parliament is in session, a flag flies from Victoria Tower by day and a light burns in the clock tower at night.

The Parliament is next on our tour. The guide informs us that this institution has been called the "Mother of Parliaments" because almost all the representative legislative bodies in the world have been copied from it. Its two houses — the House of Commons and the House of Lords — have been making England's laws for more than 650 years. Of the two houses, the House of Commons is the more powerful body. It is elected by all adult men and women in the country. The House of Lords, on the other hand, is made up of the peers, or noblemen, of the United Kingdom. It can do little more than add its approval to laws passed by the House of Commons. Many of the titles held by the noblemen, such as baron, viscount, duke, marquis and earl, have been passed from father to son for hundreds of years. Other titles are granted to reward outstanding achievements, much as American colleges and universities give honorary degrees to famous men and women.

Our walk through the Houses of Parliament first takes us to the House of Lords, a large wood-paneled room with red leather seats. At the other end of the building is the House of Commons. It, too, is a large room with blue leather benches. No British sovereign has been permitted to enter the Commons since Charles I in 1642. But the Queen traditionally opens Parliament from the House of Lords with her speech from the throne. Our tour guide also tells us

10 Downing Street is the official London residence of the Prime Minister of England.

that when a vote is taken in Commons, the doorkeeper rings a bell four times. Then, to the shout of "Division!" the ayes walk to the west lobby, the nays to the east lobby. After the count is taken to see if the law passes or not, the members walk back to their seats on the benches.

There is probably no country in the world where ancient customs are still observed so faithfully as in England. It is more than three hundred years since Guy Fawkes hatched the Gunpowder Plot, yet to this day a company of the Yeomen of the Guard marches solemnly from London Tower to the Houses of Parliament and peeps into the cellars to make sure that there is no gunpowder about, every time that the king or queen goes to open Parliament.

After leaving the Houses of Parliament, a short walk leads us to a wide street, called Whitehall. On this street are the various government buildings. In the center of Whitehall rises the Cenotaph, a simple tapered shaft of stone commemorating the dead of World War I and II. A little farther down the street, two Horse Guards stand guard in front of military headquarters. Nearby is a short, unimportant-looking street known as Downing Street. A small group of people have stopped to look at the simple house with number "10" on it. This is the official home of the prime minister of the United Kingdom.

St. James Palace in London was built by Henry VIII in 1532.

The prime minister is really the head of the British government. Although daily papers mention "lords" and "sirs," England is one of the world's great democracies, and the cradle of many American liberties. Personal rule by the King or Queen has been dead in England for hundreds of years. Today the King or Queen reigns, but does not govern. Although the British people have great affection for their monarch, they have removed from the kingship practically all political power. The ancient authority of the King or Queen has been given to Parliament and to the prime minister. Actually, the prime minister's position is similar to that of the President of the United States.

To continue our tour of Great Britain, we rent a small English-made automobile and make certain the tank is filled with gas, or petrol, as the British call it, before leaving London. Since we are doing the driving ourselves, it is important to remember to keep to the left side of the road. This is contrary to the traffic laws in our country, but the English have their own way of doing things and this is how they keep their vehicles moving. The roads leading out of London are crowded with cars, buses, bicycles and trucks, or lorries, as the British call them. Soon, however, after getting out of the Greater London area, our car can move along with less traffic as it heads toward the Midlands.

As the name suggests, the Midlands are a part of central England. This area contains many of Britain's leading industrial cities as well as the famous English countryside. Driving along the countryside, we see herds of dairy cows and flocks of sheep grazing near the road. The sheep are raised chiefly for their meat rather than wool. The British people are generally classified as meat eaters, and mutton (lamb) is one of their favorites.

Here and there are vegetable gardens where cabbage, carrots, celery, peas and beans for the nearby cities are grown. Occasionally, there are fields of wheat, oats and barley. Also, orchards of apple, plum and peach trees are sometimes seen. But even with all of its farming, Great Britain still must import a variety of foodstuffs, because of the large number of people that must be fed. As a matter of fact, fish is one of the few foods the English have in sufficient supply for the home market. The most important fisheries are on the North Sea.

English farmers utilize modern machinery and modern farm methods in their fields, but the villages are frequently quaint and old. Most of the villages started during the Middle Ages. Tracing the history of a typical village back to its earliest beginnings would most likely reveal that it started with a farm and with the dwellings of the workers who tilled

244

the farmlands. In time, the farms became grouped into manors, and under the protection of the lord of the manor a close-knit community life developed. A church was built and, of course, an inn. The primitive dwellings of the farm laborers were later replaced by more substantial cottages, just as the lord of the manor, or squire, used his riches to build himself a manor house which would reflect both his wealth and his social standing. Every century saw the village increasing in size, for it must be remembered that, until comparatively recent times, agriculture was the basic occupation of the vast majority of the English people. Almost all the farmers and their families lived in a village.

Every village we have passed through seems to have an inn. Many of these British inns also have long and interesting histories, having served travelers for centuries. Originally the only places where a traveler could obtain food and shelter for the night were religious monasteries and abbeys. Sometimes, if his social status was sufficiently acceptable, the traveler could stop at the manor lord's home. But this privilege, of course, was only for a few.

Later, there were wayside restaurants, or taverns, where a person could obtain refreshment. But the inn, as we understand the term today — a house which offers a place to sleep as well as food and drink — did not come into

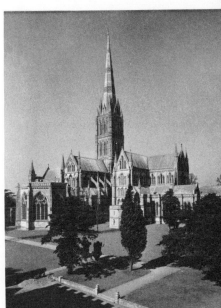

Salisbury Cathedral, in England, with its graceful spire and fine cloister and chapter house, is one of the most graceful of European church buildings.

The daffodils bloom on the banks of Ullswater in the English Lake District.

being until about the thirteenth and fourteenth centuries. After that time, the improvement of the roads and the growth of trade brought about a great increase in the number of travelers on the highways. Many of the old inns still are in business. *The Red Lion,* where we stop to eat, was founded in the fifteenth century. Most English inns have distinctive names — *The Cat & Fiddle, The White Swan, The Boar's Head, The Rose and Crown, The White Horse.* A large sign on which these symbols are brightly painted hangs over the door. This custom dates from the time when few Englishmen could read. They could, however, identify their favorite inn by the picture that hung outside.

As we eat, the innkeeper informs us that there are many old customs still followed in the different villages. "In our village near the end of the month of May," he says, "all the public officials of our village are weighed." The innkeeper carefully explains that the police chief notes the weight, and the town crier rings his bell, crying: "Oyez! Oyez! Oyez!" Then the weight of the mayor and all other elected officials is announced. The origin of this custom is not known, though it has been suggested that the mayor was weighed on taking office and again on giving it up, so that any great difference of weight might be attributed to hard work or to an idle year in office.

In a nearby town, a pancake race has taken place on the day before Ash Wednesday, the first day of Lent, for over five hundred years. Women only are eligible for this race. They must be furnished with an apron, a head-covering and a frying pan with a pancake. The race begins at noon and the pancake must be tossed upward three times in the course of the race. The winner is rewarded with a kiss from the mayor. Pancake races of this type are now held even in the United States.

Walking about the village, we notice that most of the houses are built of stone or brick, with very little wood used in their construction. This is because Britain has very few

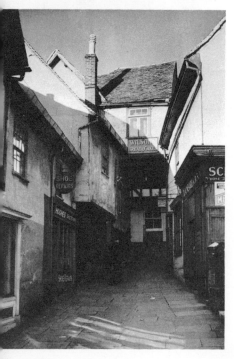

Many English villages go back to the Middle Ages and preserve much of the medieval quality. The photo shows a section of Colchester. The steps in the back date from the Middle Ages, the houses are sixteenth century.

246

Anne Hathaway's Cottage (at left).

William Shakespeare's birthplace in Stratford.

forests and thus wood is not easily available for building homes. On the other hand, stone and bricks are plentiful. Many of the roofs are made of straw. Such a straw, or thatched, roof would hardly seem able to keep out the rain. But, on the contrary, some of these roofs have kept homes dry for more than fifty years.

We decide to "post" some letters to our friends back home. The post office, however, is combined with a general store which sells anything from tea and sugar to shoelaces and peppermint lumps (candy). A shop selling antiques and local arts-and-crafts items such as hand-woven fabrics, pottery and woodcarving next attracts our attention. Ahead is the village hall, where the parish council holds its monthly meeting and decides on the laws for the village. A glance at the notice board outside the village hall shows that it is used for more than just the parish council meeting. A rehearsal for the dramatic society is announced for Wednesday night, a flower show Thursday afternoon, a jam-making contest on Friday, a cricket match on Saturday afternoon, and a father-and-son dinner on Saturday night. Life in an English village must indeed be busy!

Following our short stay in the village, an additional drive takes us to the old town of Stratford-on-Avon. After staying overnight here, we visit the birthplace of William Shakespeare, one of the greatest dramatists the world has

The tombs of the Shakespeares in the chancel of Holy Trinity Church in Stratford.

ever known. His plays have been translated into many languages and have been seen in almost every country. Many of them have been made into movies or adapted for television. We are told that Stratford has not changed too much over the centuries. Though it is more than four hundred years since Shakespeare was born there, he would still recognize many of the buildings that are familiar to present-day visitors of the town.

Our tour of Shakespeare's town starts with a visit to the gabled house on Henley Street where he was born. From there a path through the meadows leads us to the thatch-roofed cottage of Anne Hathaway, the woman who became Mrs. Shakespeare. We see many other houses built in the early seventeenth century and the churchyard where Shakespeare and his wife are buried. Later a walk along the River Avon allows us to view the large modern brick theater where Shakespearean plays are performed nightly from April to November. In the evening we go to this theater and see the play *Hamlet*. The play is doubly interesting because of our recent visit to Kronborg Castle. This Danish castle was the home of Shakespeare's *Hamlet*. However, Shakespeare called it Elsinore, which is the name of the town rather than the castle.

Speaking of castles, our next stop is Warwick Castle, eight miles from Stratford. This magnificent castle founded in the tenth century was later rebuilt by William the Conqueror. It was transformed from a fortress to a mansion in the seventeenth century. Today, it is open to the public. After going through an entrance gate, we follow a shaded walk with beautiful gardens on either side. At the end of it there is a wide green lawn and a moat that surrounds the castle. A moat is a ditch filled with water to prevent easy access to a castle built in olden times. Beyond the moat are the high walls of the castle. To cross the moat, a drawbridge must be crossed. The guide informs us that the bridge is still drawn up every evening, just as it was in ancient times. In

248

the castle itself a conducted tour through its great halls, living quarters, and kitchens gives us a good idea of how it felt to live in a castle during medieval times. Our guide even takes us down to see the dungeon, where prisoners were kept. Leaving the castle, he informs us that there are hundreds of medieval castles still existing in Britain. Many important historical events have occurred in some of these structures. Even to this day, people still live in castles. For example, Windsor Castle has been the official home of kings and queens for nearly nine hundred years.

Driving north, rural England is left behind. Ahead is the great industrial section of the country. Here are such cities as Coventry, Birmingham, Manchester, Newcastle, Sheffield and Nottingham. The latter city brings to mind the adventures of Robin Hood. To our disappointment, we learn that much of the original Sherwood Forest, where Robin Hood and his merry outlaws robbed the rich to help the poor, is used as headquarters for coal mines. Only a few huge oaks remain of what was a forest at the time when Robin supposedly lived there.

The industrial section of England is often called the "black country" because smoke from the thousands of factories seems to form a heavy black cloud over the area. While not planning to stop at any cities here, we are told that everything from airplanes, locomotives and automobiles to tiny ball bearings and costume jewelry are manufactured in England's "black country."

Continuing our journey, now toward the northeast, we cross the Tweed River and go into Scotland. Many people think of Scotland as a separate country, and indeed it was for centuries, with a line of warlike Scottish kings. Actually, Scotland is the only country in Europe that has never been conquered by an enemy. First the Romans, then the Normans, and finally the English attempted to invade and subdue the Scots. But all these invasions failed because of the fighting ability of the Scotsmen and the rugged Scot-

Some of the best farming land in the British Isles lies in Scotland.

tish hills. Scotland, of course, has now become a part of the United Kingdom. A line of British kings, the Stuarts, were Scottish.

Driving along, we pass through some of the best farming land in Scotland. These fields produce oats, barley, wheat, tomatoes, sugar beets, turnips and potatoes. The growing of seed potatoes for export is an important part of Scottish agriculture. Unlike other rectangular farm fields seen in other countries, the Scottish ones are the oddest shapes. Perhaps this is because most farms are bounded by winding country roads. From earliest time, roads have twisted and turned along the countryside, and as a public right-of-way, they must be kept. Some fields, however, are divided from each other by wire fences, others by such hedges as hawthorn. These irregular fields and green hedges add to the charm of rural Scotland.

Many of the hills in this area are covered with heather. Heather is a small evergreen plant which blooms in the summer almost everywhere in Scotland. There is an old Scottish legend to the effect that when God created the trees, flowers and shrubs, He gave them permission to select where they wished to grow. The proud pine wanted its

250

evergreen dress to be among snow and ice. The palm tree chose the tropics. The ivy selected places where it might find help to climb. The flowers and grasses spread over the entire world. At last only the heather was left. "Why do you not go forth with others and select where you want to live?" asked God.

"Dear Lord, do not be angry with me," replied the heather. "I just wanted to wait and see if there was any place where no other plants want to grow. I do see a spot on an island where there are naked highlands. May I go there?" The Lord smiled, bent down, and touching the heather, He said: "Go, and my blessing on you." And lo, lovely purplish-red blossoms burst forth and made beautiful the Highlands of Scotland. Tourists often time their visits so as to see the heather in bloom.

Our next stop is at Edinburgh, the ancient capital of Scotland. It is located on the south shore of the Firth of Forth. (Firth is the Scotch word for inlet.) Actually, Edinburgh is divided into two parts by one of the world's most beautiful thoroughfares, Princes Street. To the north of this street we find the New Town, which dates from the eighteenth century. Located here are Edinburgh's fine stores,

251

important business firms and major residential area. To the south of Princes Street is the Old Town, perched on a hill and crowned by massive Castle Rock. Many people consider this spot to be one of the most historic in Britain.

Walking across the parade grounds in front of Edinburgh Castle, and then beyond the small drawbridge, we pass through seven walls before reaching the palace building and court. St. Margaret, Queen of Scotland, died here in 1093. The tiny chapel at the very summit of the rock in the courtyard was built by her as a royal church. Close beside the chapel is Mons Meg, a huge fifteenth-century cannon which fired a salute when Mary Queen of Scots became engaged to the King of France four hundred years ago. But no event in the long history of Edinburgh Castle was more important than the birth of a son, James, to Mary Queen of Scots in 1566. For it was he who, on the death of the childless Elizabeth I in 1603, ascended her throne as James I of England. For the first time the crowns of the northern and southern kingdoms were united in one person. This led to the union of Scotland and England under a single king. Edinburgh Castle can therefore be regarded as being, in a very real sense, the birthplace of the kingdom of Great Britain.

Adjoining the castle is the Scottish War Memorial to the memory of the heroic dead of two World Wars. This memorial also pays tribute to animals of war, including the mules, horses and the carrier pigeons.

252

From Edinburgh Castle, a straight road runs downhill to the Palace of Holyrood. This is the Royal Mile, the major thoroughfare of the city before the New Town was built. There is much to be seen on the Royal Mile. For instance, we decide to visit the High Kirk of St. Giles, the principal church of Edinburgh. It is the survivor of churches that existed on the site as far back as the ninth century. The oldest parts now are the four pillars supporting the tower on which rests the spire, or Crown of St. Giles'. These are said to be part of the Norman church erected in 1120 but destroyed in 1385. The present building was erected between 1387 and the middle of the fifteenth century.

Just off the Royal Mile, on the Canongate, there is a house known as Golfers' Land. According to one story, the sport of golf was started by Scottish shepherd boys knocking small stones into crude holes in the ground with a crook (a shepherd's staff), while their flocks grazed lazily on nearby pasture lands. Whether this is true or not, golf was played in the fifteenth century in Scotland. As far back as 1457 the king made a law forbidding it because it was taking too much time away from archery. During this period man

British gunboats patrol the Firth of Forth. In the background is the famous cantilever bridge spanning the firth.

waged war with bows and arrows, and hitting a bull's-eye was more important than making a golf shot. By 1682, however, the game had become the Scottish national sport, for in that year the first international golf match took place.

According to the marker on the house, when the then Prince of Wales, later James II, was living at Holyrood, he engaged certain English noblemen in a controversy over the game's historic background, and as an outcome challenged two of them to a game. He chose as his partner an Edinburgh shoemaker, John Patterson by name. The golf match was staged at a nearby golf course. There are no details of how much the Prince contributed to the victory, but he did build John the fine house we are visiting on the Canongate.

At the foot of the Canongate is the entrance to the Palace of Holyrood, the official residence of the Queen when she is in Scotland. Since she is not there now, we can visit the palace. The rooms where Mary Queen of Scots lived fascinates us. There are many other rooms where exciting events took place in the history of this country.

In the early evening we go to a park to see Scottish folk dances. At such dances, both the men and women are dressed in skirts, but these short, pleated skirts are called "kilts" and the shawls or blankets they wear over their shoulders are known as "plaids." Each clan (the families of Scotland are called "clans") has its own colorful pattern — known as a "tartan" — for weaving cloth. (Tartans are often referred to as Scotch plaids.) The dancer's costume is rounded out by a fur pouch, called a sporran, which is worn in front and used as a purse; knee-length stockings; shoes; and a tam-o'-shanter on the head. Once this was the standard dress, but today these costumes are only worn at special celebrations.

The music for the dancers is provided by the skirling of bagpipes and the fast rhythm of drums. The bagpipe is made up of a pigskin bag and has a pipe to blow it up, much as a balloon. There are several reed pipes attached to the bag, as well. To play the instrument, the musician places the bag under his arm, and keeps blowing to keep air in it. At the same time, he squeezes the air out with his arms so that it blows the sounding pipes. While the music is playing, several kilted men and girl performers give exhibitions of Highland dancing, known as the Highland fling, or reel. Reels are danced by couples, the sets being called "four-somes" or "eightsomes," according to the number taking part. But solo dances are also very popular. Perhaps the most picturesque of these is the "Sword Dance," performed about a crossed sword and scabbard on the ground.

A Scottish military "piper" proudly shows the tartan of his regiment.

There are also several Highland sports contests which require great strength and skill. They include throwing a mighty 22-pound hammer, running, jumping and "tossing the caber." The caber is a long pole made from the trunk of a fir tree. Only a very strong man can pick it up. The object of the contest is to see how far one can toss the caber once he has picked it up from the ground.

The most common nickname for a Scotsman is "Mac," which means son. Just as Johnson and Dickson were originally the sons of John and Dick, Macdonald was once simply the son of Donald, and Macgregor the son of Gregory. The badges of the clans were — and are — sprigs of some tree, shrub or flower. The Macdonalds wear the bell heather; the MacLeods a red whortleberry; the Mackays a bulrush; the Macphersons a branch of the evergreen box. The tartans of the various clans vary greatly in attractiveness. Some are like the MacLean tartan in which the chief colors are very dark greens and blues. Some are very decorative, while others, such as the Macgregor and Macdonald tartans, are sometimes considered to have too much black and red.

After a very enjoyable time in the park, we board a night sleeper train for Hull, England. From there a channel steamer will take us to Antwerp, Belgium.

BELGIUM

One of the smallest and most densely populated nations in Europe. **Area** • 11,779 sq. m. **Population** • 9,290,000. **Language** • almost evenly divided into two language groups: Flemish (similar to Dutch) and Walloon (a French dialect). **Government** • Constitutional monarchy. **Monetary Unit** • Franc (= 0.02 U.S. $). **Chief Cities** • Brussels (capital), Antwerp, Liege, Ghent. **Religion** • majority Roman Catholic. **Mountains** • Ardennes (highest point, 2,283 ft.). **Rivers** • most important are the Schelde, Meuse, and Sambre.

(Above) The "Grand Palace" in Brussels. (Below) The "Grand Palace" in Antwerp.

CHAPTER 12

A Visit to an Old Friend

BELGIUM

After crossing the North Sea for the second time, our channel steamer ties up at a dock in Antwerp, Belgium's chief seaport and second largest city. Although about fifty-five miles from the sea on the Schelde River, Antwerp, which means "on the wharf," is actually one of the great ports of the world. It was long the center for exchange of goods between Mediterranean ports and those of northern Germany and England. Today it is connected with the Meuse River and France by a canal and the city is Belgium's leading railroad center.

Our tour in *La Métropole,* as Belgians call Antwerp, begins by visiting the dock area. Strolling along the tree-shaded streets bordering the docks, our attention is held by the loading and unloading of ships from all over the world. As might be expected in a country so highly industrialized as Belgium, its exports are manufactured goods such as metal products, textiles, lace, glassware, locomotives, chemical products and cut diamonds. To supply the factories, it must import iron, copper, cotton, wool and many petroleum

257

The Graslei, one of the oldest sections of Ghent, the famous little city in the Flemish-speaking part of Belgium.

products. It must also import flour, meat, butter and other foodstuffs to feed its population.

Following one of the narrow streets away from the docks, we come into the Market Square. There are many old buildings around the square, including the Town Hall, which were built in the fifteenth century. We enter the Town Hall and find that one splendid room opens into another. In one room, there is a tablet presented to the people of Antwerp by General Dwight D. Eisenhower for their courage during World War II. We also visit the burgomaster's (mayor's) office, the council chamber, the marriage hall where the burgomaster or one of his assistants performs the civil marriage required of every couple in Belgium. This ceremony is usually followed by a church wedding.

Antwerp's legendary beginnings are symbolized by the hands in the city's coat-of-arms. One of the burgomaster's assistants tells us, "Long ago a giant by the name of Antigoon lived on the banks of the Schelde River, near where the Market Square now stands. This evil giant took riches from all who sailed on his river and cut one hand from each person who failed to pay. Antigoon's cruel ways were, however, brought to an end by the heroic Roman soldier, Brabo, who, as we see from his statue in Market Square, gave the giant a dose of his own medicine."

Later in the day we visit the former home of Peter Paul Rubens, the great seventeenth-century painter. Several churches in Antwerp have some of his paintings. While walking about from one church to another, the sight of girls selling newspapers surprises us. The Belgian girls blow a horn to announce the latest edition of a newspaper.

Early the next morning a bus takes us on our trip south. Soon after leaving Antwerp, we find ourselves in the heart of Belgium's farm region. This loamy upland, called the Belgian plain, produces some of the world's richest yields of sugar beets, potatoes, oats, rye, wheat, flax and vegetables. The Belgian farmer has long been noted for his

258

One of scores of corner shrines placed in honor of the Virgin Mary on houses in Antwerp (above, left); at right, the picturesque Castle Walzin.

View of the Beguinage, home for the aged in Malines.

ability to make a small amount of soil produce a big crop. In the southern part of Belgium, farmers raise large numbers of sheep, hogs and cattle. Farther north, toward Holland, there are dairy farms, but, oddly enough, modern farm machinery has not replaced the huge Belgian horses. These strong horses were originally bred during the Middle Ages for use by knights who engaged in tournaments, or fought in battles.

Nearing Brussels, our map shows that the country is bounded on the north by the North Sea and the Netherlands, on the east by Germany and Luxembourg, on the south and west by France. Belgium is about the size of Maryland, and has more than three times as many people. Actually, in Europe only the Netherlands and England are more densely populated than Belgium. There are two language groups in this small country: Flemish (Dutch-speaking) in the northern part of the country, and Walloon (French-speaking) in the southern part. Many Belgians speak and understand both languages — and English, too.

The Place Royale, or the Royal Square, is the starting place of our tour of Brussels. While viewing the king's palace, we learn that only the male descendants of a Belgian

259

king can succeed to the throne. Belgium has a constitutional monarchy, like the Netherlands, and the Parliament — the Chamber of Deputies and the Senate — makes the laws and runs the government. The Parliament is elected by the people, and should any eligible citizen fail to vote, he is subject to a fine.

After visiting the House of Parliament, the magnificent Palace of Justice and other government buildings, a taxi takes us to the Grand' Place, one of the most interesting public squares in all Europe. It is difficult to describe the beauty of seventeenth-century buildings that crowd the sides of this magnificent square. A climb to the top of the tower of the Hôtel de Ville, or Town Hall, one of the finest Gothic structures in northern Europe, rewards us with an excellent view of Belgium's capital city.

Brussels has been a leading trading center as long ago as the Middle Ages. Today, canals, railroads and highways connect it with other parts of the country as well as with harbors on the sea. The name Brussels is associated with carpets, lace, gloves and cotton goods. The city is also famous for its "sprouts," or baby cabbages, which originally grew wild near this largest city of Belgium.

Renting an automobile, we head south toward France. A few miles from the city, the road takes us across the plains of Waterloo. Here, in 1815, the French were badly defeated by the combined Prussian and British armies in one of the most famous battles ever fought. Since that time the word "Waterloo" often describes any major defeat, whether it be in sports or war.

Continuing farther south, both farm and industrial areas are observed. Driving along, we practice our French: *"Parlez-vous anglais? Bonjour. Comment allez-vous? Je ne comprends pas. Je suis votre ami."* Our foreign-language practice will be handy in conversation with the people of the next country. Fortunately for us, however, many residents of France also speak English.

260

FRANCE

Although the French speak a different language from ours, they have much in common with us. The Statue of Liberty in New York harbor was a gift from the French people, sent to us in the last century as a symbol of friendship. This friendship between our two nations has existed ever since the birth of the United States as an independent nation. French ships and many French soldiers crossed the Atlantic Ocean to help us in our Revolutionary War. French engineers designed and built our fortifications. French naval forces helped to trap Cornwallis at Yorktown, which brought the war to a close. The French people were equally grateful for our help to France during two great World Wars. Thus our visit to France is to an old friend.

France is a little smaller than the state of Texas, but no nation in Europe except Russia is larger. Even more important than size is the position of France. On the north is the English Channel with the coast of England a mere twenty miles away at one point. The northern land border is Belgium, Luxembourg, and a part of Germany. On the west is the open Atlantic and the Bay of Biscay. On the south the

Except for a small, flat section bordering on Belgium, Germany and Luxembourg, France is a nation with well-defined natural mountain and river boundaries. **Area** • 212,659 sq. m. **Population** • 47,840,000. **Language** • French. **Government** • Republic. **Monetary Unit** • Franc (= 0.20 U.S. $). **Chief Cities** • Paris (capital, over 2 million people), Marseille, Lyons, Bordeaux, Toulouse. **Religion** • majority (over 95%) Roman Catholic; about 2% Protestant. **Mountains** • Mont Blanc in the French Alps (15,781 ft.) is the second highest mountain in Europe; Pic de Montcalm (10,105 ft.) in the Pyrenees. **Rivers** • four major rivers: Seine, Loire, Garonne, Rhone.

Honfleur in Normandy, France.

Father and daughter in costume of the province of Normandy, on their way to church.

green mountain ramparts of the east are high mountains — the Alps, the Jura, and the lower Vosges, from south to north — and beyond them are Italy, Switzerland and Germany. On the east France shares with Germany part of the course of the Rhine River. Two other countries that border France are so small that they look like cities on the map. They are Monaco, on the southern coast of the country near the border with Italy, and Andorra, between France and Spain.

Within France are four great river basins. In the north the Seine flows into the English Channel. In the west the Loire flows into the Atlantic. The mighty Garonne in the southwest flows into the Bay of Biscay. In the south the lovely Rhone, rising in the eastern Alps, flows into the Mediterranean. Our atlas tells us that, except for the mountain areas, most of the land is pleasantly rolling and rather fertile. Only the northern plain is flat, a fact which has played a big part in France's wars. Upon them France has been conquered often and in turn has conquered her neighbors.

Actually, the recorded history of France starts with conquest. Julius Caesar conquered Gaul — ancient France — and made it a part of the Roman Empire. When the Roman Empire fell, Gaul was left to itself for a while, but new invaders came — and went. For over forty years, beginning in A.D. 768, Charles the Great (Charlemagne) ruled over much of western Europe, but upon his death what is France today became independent. France as a nation really did not emerge until A. D. 987, when Hugh Capet made Paris the capital. In the seventeenth century, under a powerful monarchy, France became a world power with a great colonial empire. Later, France revolted against the monarchy and became a republic. The process of the French Revolution starting in 1789 was bloody, destructive and chaotic. However, it led to stability and an empire under Napoleon Bonaparte. Again France began to conquer and

262

became the heart of an empire that stretched over most of Europe.

Since Napoleon's day, France has changed its form of government several times. There have been periods when the country has been ruled by a king, but on each occasion it has returned to a republican form of government in which the French people have a part in making their own laws. The country is now called "the Fifth Republic of France."

The map of the northern hemisphere reveals that Marseille's latitude matches southern Maine in the United States, and that Paris, the capital of France, matches Gander in Newfoundland. So it would seem that France should have a climate ranging from cool to cold . . . but this is not the case. Thanks to its share of the Gulf Stream's warm currents, even the northern areas of France are seldom very cold. Southern France, which draws additional warmth from the Mediterranean, is generally hot and sunny the year around. The temperatures of Paris are very much like those of Washington, D. C.

Entering France, our travel takes us to the province of Normandy. Here are found rich pasture lands, large apple orchards, waving grain fields and ancient stone cottages with thatched straw roofs. Normandy Province is the center of France's dairy industry and of apple orchards. Cider is a popular drink here. We pass several small mule-driven carts carrying apples, vegetables, butter and cheese. Many of these carts are driven by old women in stiffly starched white bonnets, shawls of bright colors and blue aprons over wide woolen skirts. They are traveling from their little villages to the bigger towns to sell their produce in the market place.

The Normans are now mainly farmers, but they were distinguished soldiers of the past. Normandy, across the English Channel from England, has been battle-scarred by invasions in both directions for centuries. Among these were the conquest of England by William the Conqueror, and the

The country restaurant near Caen is built in the style that is typical of Normandy architecture.

Monument honoring Joan of Arc in Rouen.

From whatever direction one approaches Orléans, the Cathedral is the landmark first seen.

reconquest of Europe by the Allied Forces, by air and sea from England, during World War II. It was on the beaches of this province that Allied Forces, under the command of General Dwight D. Eisenhower, landed on D-Day, June 6, 1944. As the armies fought their way across Normandy, many ancient churches, castles and houses were destroyed. Even now there are signs of the damage done in this province during World War II.

Ahead is Normandy's capital and seagoing port, Rouen, on the Seine River. In the crooked streets of this very old city, with their quaint gabled houses, we can still recapture the feeling of medieval days when knights galloped through the streets and courtiers kneeled to pay homage to passing kings. There is a story told here about the first time the king came to Rouen. The early Normans were not familiar with the royal rules of the court, and they were told they would have to pay homage to the king by kissing his foot. The first Norman who paid homage, instead of kneeling down to kiss the king's foot, raised the foot to his mouth so roughly that the king fell over.

We see Rouen's famous clock tower with its "grosse horloge," or big clock, whose single hand has told time for more than four hundred years. In the market place is a simple tablet set in the pavement that reads, "Jeanne d'Arc, 30 Mai, 1431." It was here in the market place of Rouen that Joan of Arc, the "Savior of France," was burned at the stake on May 30, 1431. France and England both claimed Normandy. The fighting over this province lasted so long that it was called the Hundred Years' War. At a time when it seemed that the weak young prince of France by the name of Charles would be defeated, the story goes, a young shepherdess from Domremy was brought to the castle where the prince lived. She said that God had told her to lead the French army against the English and thus save her country. Charles at first refused to listen to her, but he later changed his mind and gave Joan of Arc the needed

264

men for her army. The seventeen-year-old Maid of France, as Joan was called, defeated the English at Orléans. Her army won other important battles and entered Reims on July 14, 1429. Three days later Charles was crowned King Charles VII of France. The Maid stood at his side during the coronation.

Joan wanted to go home, but the young king compelled her to go on fighting against the enemies of France. She was later captured by disloyal Frenchmen who sold her to the English. Taken to Rouen for trial, Joan was charged with being a witch. She was declared guilty by a Church court. It is said that all the members of the court were from areas under English occupation and were loyal to that country. She was sentenced to be burned to death, and it was carried out at the site where we now stand. But the French army was still inspired by the bravery of the Maid of France. They fought on until the English were driven back across the English Channel.

Following the river road toward Paris, we discover the Château Gaillard, a famous fortress built in 1196 by Richard I, the Lion-Hearted, to prevent the French king, Philip Augustus, from seizing the fertile lands of Normandy. Richard has inherited the crown of England from his father and also vast lands in France from his mother.

The Cathedral at Chartres.

The Cathedral of Toulouse.

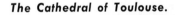

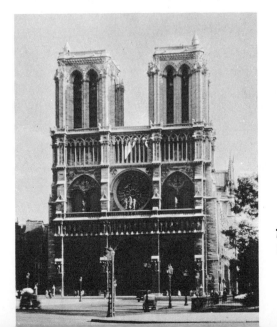

The three French cathedrals shown on this page are a part of the most famous church-architecture in the world.

The Cathedral of Notre Dame in Paris.

He wanted to hold his inheritance in both countries, so he built Gaillard on a high cliff overlooking the Seine. While Richard lived, the fortress proved impregnable, but when his successor, John Lackland, lost it to Philip Augustus, Normandy returned to the French crown. The view of the Seine Valley is splendid from this old fortress ruin.

After staying overnight in a quaint Normandy inn, we drive into Paris and go directly to our hotel near the Place de la Concorde. From our hotel window, this beautiful square with its great statues and glittering fountains lies below. For two years, during the French Revolution, the guillotine stood in the center of the square and here Louis XVI, Marie Antoinette, and thousands of other French nobles and aristocrats were beheaded. At the start of the Revolution, a statue of Louis XV occupied the center of the Place. It was taken down and a Statue of Liberty set up.

After registering at the hotel, we start our tour of Paris by strolling up the Champs Elysées, one of the most famous boulevards in the world. Along it are movie theaters, elegant shops and some of the best cafes, or restaurants, in the city. Just behind a row of trees, we sit and have our lunch at one of the sidewalk cafes. The street seems to be more like a park than a major thoroughfare.

Completing our lunch, our stroll up the Champs Elysées continues until we see the great monumental arch, the Arc de Triomphe (Arch of Triumph). Napoleon Bonaparte started this monument in 1806 in honor of his victorious French armies, but it was not finished until 1836. Under the Arch is the grave of France's Unknown Soldier, marked by an eternal flame that will presumably never be allowed to die. An elevator takes us to the top of the Arch. From here we have a wonderful view of Paris, as well as being able to notice the star-like pattern formed by the twelve great avenues radiating from the Arc de Triomphe. It is clear why the French call this spot "Place de l'Etoile," or "Place of the Star."

The Hôtel des Invalides in Paris was founded as a home for disabled soldiers. Today it contains Napoleon's tomb.

266

One thing noted about Paris is that there are no skyscrapers. The tallest buildings are the cathedrals. Apartment houses, hotels and office buildings are seldom more than five or six stories high. Paris grows outward, toward the suburbs and outskirts, where big factories are also to be found. If we were to visit the suburbs of Paris, it would reveal modern factories that manufacture automobiles, farm machinery, hardware, chemicals, bicycles, railroad equipment, shoes, cement and dyes. The city has long been famous for fine jewelry, book-publishing, cosmetics, perfumes, leather goods, and furniture. Many of these industries were started in the fourteenth or fifteenth century, when craftsmen set up their small shops in the capital city of France. In addition to being the capital of its country, Paris is called the "fashion capital of the world." Fashion experts from all over the earth come to Paris each year to view the fashion style shows put on by world-famous designers.

From the Arc de Triomphe, a taxi takes us to the Louvre. On our way there, we pass the Palais de l'Elysée, the home of the president of the Republic of France. Since this building is not open to the public, our taxi continues until it

The Arc de Triomphe in Paris is the largest triumphal arch in the world. Beneath the arch is the tomb of the Unknown Soldier and an eternal light burns in his honor.

267

The Madeleine Church in Paris, with its colonnade of Corinthian columns, takes the form of a classic temple.

arrives at the great courtyard of the Louvre and the gardens of the Tuileries. Before entering the Louvre, we take time to walk about the gardens which resemble or suggest an enormous carpeted room with a pattern of living plants. One of the most popular attractions for Parisian children is the Tuileries' pond where they sail their toy boats. In the shade of a big tree, a French Punch-and-Judy (puppet) show is in progress. This is a delight for every child as well as for parents. Guignal, the puppet hero, is a friend of all, and the interest with which his adventures are generally followed shows how dear to the heart he is to each and every one. The children in the audience take a very active part in the show by shouting directions, suggestions and warnings to Guignal. It is only when he has finally won against his wicked enemies that the audience becomes happy. We, too, are happy as we enter the Louvre.

Originally built as a fortress in the thirteenth century, the Louvre later became a palace for the kings and queens of France, but now it is the world's most famous and important art museum. In its galleries are the paintings of some of the most famous artists in the world, including Leonardo da Vinci, Van Dyck, Holbein, Raphael, Vermeer, Rubens, Velasquez and Whistler. In a room all by itself, we see the *Venus de Milo,* which is easy to recognize because we have seen numerous reproductions of this famous statue. In

268

Barges on the Seine on Quai Grands Augustins in the heart of Paris. Ile de la Cité is in the background.

Bookstalls on the Left Bank in Paris' famous Latin Quarter.

another room, the most famous painting in the world, the *Mona Lisa,* can be found. It would take years to see all the art treasures amassed in the Louvre. Since our stay at the museum is limited, we visit only the most famous rooms and galleries of this fabulous palace.

It is dusk when we arrive back at our hotel. Suddenly the lights in the city seem to go on all at once, as if commanded by signal. All the buildings and monuments are bathed in a brilliant glow. Fountains shoot up sprays of glorious color. The streets and boulevards are almost as bright as day. Paris is truly the "City of Light."

Our second day's tour of Paris starts from the Ile de la Cité. Actually, this island in the center of the Seine is where the city of Paris started. In the first century B. C., when Caesar conquered Gaul, the small island was the home of the *Parisii* tribe of barbarians. After establishing a village there, it became an important trading link in the Roman Empire. With the fall of Rome, the inhabitants called it Paris, after the barbarian tribe, rather than its Roman name, *Lutetia.* Today, besides being the spiritual and historic heart of the city, Ile de la Cité is in the approximate geographic center of Paris. It is linked to the rest of the city by many bridges.

The first place to visit on the Ile de la Cité is the Notre Dame Cathedral, a very old building in Paris and one of the

269

The magnificent Opera House of Paris, built during Napoleon III's reign, is an immense theater featuring ballet and operatic performances.

most famous cathedrals in the world. Begun in 1163, it was finished about a hundred years later. Boasting a high spire, big arches and thick walls, Notre Dame was a notable tribute to the men who built it long before the days of modern machinery.

After a tour of the cathedral's shadowy interior, we climb the 387 steps to the northwest tower. From here a fine view of the city is obtained. Below is the Seine, with small boats carrying farm produce and goods from the countryside to the capital. Some are returning with cargoes from other parts of France. Actually, though it is more than 90 miles from the sea, Paris is an important port city and more cargo comes in and out of it than from any other French port. The Seine is navigable for barges and small ships above and below the city. A canal system stretching over most of France connects Paris with the Mediterranean Sea and with larger inland cities.

The bell about which Victor Hugo wrote in his book, *Hunchback of Notre Dame,* is in the tower opposite ours. From our tower it is also possible to examine the strange-looking stone animals perched on the edge of the cathedral's roof. These odd-looking creatures are called gargoyles, and are different from any animals known. These part-bird, part-beast, part-devil figures were made as hideous as possible and put there on the edge of the roof. They were supposed to scare away evil spirits from the church. But the guide tells us that the gargoyles do perform a very practical purpose because they are also decorative waterspouts through whose open mouths the rain water that collects in the roof gutters can run out.

After leaving the cathedral, we make our way to the Pont St. Louis, the bridge connecting the Ile de la Cité to another island in the Seine, the Ile St. Louis. This small island is wholly residential and one of the most wonderful places in Paris for a leisurely stroll. Walking through its streets, we see many fine seventeenth- and eighteenth-century mansions.

270

Along both banks of the Seine River are the quays, or masonry embankments. These were built a long time ago as a mooring place for river boats. After leaving the Ile St. Louis, we decide to walk along the winding quays of the "Left Bank" of the Seine. At first there was some confusion about this name. The Left Bank section of Paris is on the south bank of the Seine, and includes the network of streets and boulevards which extend through it. The name comes from the Seine which bounds it on the north, and is the left bank facing in the direction of the river's flow.

It is on the Left Bank of the river that Paris' famous Latin Quarter is found. The Quarter is called Latin because that was the language once spoken here. In the early Middle Ages, when the University of Paris was founded here, students came from every country in Europe to study, and Latin was the common language of the students and faculty. Any outsider who was not fluent in the classic language, and who tried to intrude into the students' meeting places, was treated severely and thrown out of the Quarter. Because of the unpredictable behavior of students down through the ages, the Latin Quarter has acquired a rather happy-go-lucky reputation. The students of the various Paris universities in this section, plus young artists and writers who have yet to become notable, make the Latin Quarter a center of learning. Booksellers and publishers are located

A painter in a typical Montmartre street. Montmartre is the artist's quarter of Paris. The oriental-looking church of white stone is Sacré Coeur.

Entrance to the Louvre.

here, a logical and practical arrangement that enhances the learning atmosphere of the Left Bank.

Our stroll along the Left Bank is continued until the Eiffel Tower is reached. It is probably the best-known tower in the world. Reaching almost a thousand feet above the low roofs of the city, this metal tower was designed by Alexandre Gustave Eiffel. It was built for the Paris World Fair of 1889. For almost fifty years it was the world's tallest structure. Now, of course, several skyscrapers in the United States are higher. An elevator takes us to a platform near the very top for a spectacular view of Paris and the surrounding countryside.

From atop the Eiffel Tower, the vast military parade ground known as the Champ de Mars can be seen. It stretches all the way south more than half a mile to the Ecole Militaire. This eighteenth-century military academy, often called "the West Point of France," was established to provide officer training for the sons of poor aristocrats and for superior students from provincial high schools. One of the latter, the tower guard tells us, was its most famous graduate, Napoleon Bonaparte. His final report card carried the remark: "Will go far, if circumstances permit." Napoleon became France's greatest military leader, and as Emperor he controlled nearly all of Europe. The Ecole Militaire is now used as the Staff College of the Army and the Air Force.

The golden dome just to the left of the Ecole Militaire crowns the largest building of a group known as the Hôtel des Invalides. When originally built by Louis XIV in 1671, the Invalides was a home for disabled and old soldiers, and during the time of Napoleon it served the same purpose. Today, however, only a very small section houses some World War I veterans. The rest is used for numerous army offices and the huge war museum of France's military glory. But its chief claim to fame is that under the golden dome is the tomb of Napoleon Bonaparte.

Reaching 984 feet into the sky, the Eiffel Tower is the identifying landmark of Paris.

272

Two historically and architecturally famous French palaces: Versailles, at left, Fontainebleau, below.

The next morning we take a motor coach to nearby Versailles. The guide book states that it was Louis XIV who built a palace and a city at Versailles. He had grown tired of the Louvre as his palace and tired also of the bustle of Paris. Up to that time, Versailles had been a marshy piece of land with nothing on it but a small hunting lodge built by his father. King Louis XIV decided to set up a city entirely his own, with avenues, beautiful gardens and famous fountains. It became, in fact, the most magnificent royal palace in the world. The king and his royal family lived in the palace, as did hundreds of nobles and thousands of servants. The celebrations and receptions given at the Palace of Versailles were unrivalled for luxury and extravagance.

It was during a great banquet in this palace that Louis XVI and his queen, Marie Antoinette, were informed that the common people had begun to rise up in revolt because they had no bread to eat. "If they have no bread," the queen is supposed to have said, "let them eat cake!" The French Revolution finally caught up with the foolish royal couple and they were beheaded. The Royal Palace of Versailles was closed, to be opened nearly half a century later as a national museum.

Many of the old rooms in the palace are as they were left by their former royal occupants. It is difficult to count the bedroom suites, large and small, dining rooms, game rooms, reception rooms, music rooms, picture galleries, libraries and ballrooms. Of all the rooms, the most famous one is the Hall of Mirrors, where the Treaty of Versailles was signed at the end of World War I.

Before leaving Versailles, we go for a stroll in the palace's gardens, which are as extraordinary and significant as the palace itself. Trees are given artificial shapes; paths are literally inhabited by many statues. Because there was no river in Versailles, water was brought from miles away, just to have it perform in the elaborate fountains. The palace, gardens and fountains are beautifully illuminated at night.

Back in Paris, we go to the Gare de Lyon, and board the Paris-Côte d'Azur express train. Throughout our night of travel along the Rhône River, many cities are left behind, including Fontainebleau, Sens, Lyon, Valence, Orange and Avignon. At last our train will reach Cannes, on the French Riviera. Meanwhile, along the way are many factories that produce textiles, chemicals and various machinery. The train is also passing by many small vegetable farms and large vineyards. Among the many fine vegetables grown in this region, the potato is valued highly. The scientist, Parmentier, first made it popular as a food in France by having King Louis XVI wear the flower of the plant in his buttonhole. The grapes are the most important of all the farm products. The Rhône Valley vineyards help to make France the leading wine-producing country of the world. Fine wines are exported, but the major share of the wine stays right in France. Wine is France's most popular beverage.

After reaching Cannes, we register at the hotel where we

Harvest of jasmine flowers in Grasse. Jasmine is but one of many fragrances used to make world-famous French perfume.

have made reservations. From our room it is possible to see the beautiful harbor of Cannes with its small fishing vessels, as well as many luxury yachts. Although Cannes is an elegant resort city, the old section is still a simple fishing village. There are several other beautiful hotels, the casino, and villas on the green hills that rise from the harbor.

After spending the morning swimming in the brilliant blue water of the Mediterranean, a drive inland from Cannes takes us to Grasse. Along both sides of the road, near the town, fields of roses and orange blossoms greet the eye. During other seasons of the year, the fields are covered with lilies, mimosa, carnations, violets and jasmine. All of these flowers are grown for their essential oil, rather than their delicate beauty, because Grasse is the perfume capital of the world.

This is a photograph of Cap d'Antibes and Eden Rock, one of the many seaside resorts along the French Riviera.

At Grasse, we visit a big perfume factory. After people gather the blossoms from the fields, the flowers' petals are crushed to extract the valuable oil. It takes literally millions of flower blossoms to extract even a small amount of oil. Considering the hard work and the long period of time needed to produce it, it is little wonder that French perfume is so expensive! Even when walking the streets of Grasse, the elusive whiffs of perfume seem to follow us. On returning to Cannes, the rest of the day is spent strolling along the shore of the Côte d'Azur, or the Riviera.

The Riviera is a historical land. When Romulus was supposedly building his town on the Tiber, and Ulysses was having his adventure on the Mediterranean Sea, primitive tribes lived here in caves of the rocks, hunted in the forests and fished in the sea. Then the Greeks in 600 B. C. founded several seaports along the coast, such as Cannes and Marseille.

The next morning a motorbus takes us west to Marseille. Snaking along a winding, twisting road with the Mediterranean Sea on one side and steep rocky hills on the other, our bus passes several small villages and towns, each with its own little harbor. Every now and then, along the shore-line, or on some steep cliff, there is a beautiful pastel-colored villa, or house, surrounded by palm trees and brilliant flowering shrubs. Farther back from the road, there are olive groves and vineyards on the hillside.

Our bus driver tells us there is an old legend that explains why Marseille is a port of welcome to the people of the world and it goes something like this: In the olden times, when Marseille was a small trading port, the local chief had a beautiful daughter named Gyptis. According to the tradition of her tribe, she was permitted to select a husband of her own choosing. Most daughters of chiefs, however, selected young men whose fathers were powerful and could be helpful to the chiefs. To the surprise of everyone, however, Gyptis chose a young stranger, named Procides, who had won her heart by the lovely gifts he had brought with him from Greece. In his luggage Procides had jewels, beautiful vases, plus an orange and olive tree. Because the marriage was so successful and trees spread throughout the region, Marseille, since that day, has remained interested in everything that comes from afar.

France's second largest city is a long-time favorite of sailors around the world. Marseille plays hostess to the ships of the great steamship lines that travel the routes to Africa, India, Indo-China, Japan, Australia and all the ports of the Mediterranean. Imports include coal, copper, iron, metals, machinery, petroleum, silk, cotton, hides, rice, wheat and sugar. Raw materials brought in by sea from all parts of the world are processed in the Marseille area, thus making it a great manufacturing center. Out of the port go the great wines of France, soap and cosmetics, textiles, olive oils, leather products, tile, brick, automobiles and hundreds of other commodities.

We first visit the old harbor, or Vieux Port, with the houses close to the waterfront. Only a very few buildings date back further than the eighteenth century, since a great

276

deal of Marseille was destroyed in World War II. While much of the old has been rebuilt, it still is a place of endless interest. There are merchant ships loading to go on far voyages, or unloading varied cargoes. The water is full of shipping — trim steam yachts, sailboats, fishing boats and other small craft. The central quay is lined with little pleasure boats whose pilots shout noisy invitations to the passers-by to go on excursions — *promenades sur mer,* they call them. There is a little white dock with flags flying, from which the boats leave for the Chateau d'If. We board one of these boats.

The Chateau d'If is an old castle and prison on a tiny rocky island in Marseille's harbor. It was here — according to Alexandre Dumas' book — that the Count of Monte Cristo was imprisoned and from which he escaped by taking the place of a prisoner who had died, and being thrown into the sea in a sack. It was in the streets of Marseille that some of his adventures took place. It is a pleasant sail out to the island, and interesting to see the old castle. By the way, Alexandre Dumas is one of France's greatest authors.

The large steamers from the Americas, England, Italy and Greece dock in a new harbor built on the outer coast. It is from here that we board our passenger steamer for the Iberian Peninsula and the countries of Spain and Portugal.

View of the old harbor in Marseille. Seagoing vessels from all over the world filled it before the new harbor was built. It is now used only by fishermen and small pleasure boats.

SPAIN

Occupying the major portion of the Iberian peninsula. **Area** • 194,232 sq. m. **Population** • 31,077,000. **Language** • Spanish, Basque, Catalan. **Government** • Although again declared a monarchy in 1947, Spain is ruled by a General, Francisco Franco, who is Chief of State. **Monetary Unit** • Peseta (= 0.01 ½ U.S. $). **Chief Cities** • Madrid (capital) and Barcelona — both over one million people, Valencia, Seville. **Religion** • Roman Catholic (state religion). **Mountains** • Mulhacén (11,411 ft.), the highest; Pico de Aneto (11,168 ft.). **Rivers** • Ebro, Douro, Tagus, Guadalquivir (the only one of good navigability).

PORTUGAL

Situated in the western half of the Iberian peninsula. **Area** • 34,216 sq. m. **Population** • 9,039,000. **Language** • Portuguese. **Government** • Corporative republic. **Monetary Unit** • Escudo (= 0.03 U.S. $). **Chief Cities** • Lisbon (capital), Oporto, Coimbra. **Religion** • Roman Catholic. **Mountains** • Malhão (6,532 ft.). **Rivers** • Tagus, Douro, Guadiana.

The "Dolls' Court" in the Alcazar of Seville in Spain (picture, above left) clearly shows the influence of Moorish architecture. Photo above shows a typical Portuguese fishing village.

CHAPTER

The Iberian Peninsula

At one time, it was believed there was a land bridge connecting Europe with Africa at the point where the two continents are now separated by the Strait of Gibraltar. According to an old Greek legend, Hercules, their god of strength, was supposed to have let the ocean into the Mediterranean Sea by tearing the rocks apart between the Iberian Peninsula and Africa. He left behind the so-called Pillars of Hercules: Jebel Musa on the African side and the Rock of Gibraltar on the European side. The ancients thought that these rocks marked the western boundary of the world, and that if they dared go beyond them, they would fall off the end of the earth. Remember that in the early times most people thought the earth was flat. A few brave sailors, namely the Phoenicians, passed through the Strait of Gibraltar and braved the dangers of an unknown ocean that we now call the Atlantic.

If we are to believe this old legend, then Hercules must be thanked for making the Iberian land a peninsula. This peninsula at the southwestern tip of Europe was originally inhabited by a people known as Iberians, and was named after them. About 900 B. C. the Celtic tribes swept southward through the Pyrenees Mountains and settled in the northern and central part of the land. The Phoenicians and the Greeks established settlements along the coastal sections. The Romans conquered and colonized the peninsula in 201 B. C. They built roads, bridges and aqueducts — some of which are still in use today. The Romans also brought to the peninsula Roman law, the Latin language, and later, Christianity.

Roman rule over the Iberian lands was broken in the beginning of the fifth century A. D. by the invasion of the Vandals and Visigoths. The Visigoths from Central Europe ruled the land for nearly three hundred years. At the beginning of the eighth century, the Moors, also called Berbers, crossed from Africa and conquered most of the Iberian Peninsula, bringing Arabic civilization to the areas under their control. Many of the buildings seen today in Portugal and Spain show traces of Moorish influence. Gradually the Christians, who had concentrated in the northern portion, became stronger and began to drive back the Moors. By the end of the fifteenth century, the Moors were driven back into Africa. During the struggles with the Moors, incidentally, Portugal broke away from Spain and began its separate existence.

The people of these two countries generally have black hair, olive-colored skin and brown eyes. But the Portuguese are different from the Spaniards in many ways. They speak a different language, and have many different customs.

The Iberian Peninsula is one of the world's great natural fortresses. Some of Europe's highest mountains guard its borders and bar entry from the Atlantic and the Mediterranean. In the north, the Pyrenees Mountains form the common boundary between Spain and France, and cut off the peninsula from the rest of Europe. Spain has the highest average elevation of any land in Europe except Switzerland. Portugal is the westernmost nation on the continent.

280

The northern point of the Iberian Peninsula is about due east of Minneapolis, Minnesota, and the southern point is at about the same latitude as Norfolk, Virginia. But this does not explain the climate of Spain and Portugal, which, generally, is far warmer, sunnier and drier than most of the United States. The Iberian climate is influenced by several factors: the warm ocean current known as the Gulf Stream on its northern and western shores, the tropical Mediterranean on the south and east, and mountain ranges which rim the peninsula and split the rimmed section into high plateau areas.

While both of these countries are small when compared to the United States — Spain is about three-fourths the size of Texas, while Portugal is about the size of the state of Indiana — they once ruled a major portion of the Western Hemisphere. Spain played a leading role in the early exploration and settlement of large sections of what is today the United States. Many American place names are of Spanish origin, indicating the extensive regions of the United States that had been opened up to Western civilization by the Spaniards. Florida, Louisiana, Texas, California and many of the Western states once were Spanish territories. Among the more famous early Spanish explorers of areas now in the United States were: Ponce de Leon, who sought the Fountain of Youth and found Florida instead; Hernando De Soto, who crossed several Southern states in a three-year expedition and discovered the Mississippi River; and Francisco Vásquez de Coronado who found the Colorado River. Besides discovering the Grand Canyon, Coronado also explored much of Arizona, New Mexico, Texas, Oklahoma and Kansas. Spain also controlled, at one time, Central America, Mexico, Cuba and Puerto Rico, and all of the South American continent except Brazil. This giant colony came under the rule of Portugal. However, none of these lands is now under the rule or influence of either Iberian Peninsula country.

SPAIN

Our first stop on the Iberian Peninsula is Barcelona, in northeastern Spain. Entering the harbor, we observe ships flying the flags of many nations. The port of Barcelona is one of the best and busiest in the Mediterranean. It is also Spain's largest industrial center. On the docks, men are unloading cargoes of cotton, foodstuffs, coal and petroleum products. Ships leaving the port are carrying textiles, leather goods, chemicals, machinery, olive oil, minerals, wine, cement and fruits. An exact model of the *Santa Maria,* the ship in which Columbus sailed and then discovered America, is on exhibition on the waterfront.

We walk over to the lofty monument of Cristobal Colon. This is the real name of the man who sailed aboard the *Santa Maria* in 1492. English-speaking people gave him the name Christopher Columbus. If anyone had called him Columbus during his lifetime, he would have been unfamiliar with the name. The tall statue of Columbus overlooks the port, seemingly pointing toward unknown horizons. The lower part of the pedestal is decorated with eight bronze lions and with scenes from the explorer's life. It was to Barcelona that Columbus came after he made his voyage to America, because the Spanish King and Queen, who gave him the ships, were staying here.

After checking into our hotel, we visit the Ramblas, a

Inner court of house in Barcelona.

Port view of Barcelona.

wide avenue in the center of the city. Merchants here sell noisy parrots, sweet-singing canaries, tropical birds, dogs, white mice, guinea pigs and a multitude of other things. The flower markets along the Ramblas are well supplied with racks of many kinds of flowers, including gay roses, violets and gladioli. While in this part of the city, we decide to visit a beautiful cathedral that stands on a low hill. The guide tells us that it has been a place of worship for more than two thousand years. At first it was the Temple of Venus, later a Moslem mosque and now a grand old Christian cathedral.

Since it is lighted only from some stained-glass windows high in the walls, the inside of the cathedral is dusky and mysterious. In a crypt under the high altar lies the alabaster tomb of Santa Eulalia, the patron saint of Barcelona. This saint was one of the martyrs put to death by the Roman emperor when Barcelona was a Roman city. The choir stalls are carved and painted with the coat-of-arms of Spanish knights. "In this choir stall, the Indians whom Columbus brought to Barcelona were baptized," our guide says.

After eating lunch, we rest in our hotel room for a couple of hours. It is a custom in this country to take a siesta, or midday rest. Most shops, schools, offices and other businesses close shortly after noon for the afternoon siesta. Business resumes again around four o'clock and ends at eight. Most people do not start eating dinner until nine or ten o'clock; and even the children are rarely in bed before midnight.

Once our siesta is finished, our tour of the city continues with a walk to the Pueblo Espanol, where the customs and products of the various provinces are shown and also demonstrated. We have fun watching how olive oil is made. First, the olives are beaten off the lower branches of the trees with sticks and then they are gathered from the ground. They are then taken to a nearby processing plant, where juice, or oil, is pressed from the olives. The people

Each province of Spain has its distinctive costume, worn and shown off especially at fiestas. The girls in the picture above are from Valencia.

Milk women from Lugo in the province of Galicia.

Castanets.

Dancing to the music of guitar and castanets.

of the Iberian Peninsula partake of olive oil at nearly every meal. They cook meat, fish and vegetables in it, and they spread it on their bread in place of butter. Olives that are sold in jars are carefully hand-picked from the trees so that the delicate fruit will not be bruised. Some fruits gathered for eating are picked while comparatively green. The olives that are used for oil are allowed to remain on the tree until fully ripe.

At night in front of the Pueblo Espanol, we witness Spanish folk dances from the various provinces. These dances are generally reserved to celebrate holidays, or fiestas. The fiesta is a vital part of Spanish life. It has often been stated that "Spain lives from fiesta to fiesta!" These events are interesting and colorful, full of music and dancing. Usually they reflect a deep Spanish religious theme. There are many floats in a fiesta parade. Often, too, strange carnival figures made of wood, wax or papier-mâché are displayed. Sometimes they are twenty-five feet tall and gayly decorated. They are paraded in the streets during the day and accompanied at night by crackling and sparkling fireworks. As a conclusion to the carnival, the figures are generally burned in huge bonfires. People dance by the light of the flames.

284

In the folk-dance festival we are watching, the dancers are dressed in the costumes of old Spain. The girls look especially pretty with the long flounces on their skirts, combs in their hair and colorful shawls covering their shoulders. The young men wear stiff-brimmed hats, called sombreros, tight bell-bottomed trousers, and boleros, or short embroidered jackets. The dancing itself is to the lively rhythm of guitars and the tapping of feet. Sometimes the dancers provide their own accompaniment with tambourines or castanets. Castanets are small spoon-shaped shells, usually made from ivory or very hard wood. They are fastened to the thumb, and then beaten together with the middle fingers in the palm of the hand. A dancer holds a pair of castanets, one in each hand, and the clicking sounds they produce provide the rhythm for the dance.

After watching for awhile, we stop at a restaurant for a late-evening dinner. Each province has its own favorite dish. In Barcelona it is *arroz con pollo,* which turns out to be delicious chicken and rice. In Valencia it is *arroz valencinano,* of which the ingredients are rice, olive oil, red pepper and mutton. In Castile it is *puchero,* made with peas, beef and a special kind of sausage. As with the food of India, Spanish cooking is "hot" and spicy.

"Other countries, other tastes": **Pulpites or tiny octopuses are a Spanish delicacy on the Costa Brava.**

In the morning we head for the railway station and a train to Madrid, capital and largest city of Spain. Our map reveals that Madrid is almost in the exact center of the country. The train is driven by an electric locomotive. Electric trains operate better in Spain's mountainous country than those driven by steam.

From the train window we observe small villages spaced from ten to twenty miles apart, but since our train is an express, it does not stop at any of them. The houses in the villages seem small. Gay colors such as pink and yellow are frequent. Mr. Gomez, a passenger on the train, tells us that the walls are made of earth which has been mixed with water, then baked hard and dried by the sun. The thick walls,

The Gran Via is one of Madrid's busiest thoroughfares.

with a few small windows, keep out the summer heat and also the sharp winter cold. Some of the dwellings have only one story, while others have two. All, however, seem to have red tile roofs.

"Inside a small house," says Mr. Gomez, "there may be only a kitchen and bedroom. They have an outdoor living room which they call a patio," he explains. "I understand many of your new homes in America have patios, too."

We assure Mr. Gomez that this is true, and he continues, "Some of the larger houses have inside living rooms and several bedrooms upstairs. The floors are usually clay tile, and the walls are painted white. Many small Spanish villages have electricity, but few have any running water."

Going through a small village, we see women around a well, where water needed for cooking or cleaning is obtained. As they walk, the women balance large water-filled jugs on their heads. On the bank of a little stream just outside the village, other women rub clothes on washboards, while still others hang their wash on nearby shrubs. While thus engaged at the village well or at the outdoor laundry along the stream, the women gossip and exchange the news.

Between villages there are fields of wheat and barley, and of course, esparto grass, from which Spanish workers make baskets, rope, mats and paper. There is no modern farm machinery to be seen anywhere. The work in the fields is generally done by hand, sometimes with the help of oxen

A rare occurrence, snow in Spain. The Escorial, 25 miles north of Madrid, was built from 1563 to 1584 at the direction of King Philip II. A museum today, it was originally a royal palace, a royal mausoleum, a church, a college and a monastery.

The Royal Palace in Madrid.

The throne room of the Royal Palace in Madrid.

or mules. The farmers of the Meseta, as this vast treeless plateau is called, work very hard. They barely earn a living from their crops and farm animals.

Every now and then in the hilly portions of the Meseta, there are flocks of sheep which look like the type seen in Australia. Mr. Gomez tells us that they are merinos, and we remember that Australian sheep first came from Spain.

"In southern Spain," Mr. Gomez tells us, "olives, grapes, oranges, lemons, almonds and cork are the main crops." He explains further that Spain is the world's foremost producer of olives and olive oil, second only to the United States in the production of oranges. It is also the third largest wine-producing country in the world. Because the summers are very dry in this southern region, the water from mountain streams is used for irrigation during that season. The farmers of southern Spain are more prosperous than those of the Meseta.

After our train arrives at Madrid railway station, a taxi takes us toward our hotel. Riding along, we see why Madrid is often called a "city full of contrasts." Much of Madrid is new and clean. There are several modern skyscrapers, wide boulevards, beautiful apartment buildings and several large parks. Madrid's skyline towers are taller than those of any other European city, but in striking contrast to the newer parts are older sections with very narrow streets, ancient, often quaint buildings and plazas centuries old. Madrid, of course, is very old. It is said that the Moors, when they controlled all the Iberian Peninsula, began it with a fort built about A. D. 700. While the Spanish people were driving the Moors from their country, the former fortress of Madrid began to grow. The city became the nation's capital in 1561 and has remained so ever since.

Our hotel is on the Avenida José Antonio, the main shopping street of Madrid. On each side of this broad, sunny street are sidewalk restaurants, stores, theaters and other hotels besides ours.

Next morning, we walk to the large public square called Puerta del Sol, which means "Gate to the Sun." At one time long ago, this was the eastern gateway to Madrid. Today it is the heart, or hub, of the city from which many streets branch out. From this busy square, we take a tram, or streetcar, to the Royal Palace.

The huge Royal Palace, which at one time was one of the homes of Spanish monarchs, had been Madrid's principal building ever since King Philip II. First we walk about the beautiful park and gardens with their many fountains. Inside the palace itself are large rooms with very high ceilings. The floors are covered with thick carpets, and on the walls are hung valuable paintings and tapestries. Tapestries are heavy, hand-woven pieces of cloth, often with designs or patterns. The Royal Library has over 150,000 books and a large collection of arms and armor that had been worn by palace guards of old. We also go into the beautiful gold-and-scarlet Throne Room. This room is closed to the public only once each year, when foreign ambassadors are presented to the head of the Spanish government. Except for this occasion, and on rainy days when muddy footwear would damage the carpets, the Palace is open.

We take the tram again and go across the city to Prado Museum, one of the most famous art museums of the world. Here are displayed the paintings of the great Spanish artists, Goya, Murillo, El Greco, Velazquez, and many others.

Near the Prado is Retiro, one of Europe's largest and loveliest parks. Created by King Philip IV for the open-air theatrical performances that he particularly enjoyed, it still retains the beauty of the seventeenth century. In the park

288

are the statues of the many kings and queens of Spain. The beautiful gardens of Retiro contain trees and plants from all over the world. Strolling round the park, we see many children going into an outdoor theater. Following them through the archways, we sit down on wooden benches and watch a marionette show. Marionettes are puppets that are manipulated on a small stage by strings. While all the dialogue is in Spanish, the action and movements of the marionettes nevertheless convey the meaning of the story.

Along our tour we see many signs advertising a soccer game between a team from Madrid and one from Barcelona. The Spanish people call soccer "futbol." Our driver tells us that it is the most popular sport in his country. "Isn't bullfighting the most popular?" we ask.

"Spaniards do not consider bullfighting a sport. It is regarded as a two-act play or drama," he says. "In the first act, men on horseback, called picadors, thrust small spears into the bull to make him very angry. The second act is the battle of skill and fury between the bullfighter — called a matador — and the bull." He adds that to be a great matador requires courage, skill and grace. But we decide to watch the soccer match rather than the bullfight. Spanish "futbol" is played in the same manner as our soccer game.

Bullfighting: The matador (above) and the picador (at left) in action, and a close-up of the matador (below).

One of Lisbon's mosaic sidewalks on the Marquês de Pombal Square, seen from Avenida da Liberdade.

We take an airplane from Barajas Airport in Madrid for a short flight to Lisbon, the capital of Portugal. As our airplane approaches the city, we observe that it is located on the north bank of a river not far from the ocean. On our map, it is possible to trace the river called Tagus. This river flows past the city for several miles. Our stewardess tells us that the only way to cross the Tagus at Lisbon is by taking a ferry. It is also noticed that some of the streets are paved with black stones that seem to spell out words. "They are names of famous people in Portuguese history," explains our stewardess.

"If you could shoot an arrow from the top of the Washington Monument east some three thousand miles," she continues, "it would come to earth near Lisbon. In other words, these two capital cities are both in the same latitude. But they are not the same in climate. Portugal, thanks to its position on the western side of the Iberian Peninsula, is warmed by the Gulf Stream and has a climate much like southern California."

On landing at Lisbon's Portela Airport, we take a taxi to our hotel which is located on the Avenida da Liberdade, or Liberty Avenue. This is a very beautiful street that has many flower beds, ponds where swans swim, and eight parallel rows of trees. There are many modern buildings, wide boulevards, and beautiful parks and gardens in the new section of Lisbon. Many sidewalks are paved with small pieces of glass and stones set in the concrete. This type of artistic work is called "mosaic." Some of Lisbon's mosaic sidewalks are laid in waving black-and-white bands that look somewhat like rolling ocean waves. Jokingly, it is often said that they can make you feel a little seasick if you look at them too long. But most people think that these walks are beautiful. Each night the walks are washed and cleaned to keep them bright.

Lisbon, like most European cities, has an old section. The

290

Portuguese capital is believed to go back to the ancient Phoenicians. It is definitely known, at least, that Lisbon was a Roman town, called Felicitas Julia over twenty-one centuries ago. In the old quarter of Lisbon, the streets are narrow and twisting in many directions. Here the ancient buildings seem to huddle so close together that the roofs almost touch across the narrow alleys. While Portuguese is, of course, the official language of the country, it is fortunate for us that so many people understand English.

Walking about Lisbon, we soon learn that it is a city of hills, like San Francisco. Also, Lisbon has streetcars that travel up and down the hills, as in San Francisco. But since the streets are so winding in the Portuguese city, the ride is particularly thrilling. While walking downtown, we see an elevator that rises abruptly eight stories from the middle of the street. Getting on board, we find that it connects with one end of a bridge which extends across the rooftops to a higher level of the city. The Portuguese have tried to make hill-climbing easy in their city.

Restauradores Plaza and Liberty Avenue, notable among the squares and streets of Lisbon.

From a high point above the city it is possible to view the famous Praca do Comercio, commonly known as Black Horse Square. The entrance to this square, actually a giant courtyard next to the Tagus River, is guarded by a statue of King Joseph I riding a rearing horse. Though the statue has turned green through the years from the salt air of the harbor, its original color was black. For this reason, English sailors visiting Lisbon began calling the area Black Horse Square and the name was adopted by English-speaking visitors like ourselves. Today the square is often used for military parades, particularly to greet distinguished visitors arriving in Lisbon by ship. The ferryboat that crosses the Tagus leaves from Black Horse Square, too.

A taxi takes us to the Tower of Belem in the western part of the city. This tower was originally a fortress built in 1515 to guard the sea entrance to Lisbon. It was built here to honor Vasco da Gama, marking the spot from which he sailed away in 1497 on the voyage which resulted in his discovery of the sea route to India. Although its fancy design gives the tower a look of "wedding cake" delicacy, once it was a very good fort. This tower is shown on Lisbon's coat-of-arms.

Near the Tower of Belem is the President's Palace, painted entirely in pink. This palace is a president's home and not open to visitors, but we can watch the colorful changing-of-the-guard ceremony at the front gate. Nearby, and open to the public, is Ajuda Palace, one of the most interesting buildings in all of Lisbon. It was formerly the home of the kings of Portugal and is still used to entertain royalty. A guide takes us through its enormous and beautifully furnished rooms.

The old Palace in the village of Sintra, 12 miles northwest of Lisbon, a wealthy resort which also boasts an old Moorish Castle.

On the drive back to the hotel, our taxi driver tells us that Portugal is not an industrial nation. The means of livelihood for most Portuguese people is usually obtained from farming and from the sea. More than half of the people are farmers, growing wheat, corn, rye, rice, olives, wine grapes and fruit, or herding sheep. But despite its many small farms, Portugal is nevertheless not entirely self-sufficient in food, and must import wheat and meat from other countries. On the other hand, it exports, or sells, its fruits, notably citrus fruit, grapes and melons, to northern Europe, and a major part of its production of olive oil. There is little modern machinery employed by Portuguese farmers and most of them work with the same type of tools their grandfathers used. Farmers in the rural areas still transport much of their produce to market on the backs of donkeys or in wooden ox carts. In spite of the lack of modern equipment, these thrifty, hard-working people are able to make a fair living from their small pieces of land.

East of Lisbon on the mountain plains is the cork forest which gives this country one of its most important and

Characteristic street scene in the old quarter of Lisbon.

unusual products. Our driver tells us that workers strip the outer bark from the cork oak tree, and then dry the cork in the sun. The cork tree replaces its bark easily. We are told that cork can be taken from the same tree about every ten years. Half of the world's supply of cork comes from Portugal, and the United States is its best customer for this useful product.

While in Lisbon, we decide to see a bullfight. The aim of Portuguese bullfighting is to display skill, and here it is not the kill that counts. The bull is rarely killed. Arriving at the bull ring, we find that it is about the size of an average American college football stadium. The bullfight itself starts with a colorful parade of all the participants, accompanied by a brass band playing lively music. The cavalero, who fights the bull on a well-trained horse, is dressed in a seventeenth-century costume. He wears a bright colored silk or velvet jacket, feathered three-cornered hat, knee-high riding boots, and silver spurs. The horse, especially trained for its contest with the raging bull, is worth many thousands of dollars. The bull's horns are padded so that it cannot hurt the horse. It is an exciting contest in which the cavalero only pretends that he is killing the bull. At the end of the event, the bull is driven out of the ring without having been hurt. In Portugal, the cavalero is a national hero, similar to a big-league baseball star in the United States.

Peeling the bark of a cork tree, a first step in the manufacture of cork, Portugal's most important industry.

After several contests between the cavaleros and the bulls, the forcados, usually seven or eight men, continue the show. On foot these men confront the bulls with a mixture of skill and funny antics. The leader of the forcados teases the bull into rushing at him. Then he receives the bull's charge by locking his arms around the horns. Another forcado grabs the bull's tail while the others wrestle the animal to a standstill. Then they all let go, except the one holding the bull's tail. As the forcados race to safety, the fun begins. How can the last man release the tail and escape the irate bull? Well, we see how it is done.

Early the next morning, we rent a car and drive to the fishing village of Nazaré, which takes its name from Nazareth in the Holy Land. For centuries the Portuguese have been fishermen. Today fishing is Portugal's second largest industry. Nazaré's picturesque fishing boats catch the off-shore sardines, anchovies, tuna and other salt-water fish. For over 400 years Portuguese fishing fleets have crossed the Atlantic Ocean to the Grand Banks off Newfoundland, Canada, to catch codfish. This food, when salted and dried, is one of the most important of all Portuguese food.

On a hill that juts out into the bay of Nazaré, we see the varinas, or womenfolk of the fishermen, and the teams of oxen waiting for the boats to return. Suddenly the women start to move and, looking out to sea, we notice small dots moving toward land. As the dots move closer, we make out that they are the fishing boats coming in. These bulky wooden vessels at a distance look like melon rinds floating on the water. They are gaily painted with many-colored designs. When finally a boat hits bottom on the beach, a fisherman jumps out of the boat. A piece of rope is quickly connected from the craft to a team of oxen. The oxen then drag the boat up on the beach.

Once the boat is on land, everyone helps in the sorting of the fish, putting them in baskets. It is a colorful sight. The men wear bright plaid shirts, black trousers, and heavy, long-tasseled stocking caps. The fishwives are dressed entirely in black. They wear broad black felt hats with flat tops. As the men lay out the nets to dry, the women carry the baskets of fish on their heads from the beach to the market or to the local canning factory. The shape of their hats makes it easier for them to balance the heavy load.

Arriving back late at night from Nazaré, we go straight to our hotel and to bed. Tomorrow morning, an airplane will take us to Rabat, capital of Morocco.

Teams of oxen strain to pull a fishing boat out of the reach of tides on the sandy beach at Nazaré.

294

Across North Africa

While airborne on the way from Lisbon to North Africa, we glance again at the atlas and note that Africa is the second largest continent. Actually, it contains about one-fifth of all land on earth! Nevertheless, for such a large continent, Africa has a very short coastline. It is three times as large as Europe, yet its coastline is much shorter. The shorter coastline of Africa is due to the fact that the continent has comparatively few bays and peninsulas, and no extensions of the sea running far inland.

Along the southern coast of the Mediterranean Sea, on the continent of Africa, is a group of countries which are each similar in climate, land and resources. These North African countries include the United Arab Republic (now only Egypt), Sudan, Libya, Tunisia, Algeria, Morocco and the Spanish Sahara. With the exception of Sudan, all of these countries touch the Mediterranean Sea or the Atlantic Ocean. The people are generally similar in physical characteristics, as are their ways of living.

Our first stop in North Africa is the Kingdom of Morocco, which is located at the northwest corner of the continent

Gibraltar, the "steppingstone between Europe and Africa," is a peninsula three miles long, 1400 feet high, and seven miles in circumference. It is joined to the Spanish mainland by a low, sandy isthmus nearly a mile wide. It is Britain's oldest possession in the Mediterranean.

— almost touching Spain. It is actually about fourteen miles across the Mediterranean Sea from Gibraltar. To the north, Morocco is on the Mediterranean Sea. The coastline here is rugged. To the west, the Atlantic Ocean laps at the low sandy beaches of Morocco. To the south, the country borders the Spanish Sahara and Mauritania, while its eastern neighbor is Algeria. The size of Morocco is roughly that of California. It is about as far north of the equator as that part of the United States which stretches from northern Florida to the Virginia-North Carolina border.

Our atlas shows, or seems to imply, that the landscape of Morocco varies from beaches to plains, from snow-capped mountains and fertile valley to desert. The principal mountains are the Atlas range. Beyond these mountains the Sahara Desert stretches to the south and to the east. Along the Mediterranean coast in the north is another range called the Rif Mountains. Altogether, one-third of Morocco's territory is covered with mountains. In the hills and mountains, people tend herds of cattle, sheep and goats.

A short while after taking off, we see the famous Rock of Gibraltar. Connected with southern Spain by a sandy strip of land, the Rock, as Gibraltar is popularly called, is very steep on the eastern and northern side. To the west and south the land slopes more gradually to the water. Here the town of Gibraltar has been built. The Rock is a British possession and is one of the strongest fortresses in the world.

296

Later, while looking out the plane's window, a white city with white walls appears below us. Those towers, which rise here and there above the rest of the buildings, are the minarets of the Moslem temples, or mosques, where the priests call the people to prayer. Those trees which rise high above the flat roofs are date palms. The stewardess tells us that Rabat is one of the four imperial cities, or residences, of the King of Morocco. The other three imperial cities are Fez, Marrakech and Meknès. Rabat, however, is the capital of Morocco.

Rabat's modern section has broad avenues, many beautiful gardens, several modern large department stores, and the office buildings which are the headquarters of the Moroccan government. By contrast, in the old parts of the city, there are narrow, twisting streets, some only three or four feet wide and hemmed in by two- or three-story houses. Our walk through the native quarter, or medina, takes us past a beautiful mosque, and at our guide's suggestion, we stop to visit it. He explains that tourists may enter, provided the custom is observed of removing one's shoes at the entrance.

Northwest African nation, lying along the Atlantic and Mediterranean coasts. **Area** • about 160,000 sq. m. **Population** • 12,360,000. **Language** • Arabic, French, Spanish, Berber. **Government** • Monarchy (until 1956, a protectorate of France and Spain). **Monetary Unit** • Dirham (= about 0.20 U.S. $). **Chief Cities** • Casablanca, Marrakech, Rabat (capital), Tangier (formerly an international zone). **Religion** • chiefly Moslem. **Mountains** • Mount Toubkal, in the Atlas Mountains (13,665 ft.), is the highest mountain in North Africa. **Rivers** • Oumer Rbia, Sebou.

In the Old Section of one of Morocco's principal cities, the city of Rabat.

The inside court of the mosque is decorated beautifully with mosaics of gold, blue and green. The main prayer room is very large, but there are no seats. These are not needed since the Moslems worship on the floor. The floor, therefore, is covered with thick, soft rugs.

There are many worshippers in the prayer room, all kneeling on the rug, saying their prayers. Everyone is faced in the same direction, looking toward the east, for Moslems always pray with their faces toward Mecca, which is in that direction from Rabat. Mecca, in Saudi Arabia, is the birthplace of the prophet Mohammed, the founder of the Islam religion, sometimes known as Mohammedanism. To Moslems, Mecca is the holiest of all cities.

In the outer courtyards of the mosque, there are fountains where turbaned, long-gowned men are washing themselves before entering the prayer room. The Moslem always washes himself before he prays — even when he is out on the desert, where no water is available, he rubs his hands and face with sand. A devout Moslem prays five times a day. We see a turbaned priest away up on the gallery of the minaret calling out the hour of prayer. His words are in Arabic, but our guide tells us what they mean. He is saying: "Come to prayer! Come to prayer! Prayer is better than sleep. Come to prayer!"

Since today is Friday, the Moslem's Sabbath, our guide takes us to a spot near the Imperial Palace. In a few minutes the king rides past on a beautifully decorated horse, accompanied by a group of scarlet-clad foot soldiers, on his way to Djamea Abel Fez Mosque to preside over prayers. He is not only King of Morocco, but is also the head of the Islam religion in this part of the world.

298

Our guide tells us that it is most interesting to visit Rabat's sister city, Salé, just across the mouth of the Bou Regreg. While crossing over the bridge into Salé, he informs us that in the Middle Ages this city was the most important commercial center and port on the Moroccan west coast. European traders came here to exchange cloth and manufactured products for skins, wool, carpets, ivory and honey. In the seventeenth century, Salé became an important stronghold of pirates. The mouth of the river between the two cities afforded easy protection to the port. But the river has since filled with sand, and a sand bar has accumulated across its mouth. Today, only small vessels can enter it from the ocean.

"What an odd city!" is our first impression. The square houses with their flat roofs look like large white cardboard boxes jumbled together along narrow streets with no uniform order. A friend of our guide invites us to visit his home.

The house has blank white walls facing the street. Entering, we come into a court paved with tiles and lighted by a lantern of bright-colored glass. The court is surrounded by good-sized rooms, each of which has a low ledge running along the wall that serves as sofa and chairs. In the bedrooms there are wider ledges, upon which the residents of the house sleep at night. But the house is by no means uncomfortable. The floors are of stone and tile, and covered with beautiful rugs. The high ceilings make the rooms cool, and there is a fretwork of wood above each door for air.

Inside the walled area is a garden where there are palm trees, orange and lemon trees, tropical plants and flowers. Our host takes us up to the roof of the house, which is flat and has a little wall around it. We get a good view of the city and see that all Salé is flat-roofed. The buildings are generally uniformly low. The few that rise high above the rest are mosques.

As we stand on the roof, our attention is drawn to flocks

A Berber barber at work in the streets of old Salé.

Above, left, the market outside the walls of Rabat; above, right, entering Maknes through one of the ancient city gates.

of storks — sacred birds — perched on nests built in tree-tops, on roofs of houses, minarets and mosques. Our guide tells us that many Moroccans consider it a blessing when their home is chosen by storks for the building of a nest. When a stork abandons her nest on a house, the inhabitants consider it a bad omen.

"If storks are white and clean when they settle on a house," the guide continues, "many people believe that there will be a great deal of sunshine and extremely hot weather and that the year will be bad. But if the birds are gray and dirty, there will be plenty of rain, and the year will turn out to be a good one."

Our host offers us a cup of mint tea, a favorite Moslem drink, and as he leaves the room to obtain it, our guide whispers, "We should leave after the third cup of tea has been served." He continues by saying that on the other hand, our host would probably feel we were ungrateful if we were to depart before drinking the customary three cups. As we leave, after drinking the three cups of tea, our guide says *"Shukren, Allah ysalmak,"* which means "Thank you and good-by." Our host replies, *"Sharraft. Sharrifuna qariban. Ma'assalaama,"* which our guide tells us means, "You are welcome. Please come again. Good-by."

On leaving the house, we continue our stroll in the

300

Left: Inside the walls of the Great Mosque in Casablanca. Below: Portrait of a young Moroccan girl.

streets of Salé. How crowded they are! Unlike Rabat, across the river, there are very few motor vehicles. The only means of carrying heavy things is by donkeys or camels. The riders and other burden-bearers are constantly shouting to each other to keep out of the way. Streets are so narrow that people have to jump from one side to the other to avoid the traffic. We stop at the stand of a fruit peddler and buy figs and dates, and then go back to our hotel in Rabat.

In the morning, our guide takes us to the market outside the walls of Rabat. It is like a gypsy encampment. There are little tents scattered over the fields. Among them are men, women and children sitting on the ground or moving about, or standing in groups. They laugh, chat, buy and sell. Here two people are quarreling, there one is pulling a donkey away from another, and farther over are three long-gowned Arabs preparing their camels for a caravan trip across the desert. The ungainly animals are down on their knees, and they groan as each new burden is added.

We drive beyond Rabat to a large fruit farm that raises figs for export to the United States and Europe. When the figs are ripe, they are gathered and laid upon boards in the sun to dry, pressed into shape one by one, and then packed in boxes for shipment.

Morocco has many delicious figs; some kinds are white,

some black, some purple, and others yellow or green. The purple figs are among the best, although the yellow ones are more attractive in appearance. Fig trees are raised from seeds. The sprouts are transplanted in rows spaced sixteen feet apart or more. They begin to yield fruit in three years, and some varieties will produce two crops a year for hundreds of years. Figs are grown in different parts of northern Africa, in Spain, Portugal and Greece, and also in California.

In the morning, our trip is continued by taking a train to Casablanca, the largest city of Morocco. We pass fields of green barley, wheat and corn, and see many fig orchards, surrounded by prickly pear hedges, and groves of dark-green olive trees loaded with fruit. There are some vineyards, and lemon and orange trees, too. While some modern farm equipment can be seen now and then, much of the work on the small farms is done with crude hand tools. The plows generally have but one handle, are often little more than crooked sticks shod with iron which barely manage to scratch the surface of the ground. However, some large plows are pulled by camels or oxen.

The train occasionally crosses streams and small rivers, where we always find farmers using the water to irrigate the fields. Although a few modern irrigation systems are in use, the farmers generally water their fields as their ancestors did centuries ago. The water is raised from the stream or river to the ground levels by two wheels set at right angles to each other. These wheels are connected to a third wheel, which has clay jars tied to its rim and is so set that, as it turns, the jars dip into the water and fill. As the jars come to the top, they empty into a trough which leads out to the fields. The motive power is usually provided by a blindfolded ox, camel or mule.

After arriving at the Casablanca railway station, a taxi picks us up and drives to our hotel which faces the Place de France. This square is the hub of the city from which

302

all its main thoroughfares radiate. All around are white office and apartment buildings. Thus, Casablanca's name (meaning "white house" in Spanish) still describes it aptly, except that today many of the houses and buildings are considerably taller than was the case when Europeans named the place.

Our tour of the city starts at the harbor, which is an especially interesting place to visit. Ships from all parts of the world lie inside several jetties, or walls which enclose several hundred acres of water. The harbor is deep enough to accommodate the largest ocean liners. At one time ships could not dock at Casablanca except in calm weather, but now, because of these man-made jetties which extend out into the harbor, there is safe anchorage in any kind of weather. We stroll out on one of the jetties and watch the loading and unloading of products and foodstuffs. The chief products brought into Morocco by sea are cotton, meat, flour, farm machinery, tea and sugar. Exported are the skins of sheep and goats, the hides of cattle, and also wool, cork, wax, olive oil, almonds, eggs, figs and various kinds of fruit. Casablanca is one of the great Atlantic ports in Africa.

Like all large cities of North Africa, this city has a modern section and an old section. Turning our steps away from the harbor, we go on up into the old part of the city. Here the majority of the people are natives, chiefly Berbers or Kabyles, Caucasian tribes which have lived here for ages. Many of them have fair complexions, rosy cheeks, blue eyes and light-colored hair. Other natives, such as the Moors, are the descendants of Moslem warriors who conquered northern Africa centuries ago and who are still the ruling classes throughout the country.

Berber men as well as women wear long robes for protection against the hot sun. The men generally wear turbans, or headdresses consisting of a cap with a scarf wound around it. A few wear a fez, a brimless felt cap, usually red and often having a black tassel, which gets its name because it was

Bazaar in the native shopping district of Casablanca.

303

first made in the city of Fez, Morocco. Some of the women wear veils over their faces, a custom of the Arabs. Our guide informs us that the majority of Moroccans speak Arabic, observe Arabic social manners, wear Arabic dress, and practice the Islam religion. Only in the remote southern mountain areas are there people who still keep the ancient Berber customs and speak the Berber language.

The streets are very narrow in the old section of the city. The houses here are also flat-roofed, with white walls and with but few windows facing the streets. Many of the business streets are covered over with awnings to protect people against the hot sun. It seems almost twilight, although the glare of a hot midday sun is present on the other streets. Facing these roofed-over streets are boxlike stores, most of which are little more than holes in the walls. A merchant is in each shop, with all of his merchandise piled around him or hung upon racks overhead, each man having his own "specialty" for sale. Some are selling perfume, some rugs, some spices, and others the leather goods for which Morocco is famous. There are shoe stores and grocery stores, cook shops where meat is being broiled on iron skewers over basins of charcoal, sweetmeat shops where candies and dried fruits are kept. We buy delicious fresh dates and figs that are grown in Morocco. We also watch men working at their trades in the shops. One is weaving silk, and another making the red fez caps. In a side street boys embroider red leather slippers. Across the street are smiths hammering at jewelry of silver and gold. The native shopping district, or bazaar, as it is called, is a busy place, indeed.

Next, our tour takes us to the new part of the city, where the stores are quite modern. We walk the wide avenues of Arab League Park, which provide the city with a large patch of green in its center. Our afternoon is enhanced by a refreshing swim at a nearby beach.

The next morning we board a jet airliner at Casablanca's

304

Cazes Airport for Cairo, the largest city on the continent of Africa and the capital of the United Arab Republic, or U.A.R., formerly called Egypt.

Looking out the window, we see that much of the land is brown and barren. The stewardess says that our plane is now flying over the Sahara Desert, the largest wasteland in the world, so vast that if four mighty giants were to lift it up at the corners and drop it down upon the United States, it would not only cover our country, but in places it would also extend into Canada and the Gulf of Mexico.

The word "Sahara," which comes from the Arabic, means "uninhabited wilderness." Only a small part of it is inhabited. Oases are scattered about wells and springs, and here the land is rich and abundant with vegetation. Many oases have their little settlements, shaded by date palms and other trees.

In general, however, the Sahara is a waste of dry land cut by dry mountain chains, with many valleys and dry beds of rivers running this way and that. Here it consists of a vast plain of sand, there the land rises to a rocky plateau, and miles farther on are bleak and bare mountains as ragged and stony as the Rockies. Here the sand has blown and drifted into dunes or hills that look like snowdrifts; and there the plain is covered with pebbles and boulders, smooth round stones of many colors.

Some people look upon a desert as all low, flat and sandy, but that is not the nature of much of the Sahara. For the most part, it consists of lofty plateaus, the average height of the land being more than a quarter of a mile above the Mediterranean Sea. The desert is often called a sea of sand. It might be better to describe it as a billowy ocean of rock and sand tossed by the storms of time into all sorts of shapes. If the Sahara were *all* waste, there would be even less travel through it, but here and there, along the northern and southern edges, is some scanty vegetation which furnishes pasture for camels and sheep. Other regions are so

A camel caravan making its way across the desert.

green during parts of the winter and spring that the wandering herdsmen drive their animals there to feed. The oases are islands of green in this dry ocean, made fertile by the water from springs, wells or underground streams. Date palms, orange, lemon and fruit trees grow there, while in the desert itself one often finds ragged plants bristling with thorns.

Flying low, we see a camel caravan making its way across the desert. The camels are loaded down with cotton, palm oil, ivory and other products from the rain forests and grasslands and are carrying them to northern African cities for export to all parts of the world. Camels, often called "ships of the desert," have feet that are wide and flat, and thus are well-adapted to walking on sand. They also can go for a long time without taking food or water because they store food in their humps and water in parts of their stomachs. Most of the camels used in cargo caravans are dromedaries, or one-humped camels.

Our jet airplane lands at Algiers in Algeria, Tunis in Tunisia and Tripoli in Libya, but we do not leave the plane. Starting the last portion of the flight across North Africa, we study our atlas again. A quick look at the map of the U.A.R. may give a false impression of the country.

306

On the map, Egypt is a big country — it is roughly the size of Texas and New Mexico combined. But most of this land is barren desert; a space equal to only one-half of the state of West Virginia is inhabited. Almost all of this inhabited land lies along the Nile River, and it is one of the most densely populated regions in the world.

The Nile is the longest river in Africa, and with the exception of the combined Mississippi-Missouri in the United States, the longest in the world. It rises in the highlands near the equator, having its source in Lake Victoria, the largest lake in Africa. From this lake, the Nile is turbulent for hundreds of miles through rapids. Then it winds on its way, spreading out into a wide fan until it empties into the Mediterranean Sea. During its course, the Nile receives some large tributaries, among others the Blue Nile and the Takkaze River, sometimes called the Black Nile from the color of its waters. The Blue Nile and the Takkaze rise in the highlands of Ethiopia, where there are beds of rich soil. When the tropical rains come, this soil erodes into the rivers to

Consisting solely of Egypt, the U.A.R. is situated in the northeastern corner of Africa and the Sinai peninsula in Asia. **Area** • 386,198 sq. m. **Population** • 27,285,000. **Language** • Arabic. **Government** • Republic; from 1958 to 1961 the U.A.R. also included Syria. **Monetary Unit** • Egyptian pound (= about 1.32 U.S. $). **Chief Cities** • Cairo (capital and the largest city in Africa), Alexandria, Port Said. **Religion** • over 90% Moslem, about 8% Christian (mainly Copts). **Mountains** • Jebel Katherina (8,651 ft.) and Jebel Musa (7,400 ft.) in Sinai are the highest. **Rivers** • the Nile (about 930 miles long in Egypt) is the most important — 95% of the people live along its banks. Great dams — at Aswan, Jebel Aulia, and other spots — have been built to store the annual Nile overflow. The Suez Canal, linking the Mediterranean with the Gulf of Suez, is in Egypt and is now under Egyptian control. **Lakes** • Manzala, Burullus, Idku are salt lakes along the Nile delta.

Ancient and modern forms of transportation are in sharp contrast in the United Arab Republic. Travellers arriving by plane at Cairo's modern airport see picturesque feluccas on the Nile. These native boats have remained virtually unchanged in design and motive power since the days of the Pharaohs.

such an extent that it fills not only their waters, but later even the Nile itself. When the Nile is high, the water floods over the countryside, some of the silt descends to the bottom, and remains on land when the river recedes. Thus, the Nile has in effect built up the land of Egypt. This rich soil varies in depth from twenty to forty feet. It is said to rise about six inches every hundred years.

The good land extends as far as the line of the flooding water and no farther. Beyond, all is sand and barren rock. A man can stand with one foot entirely hidden in the richest of crops, while the other rests on the barren desert. Accordingly, along the greater part of its course, the Nile runs through a trough in the desert. The fertile strip is so narrow in places that we could walk across it in an hour, yet at other places it is so wide that it would take us about half a day to go from one side to the other. However, until it reaches the latitude of Cairo, the valley of Egypt is nowhere more than nine or ten miles wide, although it is almost a thousand miles long. Below Cairo, as already pointed out, it spreads out like a fan. Each rib is about one hundred miles long, ending at the Mediterranean. This fan is the delta of Egypt, so named from the fourth letter of the Greek alphabet, which also has a fanlike shape.

The United Arab Republic has little rain, but the Nile gives it water throughout the year, and at flood times furnishes it a meal of the rich silt which brings about a flourishing agriculture without other fertilization. However, when rains are light in the mountains of central Africa, there are no great floods. Then Egypt may suffer from famine. To control and supply water to larger areas, dams and irrigation systems have been, or are being built. We will see several of them on our journey down the Nile. But while irrigation solves one problem, it creates another. Today the Nile Valley land is farmed heavily and because the dams do not permit the river to overflow and bring the annual layer of silt, the soil is losing its fertility and productivity.

Aerial view of Cairo.

Tinsmith at work in the bazaar section of Cairo.

The time has passed quickly as our plane has made its way to our destination. A short time later, the instruction, "Fasten seat belts" flashes on, and the plane prepares to land at Cairo International Airport. On the way to our hotel, our taxi driver volunteers to show us Cairo's old section. Like the cities visited in Morocco, this part of the city has narrow, crooked streets. On many of them we notice shops selling all kinds of items, such as perfume, jewelry, leather goods and rugs. The white houses along the streets are all flat-roofed and have tiny barred windows. The new section of Cairo is like any modern city — there are wide streets, plenty of parks, and fine modern apartment houses, hotels, stores and offices. Men's fashion, as well as women's, is different in the modern section. The *galibiyeh* and the fez of the man and the *melaya* of the woman are giving way to Western dress. The *galibiyeh* is a long flowing garment that resembles a nightshirt. Most of these robes are made of striped material, with stripes of black-and-white being the more popular. The *melaya* is a long, full-sleeved black gown, flowing almost to the ground. Around their heads the women wind a black scarf. Even in the city, many men and women walk barefoot.

We also see several factories. Petroleum is now one of the major industries of the United Arab Republic. Mining industries have also increased production. Other industries being developed are food processing, chemical, and engineering. The output of medicine, fertilizers, crop sprays, and paper is constantly increasing. Heavy manufacturing industries are turning out more cars, stoves, engines and gas heaters. In this once almost wholly agricultural country, industry now accounts for more than one-fourth of the national income.

Having already visited the bazaars and native shops of Casablanca, Rabat and Salé, we decide to travel in the footsteps of the kings and people who belonged almost at the beginning of history. We shall see the Pyramids, the Sphinx and other monuments; and later, in the Museum at Cairo, the statues of the monarchs, the pharaohs who made them, and even the very kings themselves, for many of their bodies are preserved to this day.

The Pyramids have for ages been considered among the wonders of the world. They are enormous monuments of stone, built as tombs by the Egyptian rulers, four or five thousand years ago. The remains of fifty or sixty Pyramids have been found in different parts of the Nile Valley. The three largest and best preserved are here in the desert, about eight miles from Cairo, at Giza. One of these, the Great Pyramid, was constructed by Pharaoh Khufu, or Cheops, who was king of Egypt more than three thousand years before Christ was born. It is one of the most massive structures ever built by man.

On the way to the Pyramids we cross the Nile over an old iron bridge guarded by bronze lions, and ride in a horse-drawn carriage through a long avenue of acacia trees, the branches of which intertwine overhead. Shortly after leaving Cairo, the Pyramids appear through the trees. They seem small at first, but their size becomes larger as we approach. They look like three huge piles of stones against the blue sky. It is only after leaving the carriage and getting a bit closer to them that we can appreciate their

Aerial view of the Pyramids at Giza.

size. As we look up, it seems as though the whole sky is walled with stone. Surrounded by other less imposing pyramids, the Great Pyramid was once 482 feet high; and, although a great deal of it was carted away to make buildings in Cairo, it is still about 450 feet high. Its base covers nearly thirteen acres, and its top is a platform large enough to support a good-sized house. It is an almost solid mass of stone, made of great blocks which are piled up in the shape of steps, growing smaller in size near the top. The Great Pyramid is perfectly square at the bottom, carefully lined up so that its sides face directly north, east, south and west. The triangular sides rise to almost a peak at the top.

Our guide tells us that this monument was built by forced labor. It took one hundred thousand men twenty years to construct it, while ten years were required prior to that to build a road for transporting the stones. Most of the stones came from distant mountains and were ferried down the Nile. The Egyptians of this period had not yet invented wheels or pulleys, and they had no horses or other draft animals, so they moved the stone blocks into place by sliding them up huge inclined ramps. When Cheops died, he was buried with his queen inside the Pyramid, separate rooms having been made for the queen and himself.

After our visit to the Pyramids, we hire camels to carry us a short distance across the sands of the Saraha to the Sphinx, another mighty monument erected by the ancient kings. The camels are made to kneel down before us. Upon seating ourselves in the wooden saddles on the camels' back, our guide gives a signal and the camels seem to stumble to their feet. They bounce us first backward as they rise on their front legs, then forward as they get up on their hind legs, then backward again as they straighten out their forelegs. And we are off! The camels swing along with a motion like that of a boat on the waves. At first we have an uncomfortable feeling, but this passes. Travel is not too bad on the back of a camel — if the distance is short enough!

A camel driver pauses for a moment's rest before the Great Sphinx of Giza, "Guardian of the Nile Valley." The Sphinx, carved out of a mass of natural rock, with paws of masonry, is a 189-foot-long figure combining a human head with an animal's body. It has played an important role in Egyptian religion and Greek mythology.

A gold statuette of the God Amon, found in the ruins of the Great Temple of Amon at Karnak, dating from about 900 B.C.

Our camels move fairly quickly across the sand and in a short time we are in front of the strange statue known as the Sphinx. No one knows just how old it is or why it was made. It is an enormous figure, with the crouching body of a lion and the head of a man, cut out of a solid block of rock, as high as a five-story building and so large that it would about cover an ordinary city lot. The body is 187 feet long and its forelegs measure fifty feet. A man standing on the tip of its ear could not reach the crown of the head. The ears are each four feet long, the nose measures more than five and one half feet, and its mouth is so big that, if it were open, an ox or a camel could be put inside it. The face of the Sphinx is now somewhat mutilated, for it has been worn away by the sands of the desert during the past five or six thousand years.

Returning to Cairo, our tour of ancient history continues with a visit to the museum, where scores of mummies which have been found in tombs are on exhibit. These mummies are the real bodies of the ancient kings, or pharaohs, as they were called, so treated with ointments that they have not crumbled to dust. The limbs are wrapped around with many cloths. Some faces are so lifelike that it seems as though they might talk. In other rooms are articles taken from the tombs. There are gold bracelets and rings like coiled snakes, similar to the jewelry of today. There are fishhooks such as the ones in use now, writing materials, and other things which show us that the Egyptians of four thousand years ago were not much different from us.

In the evening, antiquity is left behind as we visit the tallest concrete structure in the world, the new 630-foot Tower of Cairo, located on Gezira Island in the middle of the Nile. This impressive modern-looking tower features an unusual restaurant at the top which revolves 360 degrees, affording us a panoramic view of the city, the Pyramids, the Sphinx and the desert beyond.

After spending two days in Cairo, we board a river

steamer for a trip up the Nile. Our boat moves along past farm fields and small villages. The fields are enclosed by low mud walls, which keep the water from running off into the river. The crops are spread out before our eyes in a many-colored patchwork, through which run roads, paths and silvery canals. That field of whiteness in the distance is Egyptian cotton. The green expanse at the left is clover, which grows here as luxuriantly as anywhere in the world. Farther on are corn and sugar cane rising and falling under the wind from the desert. As our steamer slowly moves past pastures, many animals are observed, each tied to a stake or watched by a herdsman. There are camels, donkeys and water buffaloes; there are flocks of fat sheep and goats, and here and there a horse or mule.

In the fields, farmers are hard at work, most of them using very crude tools. These farmers and field workers, known as fellahs, form about three-fourths of the whole population. They are the descendants of the ancient Egyptians mixed with the various races which have conquered the country.

The fellahs live in villages and travel to the fields to work their farms. The villages are sometimes shaded by date palms, but often they have no trees whatsoever. There are no yards or gardens. The houses are square huts made of mud or sun-dried brick, the roofs of straw or palm leaves are flat, the walls are thick, and there usually is just one door. Most houses are of one story, and few have more than two small rooms. Near the roof are little square holes which admit the air, and also serve as windows.

We learn that the furniture in most of these houses consists of little more than a few mats, a copper kettle and some earthenware pots. The bed is a ledge, built in the side of the room, and covered with a cotton mattress. Fires are not needed for heating, and the cooking is usually done out of doors on little stoves of burnt clay. The ordinary food is a coarse bread of corn, wheat, or millet made up in round,

Above, Egyptian Cat Goddess from about 600 B.C., and below, golden hair ornaments from about 1500 B.C.

flat cakes. The fellahs eat vegetables, eggs, cheese and dates; but they seldom have meat. They sit about on the ground at their meals. They rarely have forks, and nearly everyone eats with his fingers. Cattle and other farm animals feed out of doors all the year round, and are often taken into the house with the family at night.

As our steamer continues along, we notice many interesting methods employed by the farmers to lift water from the level of the irrigation canals to the level of their fields. Here are two men standing knee-deep in the canal with a basketwork bucket hung by rope between them. They are scooping the water from the canal into the bucket. With a swinging motion, they cast it into another canal higher up. In the end, it reaches the fields. That is one method of irrigation which is used widely in Egypt.

There are many other methods of irrigation, and among them is the great wheel with jars attached to its rim, such as was seen in Morocco. The wheels move about in the wells or canals, and as they turn, raise the water and pour it into troughs, through which it flows over the fields. An animal keeps the wheel moving, and a boy or girl runs along behind to use a whip when needed. There are more than fifty thousand such wheels in lower Egypt, requiring about twice that number of buffaloes and donkeys, usually blindfolded, to keep them in motion. At a few places we see some gasoline engines pumping water from the canals.

The climate grows warmer as we go up the river, and the difference affects the seasons of seedtime and harvest. Generally three crops are grown. The winter provides a grain crop. This is sown in November and harvested in May or June. The summer crop is sown in March, April and May, when the Nile is low, and is harvested in October and November. It yields cotton, sugar and rice. The autumn crop, which is sown in July and gathered in September and October, consists of rice, corn, millet, watermelons, cantaloupe and vegetables. Other crops include dates and citrus

314

fruits such as oranges, lemons and mangoes. The mango tastes like a combined orange and cantaloupe, sweet and juicy.

In the delta vast quantities of cotton are produced, as well as rice, wheat and corn. Cotton is the most valuable crop, being exported throughout the world. Egyptian cotton has a fiber which is very desirable for certain kinds of cloth. Much of it is imported by manufacturers in the United States.

Stopping at a small village to pick up some passengers, we stroll about the village and stop at a grove of date palm trees. With our guide serving as an interpreter (most people of Egypt are Arabic-speaking Moslems), we learn from a farmer how dates are grown. We pick some dates from the younger trees and bite into them. The ripe dates are delicious, but the green ones pucker the mouth like unripe persimmons.

The date palm, although it thrives on the dry air of the desert, must have plenty of water about its roots or it will die. The Arabs call it the queen of trees. It is said that the palm tree must have its head in the burning sun and its feet in running water. For this reason the orchards are irrigated. Ditches are dug around the trees to keep the roots moist. The date trees is usually grown from one of the suckers which sprout from the trunks of the older trees. The suckers

315

are taken off and planted. If watered well, they strike root at once, and within four or five years begin to have fruit. They are in full bearing at about eleven years, after which they will each yield a hundred pounds or more of dates a year for about a century.

Along the Nile the date palm begins to blossom in April, great bunches of beautiful flowers sprouting out of its top. The blossoms fall after a time and green dates appear. As the summer goes on, they change to a reddish or yellowish color, and grow brighter until they are ripe, when the yellow dates are the color of amber and the red dates are brownish or black. As the fruit ripens, the flesh, which was at first unpleasant to the taste, changes and becomes very sweet. The dates shipped to the United States are generally sweet dates. Before being exported they are allowed to dry on the trees. They shrink as they dry and after a week or so are ready to be picked and packed for the market. Dates are exported in bags or long wooden boxes, the choicest varieties being repacked before they go to Europe or the United States.

Along the Nile, we also see the ruins of several old temples. At Luxor, there is the Temple of Karnak and its famous Hypostyle Hall, with the largest single chamber of any temple in the world. Within the walls of this temple there would be room for three of the biggest cathedrals we have already seen — Notre Dame of Paris, St. Paul's of London, and St. Peter's of Rome. The central columns, or

Native village in an oasis near Memphis, Egypt.

At left, hieroglyphics on the wall of the ruins of the Great Temple of Amon at Karnak, and, (below) close-ups of pillars of the temple, showing carvings of lotus and papyrus, ancient symbols of Upper and Lower Egypt.

supports, of the Temple of Karnak are seventy feet tall, and so large that fifty of us could stand on top of one of them. Also at Luxor, we view the Temple of Amun (also called Amon and Amon-Re) and its two-mile avenue of ram-headed sphinxes. Present-day Luxor is on the site of the ancient city of Thebes, which was the capital of Egypt for many centuries.

At Aswan, we see the world's longest dam, more than a mile from end to end. The dam supplies electrical power to the United Arab Republic's industry and serves to keep the annual flood waters in check so that they may be used for irrigation the year round. One of the finest of the ancient temples that lined the banks of the Nile, the Temple of Isis, is now completely covered by the waters of the lake which the Aswan Dam created. We are told that when the flood-gates of the dam are open to provide needed water in the Nile Valley, the temple with its beautiful columns and statues emerges briefly from the water. It is then covered again with the rising waters.

Farther upstream, we see men and machines working on

317

the new Aswan High Dam, which when completed will be the greatest dam in the world, as well as being the largest man-made structure on earth. The High Dam power station will triple Egypt's electrical output and lower the consumer cost of electricity by one-third. Branch lines will carry power along the Nile Valley and through the delta region to provide energy for a new industrial area in Egypt's eastern desert and enrich the new agricultural region of the western desert. The lake, two thousand miles in area, will become a breeding-ground for fish and help provide more food for the people. But because of the High Dam and others that are being built along the Nile, many more of the ancient temples are in danger of being drowned by new artificial lakes. An international organization has been formed for the purpose of moving these art treasures out of the river valley and placing them on higher ground.

We visit one of the Egyptian treasures threatened by the High Dam. It is the Temple and Colossi of Rameses at Abu Simbel. Carved out of the face of a rock mountain by skilled stonemasons, these beautiful monuments took twenty-five thousand workers twenty years to complete. The two temples are located on the west bank of the Nile in lower Nubia, eight hundred miles south of Cairo. Pharaoh Rameses II ordered the Great Temple built to honor the Sun God Ra Horakhti, and, like all pharaohs, to honor himself as "the living God." The smaller temple downstream was dedicated to Hathor, Goddess of Love, Music and the Dance, and also to Rameses' Queen, the lovely Nefertari. While the smaller Temple of Nefertari has been known to history for many hundreds of years, the Great Temple of Rameses is a comparatively recent discovery. A surprised Swiss traveler, exploring the Nefertari monument in 1812, noticed what turned out to be a stone head protruding through a nearby sand dune. The occasion marked the start of a hundred years of digging, culminating in the exposure of four Colossi and the Great Temple.

318

When we recall the simple tools of the builders, the size of Abu Simbel is almost unbelievable. Guarded by four giant statues of Rameses II, each sixty-seven feet tall, the Great Temple is one hundred and eight feet high, one hundred and twenty-five feet wide and extends more than two hundred feet into the mountainside. Entering the great hall, we are amazed by the sense of power and strength emanating from eight statues of Rameses. Each one is thirty feet high, standing erect against the wall. In the main chamber, somehow miraculously preserved through the ages, a colorful painted wall depicts the courage of Rameses in his battles to overcome the Hittite enemy. Mysterious passageways lead into lesser halls, then into the inner sanctuary. Here one comes face to face with four larger-than-life statues: the god Ra Horakhti, the sun god to whom the temple was dedicated; Amun, God of Thebes; Ptah, God of Memphis; and Rameses himself. Three hundred feet to the right, downstream from the Great Temple, stands the Temple of Nefertari, known also as the Small Temple of Abu Simbel. Forty feet high, ninety feet wide and seventy feet deep, this temple contains six 33-foot-tall statues of the king and queen, alternating across the front part of the building. The structure boasts many interesting features, including a hieroglyphic inscription (ancient Egyptian writing) that tells of the coronation of Queen Nefertari.

Head of Nefertiti, queen of King Akhenaton, and reputed to be one of the most beautiful women of ancient times.

The valley narrows as we go southward. We are often close to the desert and sometimes between rocky hills and strips of green marking the banks of the Nile. Everywhere half-naked men and boys are raising the water and pouring it into ditches, through which it is conducted over the land. Everywhere are the same kind of mud villages shaded by date palms that we saw in Lower Egypt.

Later on, we must leave our boat and take a motor bus to Khartoum, capital city of Sudan. This ends our tour of North Africa. Now Africa south of the Sahara remains for us to see and explore.

Victoria Falls in Southern Rhodesia, Africa.

Africa South of the Sahara

UGANDA

Lake-filled country in Central Africa. **Area** • 93,981 sq. m. **Population** • 7,016,000. **Language** • Luganda, Bantu, Swahili. **Government** • formerly a British protectorate, Uganda became an independent republic in 1963; member British Commonwealth. **Monetary Unit** • East African shilling (= about 0.14 U.S. $). **Chief Cities** • Kampala (capital), Jinja. **Religion** • Christian, Moslem. **Mountains** • Ruwenzori (16,-795 ft.), Mount Elgon (14,178 ft.). **Rivers** • Victoria Nile, Albert Nile. **Lakes** • over 13,000 miles of lakes, most important are Lake Victoria Nyanza (world's second largest fresh-water lake) and Lakes Albert, Edward, and George.

From Khartoum, we board an airplane which takes us to Entebbe, which was the capital of Uganda before the country gained its independence. (Kampala is its capital now.) Our stewardess informs us that we are leaving the cradle of civilization, as Egypt is often called, for the lands of people who are among the most primitive on earth. Africa has more kinds of people and races of people than all the other continents put together. Its more than two hundred million people are divided into thousands of tribes that speak over seven hundred different languages. Africa is also the continent of new countries. Guinea, Ghana, Republic of Congo, Mauritania, Niger, Togo, Nigeria, Cameroon, Mali, Tanganyika, Ivory Coast and Sierra Leone are some of these countries.

Everything in Entebbe is new and different from what we expected before we arrived. Entebbe is not very far from the equator, but the weather is pleasant, and the

320

breezes from Lake Victoria are cool. We are on a high rolling plateau with mountains rising here and there far above it. To the east and south is Kilimanjaro, one of the tallest mountains in Africa and notable among the great mountains of the world. Kilimanjaro is only a few miles south of the equator, but its top is so high that it is always covered with snow. The natives who live in the tropical lowlands, where snow never falls, cannot understand what the white peak means. It is said that they believe Kilimanjaro is capped with molten silver, and that if they could climb to the top they might bring back a store of that precious metal. Farther northward, between us and the coast, is Mount Kenya, and on the west, on the other side of Uganda, are the Ruwenzori Mountains.

All the land about us is far above the level of the sea. It consists of rolling plains, with gorges here and there running through them. There are great troughs and basins in which are some of the largest lakes of the world, such as Lake Tanganyika, lying between the Republic of the Congo, Burundi, and Tanganyika; Lake Edward and Lake Albert on the west of Uganda; and Lake Victoria, where Kenya, Uganda and Tanganyika come together squarely on the equator. Lake Tanganyika is the world's longest lake, four hundred miles long from north to south.

Lake Victoria is larger than Lake Huron, almost three times the size of Lake Erie, and ranks just behind Lake Superior as the largest lake in the world. Its waters have a deep-blue color when seen from a distance.

The banks of Lake Victoria are grassy hills and rugged rocks. In some places near the shore the water is shallow, and there we see beds of papyrus reeds, the homes of hippopotamuses and crocodiles. There are many large islands, some of which are inhabited by natives, and also floating islands of papyrus reeds, patches which have been torn loose from the bed of the lake and which move to and fro with the current. Over a new hydroelectric dam in Uganda, the

Moving day in Kigezi, Uganda. The children join others at the end of the line, leaving their old home in the overpopulated Kabira district.

321

waters of Lake Victoria flow northward to create the mighty Nile River. Uganda is one of the smallest countries in Africa. It is about the size of the state of Wyoming.

From Entebbe, we take a side trip into the Ituri Forest, in the northeastern corner of the Republic of the Congo, which is so-called "pygmy country," because that is where these small people live. To get there, we travel by bus and then by sedan chair. The bus is not like the ones to which we are accustomed; it is just a truck fitted with wooden benches and canvas roof to protect the passengers from the sun. On the front and side of it is a legend that reads, "Hope we make it!" On the other buses are other mottoes or messages such as, "Safe Journey," "God is Love," and "In God We Trust, But Don't Trust Women." Each bus owner selects something appropriate and paints it somewhere on his truck as a means of identification.

After a bouncing journey along a dirt road, we stop at a small village in Uganda. The people of this part of the country have one of the highest cultures among native tribes of central Africa. They are polite, neat and clean, and they wear clothing of bark cloth or cotton. Some of them, however, take their clothes off when they are at work in their huts. This, we presume, is done to keep their clothing clean.

Their huts look a bit like haystacks in shape, rising from the ground in a cone. The doorway is cut in the side of the hut, with a bonnetlike projection over it. The houses have a framework of wood, covered with reeds. The walls are thick, and the houses are comfortable.

Entering one of these homes, we find that the roof is supported by poles. These are so arranged that they divide the interior into two apartments — front and rear. In the back, around the wall, are bunks in which the family sleep at night. The front room is where the cooking is done. The floor of the house is the ground. It is covered with soft grass, a new carpet of this kind being spread upon the old when it becomes dirty or wet. There is little furniture in the house.

Tribal chief from the Republic of the Congo.

322

The ordinary family is satisfied with a few wooden stools, a half-dozen earthenware pots, some wooden bowls, and basins made of wicker or grass.

The village is situated in a grove of trees surrounded by pasture lands. The people have cattle, sheep and goats, they raise chickens, and have dogs which seldom bark. Nearly every family has a garden of sweet potatoes and other vegetables, and some have patches of grain, sugar cane, and coffee plants.

Later, our bus makes another stop at a village in the Congo, and here we meet our guide and porters. For the four-mile trip to the pygmy village, our means of transportation are sedan chairs, which are borne on poles by porters — a comfortable way of traveling in the jungle forest!

Ngombo natives performing a war dance.

We finally arrive in the village. The pygmies are the smallest full-grown people in the world. The men are about four feet six inches tall and the women are still shorter. Many of the women are under four feet in height, and some are only a little taller than three feet. Still, they are well-formed, and otherwise look like normal men and women. Some pygmy men have beards. Many of the little women go about carrying their babies on their backs or astride their hips. These people wear little clothing. The men have only a strip of cloth about the waist, and the women a short petticoat of leaves or an apron of bark. Some of the pygmies pierce holes in their upper lips and put porcupine quills or the teeth of various animals in them.

The pygmies are comparatively primitive. They seldom clear the land, and have no farms or gardens. They hunt and trap, and dig roots for food. Their villages are usually not far away from the settlements of other tribes. In such localities the pygmies often trade for corn, tobacco, bananas, sugar, salt, and also iron to make tips for their spears.

In this pygmy settlement, the ordinary hut is seldom more than four feet in height and four or five feet in diameter. It is often made in oblong shape, being formed of branches stuck into the ground and tied together at the top, then thatched with grass or leaves. The doors are so low that the pygmies must crawl to get in. These little people sleep on the ground or on beds of leaves spread out inside the hut. Some of the huts have two doors, one in front and one in back, so that the residents may escape when attacked.

The pygmies use poisoned spears and arrows. A scratch from one of them will often cause death. The men are skillful bowmen, shooting arrows at such a fast rate that the first one will often not have fallen to the ground before the third has left the bow, and they are also expert trappers and hunters. They catch all kinds of birds and trap elephants in pits dug in the ground. They shoot into the eyes of the elephants with their little arrows, blinding them; and then follow them until they fall.

When eating-time comes, we are glad that our guide brought our own food. The pygmies eat flesh of all sorts except that of man. They are fond of monkeys, antelopes, rats, birds and reptiles. They eat termites, white ants, bees, caterpillars and certain beetles. They roast their meat on the coals and smoke some of it to preserve it for future use. The women usually do the cooking and the gathering of berries and honey. The men hunt, fish, trap and fight. The boys are constantly practicing marksmanship with bows and arrows, and as soon as they are considered old enough, they are allowed to participate in a hunt.

The pygmy tribes have no common language, but they usually speak, more or less imperfectly, the tongues of the neighboring tribes. They are elfish and full of fun. They are fond of singing, and have drums made of sections of a hollow tree, covered with monkey skin. They are intelligent and quick to learn, but are timid and afraid of all other tribes except their own. Our guide tells us that they try to return kindnesses, but are spiteful when ill-treated. They will wait a long time, if need be, to avenge wrongs. They seem to be like gnomes and sprites described in fairy stories.

Natives of the Congo making corn flour by pulverizing the corn seeds in wooden containers.

324

While Nairobi is a fairly modern city, many tribal villages in Kenya still look like the Masai village in our photo.

KENYA

We travel from the pygmies' settlement back to the village, and stay there for the night. The next morning a native bus — this time our driver's motto on the side of the bus is "Bounce Along to Heaven" — takes us back to Entebbe. From there we travel about twenty-five miles by a "modern" bus to the nearest railroad, where we board a train and then travel all the way to Nairobi, the capital city of Kenya. Looking out of the window, we see a safari on its way into bush country. A safari is a big-game hunting trip through the wilds of Africa. There are a great variety of animals in Kenya. Lions, elephants, rhinoceros, leopards and hippopotamuses are all prime targets of most big-game hunters. Other animals hunted include zebras, giraffes, hyenas, gazelles and many kinds of antelope.

Elephants are found both in Asia and in Africa, but the largest and fiercest come from Africa — especially from the region in which we are now traveling. The African elephant differs from its Asiatic brother in that it has larger tusks, a more sloping forehead, and wide, flapping ears. Remembering our stay in India, we recall that the elephants of Asia are sometimes caught and tamed. They are used as beasts of burden and are made to work in the lumber yards. In parts of India, Burma and Siam, people travel from place to place seated upon them, and the rajahs or princes ride them

On the Eastern coast of Africa, this former British colony became independent in 1963. **Area** • 224,960 sq. m. **Population** • 8,847,000. **Language** • Swahili, Bantu, English. **Government** • republic. **Monetary Unit** • East African shilling (= about 0.14 U.S. $). **Chief Cities** • Nairobi (capital), Mombasa. **Religion** • tribal religions, Christian, Moslem. **Mountains** • highest is Mount Kenya (17,040 ft.), Mount Elgon (14,-178 ft.). **Rivers** • Tana. **Lakes** • Rudolf, Baringo, Magadi, and northern shore of Lake Victoria Nyanza.

325

African elephant in Nairobi National Park.

when they go about in state. The African elephant seldom becomes tame. It lives in the forests or on the plains of the wilder regions of the continent. Hunted for its ivory tusks, this elephant was gradually being exterminated in some regions until protective laws were enacted. In most regions of Africa today only a certain number of elephants can be killed each year. In other words, they are being protected against extinction.

Along the way our train passes several mounds thirty to forty feet thick and from ten to fifteen feet high. The conductor tells us that each of these mounds is an ant hill, the home of thousands of ants. It is a network of tunnels, galleries and chambers, arranged in levels, some of which are far below the ground. Each mound might be called an ant apartment house. The ants have a queen who is waited upon by the workers in the basement of their house. The queen lays all the eggs of the colony, and as these are laid, her subjects carry them off to the nurseries to hatch them. In some colonies there are soldier ants which guard the queen, and the working ants labor under the supervision of the soldiers.

The most ferocious creature in this part of the country is the driver, or safari, ant. A bite from one of them stings like a needle. These ants are so tenacious that we can pull their bodies apart, but their jaws still stick in our flesh. This terrible driver ant should be given a wide berth at all times. The insect does not weigh as much as the smallest pea, yet lions, leopards, and even elephants rush to get out of its way. Driver ants move in vast numbers, in regular order, from place to place, looking like a strip of black ribbon as they cross one's path. If they meet anything living, they throw themselves upon it and bite it to death. They tear the flesh bit by bit from the bones, and in a short time reduce it to a skeleton. When they attack a hut, not only the people, but even the rats, mice and insects run out, for no creature is willing to fight the terrible driver. If they get

326

upon us, we are told, the best thing to do would be to rush for the nearest stream and dive in. The ants do not like water, and they will let go when it touches them. On the other hand, there are crocodiles in the waters around here. Maybe we are "better off" as passengers here on the train than out there on the safari.

Finally, our train arrives at Nairobi, a very modern city that was never intended to be a city at all. It began life as a railway camp on the rail line that we have been traveling, but railroad engineers, surveying the highland country, discovered large areas of rich, empty land with a climate suited to cultivation by Europeans. So Nairobi grew up with Kenya, and is now the center of a prosperous farming and grazing country. Kenya is about the size of Texas.

While here, we decide to take an "automobile" safari into Nairobi National Park, one of Africa's finest game preserves. An African game preserve is a zoo in reverse. The animals are free to roam anywhere, while people, staying in their cars, are more or less "behind bars." We are warned that it is very important to stay in the car, for the animals are not tame. Somehow, most animals do not associate people with automobiles, so it is possible to drive within a few feet of a herd of antelope, or a group of lions. Rounding a bend on a dirt road, we observe a pair of lions rolling in the dust like playful kittens. Our guide honks the horn. The lions get up and move slowly into the bush. The lion had smelled the car, and his nose told him that it was not good to eat. He might have reacted quite differently to the smell of a man. That is the reason for the rule requiring visitors to stay in their cars. Lions are dangerous, even on the outskirts of a modern city like Nairobi.

Native caravan. Whatever is heavy is carried on top of the head.

REPUBLIC OF SOUTH AFRICA

Most industrialized and richest of the nations of Africa. **Area** • 472,494 sq. m. **Population** • 17,075,000. **Language** • Afrikaans (a kind of Dutch dialect), English and many tribal dialects. **Government** • Proclaimed a republic when it left the British Commonwealth in 1961. **Monetary Unit** • Rand (= 1.40 U.S. $). **Chief Cities** • Johannesburg (over one million people), Cape Town (legislative capital), Durban, Pretoria (administrative capital). **Religion** • majority Protestant (mostly Dutch Reformed); about 5% Roman Catholic. **Mountains** • Drakensberg Range rises to over 11,000 feet. **Rivers** • Orange, Vaal — neither of which is navigable.

Next morning we board an airliner at Embakasi Airport in Nairobi and then fly southwestward to the city of Johannesburg in the Republic of South Africa. This country is almost three times as large as California. The land and climate are also similar. However, the weather in South Africa during winter months is not so cold.

Mr. Ayer, a passenger on our plane, tells us that South Africa has about two-thirds of all the railways and automobiles on the continent. More newspapers, libraries, colleges, modern cities, telephones and industrial plants are found here than in any other African country.

Farming is an important occupation in South Africa. Corn, wheat, sugar cane, tobacco, tea, cotton, oats, citrus and other fruits — apples, pears, plums, and grapes — grow well on the moist lowlands. Sheep, goats and cattle graze on the drier lowlands and plateaus. Another important livestock animal in South Africa is the ostrich, once raised for its feathers to adorn women's hats. Ostrich skins are now sold for the manufacture of fancy leather goods.

The principal industry of South Africa is mining. Gold, diamonds, coal, uranium and iron ore are the important minerals. Silver, copper, platinum, tin, chromite, zinc, asbestos, mica, lead and a number of other minerals are known to exist. No other nation in the world produces as much gold or as many gem diamonds as South Africa. The headquarters of the gold mining industry is in Johannesburg. "I am an engineer for one of the mines," our fellow passenger explains. "If you wish, tomorrow I will show you how gold is mined."

Johannesburg is the largest city in Africa south of Cairo, and looks like almost any city in the United States. It has tall office buildings, modern apartment houses, luxury hotels, fine public schools, museums and libraries. The principal streets are wide and tree-lined.

The next morning we meet Mr. Ayer at his office. He tells us that gold around Johannesburg lies in veins or strata

The Republic of South Africa is a country full of contrasts — contrasts in the legal, economic and cultural possibilities and position of the minority white and majority black population, contrasts between rural and city life. Above, a native village in Swaziland, a province of the Republic of South Africa. At right, Jeppe Street in the white quarter of Johannesburg.

(Photo, left): Surrounded now by the town of Kimberley, South Africa, the "Big Hole," as it is known locally, is the largest man-made excavation in the world, about 1,500 feet in diameter at the surface and 1,300 feet deep. The depth of the main rock shaft is 3,250 feet. The Kimberley Mine was discovered July 16, 1871. From 1888 to 1914, about 16,000,000 tons of "blue ground" (diamond-bearing rock) were taken from the mine and yielded 6,404 pounds of diamonds. It is estimated that diamonds taken from this mine since its discovery represent about $800,000,000 at today's prices.

which run a long distance down into the earth. It is mostly in crystals or flakes so small that they cannot be seen with the naked eye and mixed with a vast amount of quartz pebbles which are cemented together with sand and other rocks. The pebbles look like raisins in a plum pudding. The gold is not found in the pebbles, but in the other part of the pudding. The rock is very hard, and it has to be taken up to the surface. It is then pounded to powder before the gold can be obtained.

The mining is done by sinking a shaft, or great pit, down through the veins. Tunnels are dug into it so that the precious rock can be broken down and brought to the surface. There it is put into stamping mills and crushed to powder. Later, at the smelting plant, the gold is separated from the crushed powder.

Mr. Ayer takes us down into a mine. It is almost six thousand feet deep, but thanks to air-conditioning, the temperature is bearable. If the mine were not air-conditioned, the temperature would be over 110 degrees. The mine is lighted by electricity.. The precious rock is broken free by huge electric drills, then loaded on cars and pushed along a railroad track to a shaft where an electric elevator brings it to the ground surface. Walking through a long tunnel, Mr. Ayer says, "Johannesburg is literally built on top of our gold mine. There are probably more tunnels and mine shafts a mile or more deep under the city than there are streets on the surface."

From the mine we go to the crushing mill, to the smelting plant, and finally into the offices of the superintendent. Here Mr. Ayer shows us bricks of pure gold in a big safe.

Headgear of a rickshaw boy in Durban, one of the bigger cities in South Africa. A rickshaw is a man-drawn two-wheeled vehicle for transporting people.

Johannesburg in the distance, the gold mine on the reef in the foreground.

In the morning our airplane leaves Jan Smuts Airport for Léopoldville, the Republic of the Congo's capital and largest city. While en route, our stewardess alerts us to the fact that our plane will soon be flying over Victoria Falls, the world's mightiest waterfall. She says that when David Livingstone, the famous missionary and explorer, first went into the wilds of the country now known as Southern Rhodesia in 1855, natives told him tales of a mysterious place down the Zambesi River which they called "the smoke that thunders." Dr. Livingstone followed the natives' directions for getting there and soon found one of the great natural wonders of the world. He named the waterfall in honor of Queen Victoria of England. As our plane dips low over the falls, we see the towering column of white spray of the most famous of Africa's many waterfalls.

Looking at our map, we see that the Congo lies on the equator. For that reason, it is hot the year round. It has about one-fourth as much land as the fifty states in the United States. Most of the area is a large basin drained by the Congo River and its tributaries. The Congo River, while not so long as the Nile, is greater in volume than any other river in Africa. More water flows in this river than in the Mississippi.

The main exported products of the Congo are from agriculture and mining. Some of the crops are vegetable oils, coffee, cotton, rubber, cacao, bananas and yams. The main minerals produced are copper, diamonds, uranium, tin, cobalt, tungsten, manganese and gold. Several new factories have been started in recent years.

As our plane lands at Léopoldville, it is apparent immediately that this city is the hub of the Congo's transportation and its governmental and manufacturing life. Léopoldville, named after King Léopold II of Belgium, has grown from a primitive trading station in 1887 to a thriving city, a center of learning and trade, boasting an excellent African university. Airlines, roads and railways link the capital with

Central African nation, covering two-thirds of the Congo basin. **Area** • 904,-754 sq. m. **Population** • 15,007,000 (for African population only). **Language** • over 200 dialects are spoken; principal ones are Swahili, Luba, Kongo, and Ngala. **Government** • independent republic since 1960, before that a colony of Belgium. **Monetary Unit** • Congo Franc (= about 0.02 U.S. $). **Chief Cities** • Leopoldville (capital), Elisabethville, Stanleyville. **Religion** • mainly tribal African religions; some Christian (mostly Roman Catholic). **Mountains** • Mount Margherita (16,795 ft.), Mount Karisimbi (14,787 ft.). **Rivers** • the Congo, second largest in Africa; Lualaba; Kasai; Uele; Kwango. **Lakes** • Tanganyika (boundary between Congo and Tanganyika), Leopold II, Tumba.

Aerial view of Léopoldville, capital of the Republic of the Congo.

the interior and tall buildings arise from the muddy banks of the Congo River. As a taxi takes us on a short tour of the city, the broad streets, modern stores, new apartments, government offices, and air-conditioned hotels give us the impression that Léopoldville is a thriving city.

NIGERIA

West African country, with the largest population in Africa. **Area** • 372,674 sq. m. **Population** • 37,213,000. **Language** • Arabic, English, native languages. **Government** • Federal republic within the British Commonwealth (became independent in 1960). **Monetary Unit** • Nigerian pound (= 2.80 U.S. $). **Chief Cities** • Ibadan, Lagos (capital). **Religion** • Moslem (majority), Christian, native religions. **Mountains** • Bamenda, Shebshi, and Alantika ranges rise up to 7,000 ft. **Rivers** • Niger, Benue.

Unfortunately, our stopover at Léopoldville is only a short one. After leaving the airport, our plane flies northwest across the jungles of the Congo and Gabon, and then over the Gulf of Guinea. Our next stop is Ibadan, Nigeria. It is the most populous city built by Africans south of the Sahara — Johannesburg was built by Europeans — and it is also the largest Negro city in the world.

From the air, Ibadan looks like a maze of corrugated tin roofs, which are really the city's trademark. It might well be called the "city of tin-tops," for almost all of the houses are built of mud and plaster with corrugated iron roofs for protection against the sun and rain, and against fire. Like most West Africans, the people of this city generally build their homes around a large common courtyard. Ibadan is made up of thousands of family and communal compounds.

In striking contrast to the tin roofs of the older portions of Ibadan are the new modern office buildings and those of University College and University College Hospital. These are constructed of steel, concrete and glass. Unlike most large cities of the world, Ibadan is not situated on any body

The walled city of Kano, Nigeria.

of water. It has grown to its present size on its own merit as a commercial trading center.

While our stopover in Ibadan is only for an hour, we learn a great deal about this country that has been independent only since 1960. Nigeria is about the size of Arizona and Texas combined and is one of the wealthiest and most progressive nations in Central and Western Africa. It extends about five hundred miles from north to south, and thus has a varied climate. Along the coast the climate is hot and rainy, and much of this land is jungle. The major agricultural export crops are cacao and palm oil. Palm oil is used to make margarine, soap, and some medicines and explosives. The natives raise cassava, yams, rice and corn as food crops.

Northern Nigeria is quite different from the land along the coast. Instead of heavy forests, grasses become the natural vegetation. The climate is warm, with alternating wet and dry season. The farmers raise peanuts, millet, sorghum, cotton and corn. Much of the peanut crop is exported. Many of the people who live in this region are Moslems who raise sheep, goats and cattle.

While driving back to the airport, our taxi passes a big field where boys are playing soccer. The driver tells us that soccer, cricket, basketball, tennis and boxing are very popular sports.

The bronze head of a native made in Benin, Nigeria, in the seventeenth century, is now on display in the Museum of Primitive Art in New York.

LIBERIA

The next stop on our tour of Africa is Monrovia, capital city of Liberia. As soon as the plane touches the ground at Roberts Field, we are in a country that was for over a hundred years the only Negro republic in Africa and, except for Haiti in the West Indies, in the whole world. About the same size as our state of Ohio, Liberia stretches along the coast for about three hundred miles from Sierra Leone to the Republic of the Ivory Coast. The country got its start in 1822 when the shipload of freed American slaves landed

On southwest coast of Africa, one of the few African countries never to have been a colonial possession. **Area** • 43,000 sq. m. **Population** • about 2,500,000. **Language** • English, native languages. **Government** • Republic. **Monetary Unit** • Liberian dollar (= 1.00 U.S. $). **Chief Cities** • Monrovia (capital). **Religion** • Christian (majority Protestant), tribal religions. **Mountains** • some mountain ranges rise up to 6,000 feet. **Rivers** • Lofa, St. Paul, Cess, Cavalla.

on what was then called the "Pepper Coast," because pepper-seeds could be found growing wild. (Europeans delighted in hot spices at that time and gladly paid a high price for the African pepper-seeds.) The colonists called their new land Liberia, meaning "land of freedom."

But like the colonists in the New World, they had many problems. The local natives, like some of the Indian tribes, were hostile to the new settlement and attacked it at every opportunity. It was during one of these attacks, on December 1, 1822, that Liberia's favorite heroine came into being. When the gunner firing the big cannon was killed, a woman named Matilda Newport took his place and continued shooting the cannon until the natives were driven off. Since that time, December 1 has been a national holiday in Liberia. It is called Matilda Newport Day.

After a number of fierce battles, peace was finally attained in Liberia. More and more freed slaves arrived from the United States and the settlement grew. On July 26, 1847, the American-born Negroes drew up their Constitution, basing it on that of the United States. They proclaimed their land the independent Republic of Liberia. The settlement of Monrovia, named for the American President, James Monroe, became the capital. Many of the villages and towns have names such as Charlottesville, Memphis, Bunker Hill, Philadelphia and Hartford. One part of the country is called Louisiana, while another is known as Maryland. Independence Day, Decoration Day, Flag Day and Thanksgiving Day are celebrated. The likenesses of several United States Presidents have appeared on Liberian postage stamps. The official language of the country is English and the United States dollar serves as the basis of its currency. Liberia might be said to be a bit of the U.S.A. transplanted to the African coast.

Riding from the airport to our hotel by bus, we pass the bathing beaches, modern capitol building, the new city hall, the National Museum, and the president's home. The streets

334

in this part of the city are broad and well-kept. After changing to cooler clothes, we leave the hotel and walk to the native market, the great "supermarket" shopping center of the Liberian people. All West African cities have such markets where local housewives come to buy the necessities of their daily lives.

Early in the morning, the merchants — usually women — bring their goods to the market square and spread them out on the ground or in little huts. The buyers begin arriving almost as early as the sellers. Many of them have started before dawn from remote, outlying villages. Buyers are mostly women and girls, some quite well dressed in brilliant costumes. Others have only a cloth about their bodies, fastened tightly under the arms and falling to the feet. Some carry babies astride the hip, and others have them slung on their backs. On their heads they balance large baskets with produce from their farms which they wish to trade for other things they need. We observe that soda pop and American cola drinks are popular with the Africans. If a woman shopper can spare a few coins, she usually stops at a soda stall to refresh herself.

Fruits of all kinds, spices, herbs, beans, rice, yams, vegetables, peanuts, smoked fish and dried meat are displayed. These foods are in wooden bowls, woven baskets or makeshift trays of banana leaves, skins and fragments of heavy paper. Over there women are selling fuel, native medicines and hardware. Others sell pipes and tobacco. Here is a girl with musical instruments on display and there is an old woman who has many quacking ducks for sale. In other places they are selling jewelry of ivory and gold, bright-colored clothes, cooking pots, mirrors, tools, buttons, beads and many other items. There are generally no fixed prices in a native market. We witness a woman haggling for half an hour over the price of a bottle of palm oil — for which the shopper has brought her own bottle. Bargaining is considered half the fun of going to market in Africa. We learn

Tapping a rubber tree in Liberia. A few drops of ammonia poured into the collection cup of a tapped rubber tree keeps the raw rubber in a liquid state.

335

also that West Africa is the only part of Africa where women play an important part in the world of business. Many of the women merchants have gone into other kinds of business, such as constructing houses and office buildings, and exporting native products to foreign countries. Some of them are quite wealthy.

One of the interesting things to watch in the market is the native craftsman at work. Sometimes in an open stall, or more often in the middle of the milling crowd, he uses those materials for his work that come most readily to hand. In the stall ahead of us is a man working with wood. He uses a knife, a chisel and a small ax to cut the wood and shape the object. He bores holes with a red-hot poker. After the work is finished, he smooths and polishes it with ashes, soot and mud. If a piece is to be darkened, he does this with wood-smoke, or sometimes with the blood of animals. Other craftsmen are making things from iron, clay, bone and gold, and weaving baskets of grass mat.

In the afternoon, we drive out to a nearby rubber plantation. Unlike the jungle rubber trees that will be seen during our visit to South America, the man-planted plantation rubber trees are in straight, well-kept rows. Men gather the sticky milk-liquid, called latex, from containers fastened to the tree and pour it into a bucket. In turn, the bucket is poured into larger containers and the latex is taken to a nearby processing plant where it is converted into crude rubber. The export of crude rubber is Liberia's biggest business.

After an overnight stay in Monrovia, we go back to the airport and board a helicopter for a flight over the interior of West Africa. Since there are few roads and only one railroad into the interior of Liberia, we decide that a low-flying helicopter is the best way to travel.

Almost as soon as the helicopter is in the air, we see what seems to be a solid green blanket beneath. Our pilot tells us that the jungle forest region of West Africa is below us.

A native tanner at work.

It extends inland from the Atlantic Ocean from fifty to three hundred miles and ranges from Senegal to Cameroon. The trees are so dense that they form almost a solid carpet of vegetation. On the jungle floor unseen by us are apes, chimpanzees, bongos, okapis, gorillas, baboons and the other animals. As the helicopter comes down close, we see through our binoculars families of monkeys, sometimes a hundred or more in a group, swinging through the treetops on vines, or leaping about as nimbly as trapeze artists in a circus. The baby monkeys ride piggy-back, their little arms clutched firmly around their mother's neck as she hurls herself through the air about 150 feet above the ground.

Native "blacksmith" puts a keen edge to a new spear blade.

Suddenly, a river appears ahead and along its bank a small native village is seen. It has just one street with a row of tiny houses on each side. The houses, or huts, are made of thin strips of wood fastened between posts set in the ground, and its walls are partly plastered on the outside with mud. There is only one doorway, but no door, and no windows. The roof is thatched, or covered, with a thick layer of palm leaves tied with vines. Our pilot tells us that palm leaves make a very good roof because they are smooth and slippery, and the rain runs off them quickly.

One of the first things we notice in the village is that everyone seems to be outdoors — the children are playing in the street, the grownups are sitting outside their huts. Some of them are just sitting and talking, or looking up at our helicopter, others are busy at some kind of work. Nearly everything that goes on in the little village takes place in the street. The huts in the village are really only bedrooms for the families. The people sleep indoors on beds of leaves, but in the daytime they stay outside. They eat outdoors, and even when it rains they sit under the eaves instead of going inside.

At the far end of the street is the village garden. Here corn, fruit, peanuts, yams, beans, onions and other vegetables are grown for all the villagers to use. The entire population works together and everyone has a job to do. Boys

Ivory scabbards.

and girls feed the chickens, take care of their younger brothers and sisters, and help their mothers weed the village garden. The men take care of building or repairing houses, and do the hunting and fishing. The village is ruled by a chief who is in charge of everything. In addition, there is usually a "medicine man," who is the doctor and religious leader of the village.

Continuing above the river, we see many crocodiles either swimming or sunning themselves on the banks below. The crocodile, like the American alligator, is a large reptile that lives mainly on fish and animals, but it has been known to eat humans. Our pilot flies low over the water. He points out a hippopotamus with only its eyes and nostrils showing above the water. Then the "hippo" disappears, and it seems a long time before its head can again be seen. We learn that it can stay under water without breathing for eight to ten minutes at a time, permitting it to eat water plants that grow on the bottom of the rivers. Each hippopotamus eats an average of five to seven bushels of such plants or grass every day. Later on we see several of these huge animals standing on the river bank. It would be dangerous for anyone in a small boat to meet one of these big creatures.

As we head farther inland, the jungle begins to thin out. Large patches of land have been cleared of trees and turned into farms or plantations where coffee, peanuts, cocoa, palm oil and bananas are the principal commercial crops. They are sent down the rivers to port cities for export.

Another of West Africa's valuable exports is the fine hardwood that grows in the forest. African mahogany, ebony and teak are shipped all over the world to be made into fine furniture. Still another resource of this region is such valuable minerals as gold, tin, iron, diamonds, zircons, copper, lead, silver, platinum and uranium. At the present time, however, little mining is being done because of transportation difficulties or other problems of production. When solutions are found, the jungle wilderness land may prove

SENEGAL
Newly independent West African state. **Area** • 75,750 sq. m. **Population** • 3,360,000. **Language** • French, native languages. **Government** • Republic, within the French Community. **Monetary Unit** • C.F.A. franc (= about 0.002 U.S. $). **Chief Cities** • Dakar (capital). **Religion** • Christian (mainly Roman Catholic), Moslem, tribal religions. **Mountains** • none, land is mostly flat. **Rivers** • Senegal.

338

to be one of the greatest sources of wealth that the world has ever known.

Turning northward, we see that the land becomes even less wooded. Instead of dense forests, there are smaller trees and tall grass. Our pilot tells us that we have reached the grassland region of West Africa. During the warm rainy season the grass grows very long, but during the dry season it dries up.

Flying fairly close to the ground, our helicopter frightens several herds of giraffes, gazelles, antelopes and zebras. There are more kinds of animals in Africa than anywhere else in the world. The grassland region has the biggest share of these animals. Our pilot tells us to look for the "king of beasts," but because the lion's fur is almost the color of the tall, dry grass, we cannot see any lions as we fly by.

Flying over a grassland native village, we see that it is similar to ones seen in the jungle except that these houses are bigger and the roofs are made of grass. These houses are usually divided into two parts, one for sleeping and the other for cooking and eating. Nearing the Atlantic coastline again, we fly over several good-size farms that raise corn, yams, millet, cotton and peanuts. There are also flocks of sheep, cattle and goats grazing on the grassland below. Ahead, on the horizon, appears Dakar, the capital city of Senegal. Before landing at Yoff Airport, our pilot points out Cape Verde lighthouse, the westernmost point of the continent of Africa. Tomorrow a freighter will take us back to the Western Hemisphere — to South America.

Native fishing: Fish are driven into baskets by the rushing river waters. The baskets hang from poles in the middle of the river.

We have selected a freighter for our trip.

Down the South American Coast

On occasion, during our trip around the world, we have traveled on several types of ships and boats. For our journey to South America, we have selected another type of vessel, a freighter. It carries only a few passengers, since most of the space is used to carry cargo — the goods that ships take from place to place.

Accommodations aboard the freighter are most comfortable, but much simpler than those found aboard the passenger liner we took from Greece to Italy, where there were such conveniences as swimming pools, theaters, dining rooms, sports deck, observation lounge, ballroom, health baths, gymnasium, shops and a hospital, to say nothing of children's playrooms and kennels for dogs. For recreation aboard this freighter, the grandeur of the sea and friendly talks with the crew members may have to suffice.

The crew members are real world travelers, having seen

340

most of the seaports of the world. From them we learn many things about traveling, ships, and the customs and language of the men whose life is the sea. "Sailing ships are seldom used today," the first mate says, "but it is still the tradition of sailors to say that a ship 'sails,' even though she has no sails aboard." Apparently it is also traditional to use the letter "a" as a prefix for "on" or "in," as in *amidships* — meaning on or in the middle of a ship; *aboard* — on or in a vessel; *astern* — meaning on or in the back.

A sailor also always refers to a ship as she. No one knows why, but one theory is that the early Greeks gave their ships female names to honor Athena, the goddess of wisdom and warships. Also, anyone who calls a ship a boat is immediately labeled a landlubber — a shore person. Boat is a term used only for small craft, usually propelled by oars, outboard motors or small sails. We also find out that the tradition of the sea has some noble customs. For example, it is traditional for all ships to come to the aid of another in time of peril. When an SOS (the international distress signal) is sent out over a ship's radio, all vessels nearby immediately change their course, or direction, and come to the aid of the ship in distress. When rescue is necessary, it is traditional that women and children are the first to be saved. Also, it is traditional for the captain of a sinking ship to be the last person to leave it.

Walking about the deck, one of the crew members tells us how to identify the nationality of a ship. He points to a passing ship and says, "The flag of her country flies from a staff at the extreme stern of the ship. The foremost mast carries the flag of the first country to which the ship is bound." He adds that some vessels fly a private "house" flag, indicating the ship's owner or charterer, from the aftermost mast, and that smokestacks are also marked to indicate the shipping owner's line.

Back in our cabin, we decide that it would be well to take a good look at a map of South America. A study of it reveals that the continent can be divided into two parts: tropical and temperate South America. In the tropical portion are the countries of Venezuela, Colombia, Ecuador, Peru, British Guiana, Surinam, and French Guiana. The temperate zone of South America includes Argentina, Chile, Uruguay, and Paraguay. Brazil is both in the tropical and temperate areas of the continent.

Tropical regions are generally hot and quite rainy. However, this is not always so. In one country on our journey through South America we can have a snowball fight right on the equator. But the temperate-zone countries have well-defined warm and cool seasons, just as in the United States. South America is in the Western Hemisphere, but it is also in the Southern Hemisphere. Thus the temperate-zone seasons in South America run counter to ours.

BRAZIL

The fourth largest country in the world and the largest in South America. **Area** • 3,287,842 sq. m. **Population** • 77,521,000. **Government** • Federal republic. **Monetary Unit** • Cruzeiro (= about 0.0005½ U.S. $). **Chief Cities** • São Paulo and Rio de Janeiro (both over 3 million people), Recife, Salvador, Pôrto Alegre, Belo Horizonte, Santos. Brasília, the new capital, was founded in 1960. **Religion** • majority Roman Catholic. **Mountains** • Pico da Bandeira, the highest, is 9,462 ft. **Rivers** • Amazon, one of the world's longest rivers; Río de la Plata; Paraná (one of whose tributaries forms the Iguassú Falls, higher and wider than Niagara); São Francisco. **Lakes** • Lagoa dos Patos is the largest.

The first country we plan to visit in South America is Brazil. It occupies nearly half of the continent of South America and is one of the biggest countries in the world. The United States, without its newest states of Alaska and Hawaii, would be smaller than Brazil, while the frozen islands of the Arctic would have to be added to Canada in order for it to be a much larger area. In all the world, only the Soviet Union and China have more land. If Brazil could be placed upon Europe, it would cover much of the continent. Brazil has a common border with every South American nation except Chile and Ecuador. Our freighter is going to dock at Belem, the chief seaport on the Amazon River.

Our steward asks us, "Do you know how the Amazon River gots its name?" Answering that we do not, we are then told the following story: In about 1541, a young Spaniard named Francisco de Orellana traveled the entire length of the river, looking for passage to the Atlantic Ocean. One day, Orellana and a few of his men went down one of the branches of the river seeking food. Soon Orellana and his men were surrounded by a party of warlike Indians. Some of the fighters were very tall women. Orellana had heard stories of a tribe of mighty women warriors, called Amazons. He thought he had found them, so after the Indians had let him and his men go free, he named the river after the Amazons.

The Amazon is rightly called the "King of Rivers." The source, or start, of this river is in the Andes Mountains and it flows eastward for about 3,800 miles. As the Amazon flows toward the Atlantic Ocean, it is joined by many other larger rivers and streams. These winding rivers and streams, upon which boats can travel, are so many and so long that if they were put end to end they would reach all the way around the world at its widest part, and flow on several thousand miles still farther. Unlike most river mouths which serve as an inlet for the ocean, so much water flows out of the Amazon River that it turns the ocean into fresh water for many miles.

It is only a short distance from the mouth of the Amazon to the city of Belem. As we leave the ship, our steward advises us not to forget to take our raincoats with us. Almost every day in the early afternoon, it rains for an hour or so. Then the skies begin to brighten, and it becomes as clear as it was in the morning. The natives in this region arrange their business according to the rain schedule. Belem is only a few miles south of the equator.

Since the river steamer that is going to take us up the Amazon River is docked on the other side of the city, we hire a taxi. On the way there, our taxi passes many large mansions, an old cathedral, a large municipal theater, and the Bosque, a section of jungle kept as a park right in the center of the city.

Going up the Amazon, our steamer passes through thick forests. These forests, however, are unlike those we saw in the United States. Forests as we have known them are

Brazilian toucan.

Brazil nut.

Brazilian ant bear.

groves of maple, oak, pine and other trees. They are enjoyable places where people may camp and spend their vacations. The forests along the Amazon, on the other hand, are tangled and the trees are close together, much like the forests of Central and West Africa. The leaves of the trees and vines are so intertwined that in many places the rays of the sun never reach the ground. Such dense jungles are often called rain forests.

The trees of these forests are important to the people of Brazil. Actually, one of the trees gave this country its name. The valuable red dyewoods in its jungle forests were already known in Europe as brazil because the brilliant red color was like braza, a live coal. The dye came from a tree known as Brazilwood. Thus, when the Portuguese found these trees growing in large quantities, they called it the "land of brazilwood"; later, simply "Brazil."

Besides dyewoods, there are a number of other trees whose products are useful to man. There are giant trees that bear the "wrinkle"-shelled nuts called Brazil nuts. These nuts are very rich in oil, and are gathered for that purpose as well as for their sweet and nutritious white meat. Moving slowly along the Amazon River, we also see many cacao trees, from which comes the chocolate used so frequently in cakes, candies and desserts.

Palm nuts and babassu are large lemon-shaped nuts that contain oils which are used in the making of margarines, soaps and medicine. The oily seeds of the oiticica tree produce yellow drying oil for paints and varnishes. The leaves of the carnauba are used in the manufacture of fine furniture, shoe and automobile polishes. Carnauba wax is used in the making of phonograph records, lipsticks, candles and

344

many other things. We also see several silk cotton trees from which is obtained kapok, which is used in life preservers. There are many mahogany trees in the Amazon basin. Some of the finest furniture is made of mahogany. Rubber trees are also plentiful.

Many miles farther along the river, the steamer stops at a rubber camp to pick up some balls of crude rubber. We are told that every morning the workers in the camp set out for the forest. They each have about 150 trees in the jungle to "work." When one of the workers comes to a rubber tree, he makes a V-shaped cut in the soft bark with a long, sharp knife and then places a cup under this cut so that the milky latex can drip down into it. By noontime he has finished this part of his job, and he returns to the camp to eat and have his siesta.

A Brazilian buyer weighs "biscuits" of wild rubber.

Later in the afternoon he follows the same path through the jungle. This time he collects the milky latex from the cups that he hung earlier on the rubber trees. Returning to the camp, he pours the latex a little at a time upon a wooden stick, which he rotates over a fire of oily palm nuts and leaves. In the hot smoke the latex darkens and hardens. Continuing this operation of pouring and turning, he builds up a big ball of crude rubber. When the ball is about the size of a man's head, he cuts it so that he can pull it off the stick. The ball is now ready to be shipped to manufacturers to be made into overshoes, automobile tires and many other useful articles.

In earlier times, the area around Brazil was where the best rubber trees grew, but some rubber-tree seeds were taken out of the country by an Englishman and planted in the far-off Asian countries of the Malay States, Ceylon, and the British East Indies. Because plantation rubber is superior to wild rubber, Brazil today supplies only a small part of the world's needs. In parts of Brazil, plantations such as the one we saw in Liberia are being started. Today, most natural rubber still comes from southeast Asia.

Farmer near the Amazon basin at work trying to rid his field of nut grass which chokes out his corn and rice.

During our trip upriver, many brilliantly colored butterflies flutter over the open decks in the daytime, and giant moths at night. It is said that there are more than fifteen thousand varieties of butterflies and moths in the Amazon Basin. Butterfly collectors from all over the world come to this region to add to their collections. The birds of the Amazon are as brilliant and beautiful as the butterflies. The multicolored parrots chatter and seem to call to us from their homes in trees along the river. Scarlet ibises, green parakeets, turquoise lovebirds, pink flamingoes, red-and-blue macaws, and the large-beaked blue-and-yellow toucans fly about near our steamer or watch us from the river's bank. To add more color to the gloom of the dense rain forest, there are hundreds of varieties of orchids clinging to the branches of trees along the edge of the Amazon. We even see several rare golden orchids, found only in this river basin.

There are animals and reptiles along the Amazon, too. Monkeys swing from tree to tree, and can be heard chattering from sunup to sundown. We also see many strange wild animals, such as the jaguar, a large catlike animal; the leopard; the tapir, a pig-like animal with a long nose that moves about like an elephant's trunk; the anteater, a creature that has a long pointed nose like the nozzle of a vacuum cleaner and a sticky two-foot tongue that catches ants and other small insects; and the sloth, perhaps one of the strangest of animals — it swings like a hammock from the underside of a tree limb, cradling its baby on its stomach. As our steamer plows the water, crocodiles are seen along the banks of the river, large turtles swim by in the water, and anacondas — snakes which are fifteen to twenty feet long and two to three feet around — sun themselves in the mud, or hang from trees, waiting for evening when they can catch animals coming to the river's edge to drink. The wild animals will let us alone as long as we stay in our boat, but the flies, mosquitoes and other insects are annoying, indeed. They are with us both night and day.

Brazilian Indian with blowgun.

346

Along the river banks, we often pass native Indian huts. The floor of each house is set on poles to raise it above the ground, thereby preventing flood waters and animals from coming into the hut, and the walls are generally open to permit the free flow of air through the home. The roof of the hut is rather steep and covered thickly with palm leaves so that it will shed the rain. These huts are not built to last very long, since the Indians move from place to place in search of food.

Much of the Indian family's food is fish from the Amazon River, or wild pigs and other animals from the nearby forests. The natives use blowgun-darts for their hunting of jungle animals, and spears for fishing. They also throw a root-poison into a pool of water, whereupon the fish become dazed and float on the surface. The Indians then gather as many fish as they need and leave the others for the next hungry day. The fish soon recover from the poison and are as lively as ever. One fish the Indians do not want to catch is a piranha, a "cannibal" fish that will attack anything in the water. It averages about one foot in length and is equipped with two rows of razor-sharp teeth. One bite will cut out a piece of flesh about a half-inch thick. Once it draws blood, other piranhas are attracted. They can strip to a skeleton an animal, or even a man, in a matter of a few minutes. Even when these fish are caught and dropped on shore, they will continue to attack, snapping at rocks and the ground itself.

347

The Indian women are the farmers of the family. They grow beans, corn, sweet potatoes and other vegetables, and raise chickens and pigs. They also gather the poisonous potato-like roots of the manioc plant. The poisonous juice must be squeezed out before its starchy root can be eaten. The natives also make the root into flour for bread, which is one of their most common foods. Women make finely woven baskets and decorate gourds, and sell them to passengers on passing river steamers. Because this a very hot climate, the members of the Indian family wear few clothes.

We have crossed the equator several times, but our trip up the Amazon marks the first time that we have remained near it for any length of time. Days are all about the same length and approximately the same temperature prevails throughout the year in the Amazon Basin. Nights are much cooler than days. Near the equator, the sun "rises" and "sets" at almost the same time every day.

After a six-day journey, the ship turns from the yellow Amazon into the blue-black waters of the Rio Negro River for the nine-mile trip to the city of Manaus. This both primitive and modern city, over nine hundred miles from the mouth of the Amazon River, is built on a cliff in the middle of the rain forest. Most people in the city live on land, but some live in small floating houses, or *flutuante,* built on rafts. The people who live on land generally have electricity, telephones and water systems in their houses. The "water people" have more primitive accommodations.

Manaus has a radio station, mosaic sidewalks like those of Lisbon, movie houses and streetcars. There are, however, no railroads or highways leading from it. Almost all of the travel and transportation is done by airplane, ship or small boat. Manaus is really a trading post. It is a collecting point for Amazonian products like rubber, Brazil nuts, cacao, lumber, fruits and nut oils for shipment to Belem and to the rest of the world. Here are seen traders, hunters, Indians, and trappers — people of all colors and races.

Rio de Janeiro, as seen from the cable-car station atop Sugar Loaf Mountain. The famous statue of Christ is on the mountain in the background.

348

After an interesting stay in Manaus, we board an airplane for the city of Rio de Janeiro. Our plane makes a stop for passengers at Brasília, the new capital of Brazil. This city, like Washington, D. C., has been methodically planned as the nation's capital. Unfortunately, our travel schedule does not call for a visit to Brasília, but the beauty of the new capital city is evident from the airborne plane.

The airplane approaches Rio from the sea. Rio, as it is usually called, is a large city and one of the most beautiful on earth. It was Brazil's capital city until 1960. On our left is a rounded peak, known as Sugar Loaf Mountain, which seems to stand guard at the harbor's entrance. At its feet lie the many small islands that dot Guanabara Bay. Inland and on the opposite shore is another peak, called Corcovado (Hunchback) Mountain. Rising from the top of this mountain is a statue of Christ, a hundred feet tall. The outstretched arms of the figure form a cross. This monument is so high above the city that it seems to guard every house and person in the vicinity.

Church of Our Lady of Penha, Rio de Janeiro. A climb is necessary to attend the service.

Our stewardess tells us that Rio de Janeiro means "River of January." It seems that an early explorer thought that Guanabara Bay was a river and he made his discovery during the month of January. As our plane comes in for its landing, we are able to see how the explorer made this mistake. The sparkling blue bay sweeps inland for more than twenty miles and in doing so, it breaks the shoreline into several crescent-shaped sandy beaches.

After our plane lands at Rio's Galeao Airport, we take a taxi to the city itself. The main street sidewalks are paved in mosaic patterns of black and white stones laid out in various patterns. Walks of this type are Portuguese in origin. We must remember that Brazil was a Portuguese colony from the sixteenth to the nineteenth century. Portuguese is still the official language of this country.

Many of Rio's streets seem different from city streets in the United States because of the tall, royal palm trees that line and shade them. These trees are perfectly straight with smooth trunks and have a crown of leaves at the top, a sight which has caused them to be called "the feather dusters of the gods." While walking through the Botanical Garden, we see the historic royal palm, said to have been planted by the Portuguese king, Dom João VI. Brazilians say this is the mother of all the palms in Rio.

On the Avenida Rio Branco — Rio's finest street — are beautiful marble mansions built in the eighteenth century, now standing next to modern skyscrapers. World-famous shops, hotels, and sidewalk cafes line this long, beautiful boulevard. Later, while driving along the waterfront, our bus passes white sand beaches where people swim and enjoy the sun. Since the temperature rarely gets very cool in Rio, people use the beaches the year around. Riding about the city, we see big pineapples made of stone, or of yellow or blue porcelain, on the gateposts in front of many of the houses. These are not there merely as a decoration. The ornaments are symbolic of the Brazilian's welcome. Rio is not a new city in the Western Hemisphere. It was actually settled sixty-five years before the Pilgrims landed on Plymouth Rock.

While in Rio, we decide that it would be exciting to take a ride in the famous "basket car." This is a big brother of the cable car ride we took while in the Blue Mountains of Australia. Once in the cable car, we go off through space as it moves over the trees. The car comes to its first stop

Sugar Loaf Mountain, Rio's outstanding, and most famous landmark.

350

on the top of a very steep hill, which is about seven hundred feet high. Leaving the car, we walk across to the other side and take another car. Again it moves out over the tree-tops and glides through space. Finally it stops on top of Sugar Loaf Mountain.

From Sugar Loaf, we see the ocean, far out, the entrance to the harbor and the harbor itself. There are many ships in the harbor. They bring automobiles, trucks, machinery, oil and many other things to Brazil. They carry away cargoes of cacao, coffee and cotton, and such minerals as iron ore, manganese and quartz, to supply the needs of other nations of the world.

Continuing our tour southward, we board an airplane for São Paulo. Below the plateau over which our plane is now flying is a narrow coastal lowland. On this coast and in the highlands live most of the people. Few countries can match the length of Brazil's coastline, which is much longer than both the Atlantic and the Pacific coasts of the United States. Our airplane heads away from the coastal region toward the highland and soon lands at São Paulo Airport.

São Paulo is the largest city in Brazil and is one of the fastest-growing large cities in the world. It has skyscrapers, factories, textile mills, warehouses, packing plants and the finest of stores. The streets are crowded with people, cars, buses and trucks. Inasmuch as the buying and selling of coffee is the leading business, the city is often called "the capital of coffeeland."

A special sightseeing bus to a coffee plantation, or *fazenda,* as it is called, is leaving in a few minutes from in front of our hotel. Driving out of the city, we see coffee trees on both sides of the road. Our guide tells us the story of coffee. "Hundreds of years ago, the people of North Africa drank a beverage they called kaffa," he explains. "The French liked the beverage, too, and from France it spread throughout Europe. The British and Dutch wished to enter the very profitable coffee trade, so they started

São Paolo is a beautiful modern city. This is a view of the new Municipal Library.

351

plantations in their tropical colonies in Asia. Many years later, Brazil obtained its first coffee plants from Dutch merchants in Amsterdam and Surinam. In Brazil the trees grew well and young trees were planted throughout the region.

After an interesting ride, we pass through a gateway and drive to what looks like a park. The bus stops near a beautiful big house, the home of the *fazenda's* owner. In the distance are hundreds of workers' cottages, a store, a hospital, a church, a school and other buildings that make the *fazenda* practically a small town.

São Paulo is in the temperate zone of Brazil; thus it is early spring here. The coffee trees are covered with fragrant white flowers. Our guide informs us that the coffee berries will be ripe about six months from now. Then men, women and children will pick the bright red "cherries," as the Brazilians call them. Since a full-grown coffee tree is only about six feet high, ladders are not needed. Sheets are sometimes spread under the trees to catch any berries that drop during the picking job. Afterward, the berries are shaken through sieves to separate them from twigs and leaves. The berries are then put into a machine where the pulp is separated from the two small half-round seeds which lie "face to face" inside each coffee berry. These twin seeds, called coffee beans, are then washed and placed on concrete drying floors.

The drying floor of the *fazenda* we are visiting covers many acres and can hold thousands of pounds of coffee beans. Men with wooden rakes will turn them over and over to dry them in the sun. Since the coffee harvest comes in the dry season, there is then very little chance of rain. At first the beans are gray-green in color. They turn dark brown only after roasting at a later time. After the beans are dried, they are packed in cloth bags and taken by the railroad to the seaport city of Santos. The bulk of the world's coffee comes from Brazil.

On our return to São Paulo from the *fazenda,* our bus

Coffee beans are spread out on great slabs of concrete to dry in the sun.

stops at the snake farm of the Butantan Institute, where snakes are kept in a grassy place enclosed by a low concrete wall and a ditch of water. In this grassy enclosure, small dome-shaped houses have been built in the midst of green lawns. At the Institute, the poisonous snakes have their poison taken from them and it is then made into a serum. The serum, injected into a victim after a snake bites, often saves that person from death.

We are lucky to arrive at the "farm" just in time to see the poison being taken from a snake. Safely behind the fence and ditch, we watch as a man who knows how to handle snakes picks one up on a stick. He grabs the snake from behind the head in such a way that the jaws are forced open, then gently squeezes the reptile's head. From its two teeth, or fangs, which the snake uses for biting, big yellow drops of liquid appear. This liquid, which could kill a man, is caught in a glass bottle. The snake is then put down by his house. The poison is taken to the laboratory for processing into life-saving serum. (At this particular farm, snakes are milked, rather than cows.)

Leaving the airport at São Paulo, our airplane flies south across some of Brazil's richest farmland. Cotton, corn, wheat, cattle and sheep are raised here. A little later we fly over Uruguay. This smallest of the South American Republics, about the size of Oklahoma, occupies a little corner between Argentina and Brazil. It is one of the most prosperous of South American countries. The country's wealth does not come from manufacturing, nor does it come primarily from farm crops. Most of the land is used to raise cattle and sheep. In fact, livestock outnumber the people of Uruguay by more than twelve to one. For its size, this country has more sheep and cattle than any other country in the world. Wool and beef are therefore Uruguay's most valuable exports. In the spring the Uruguayan prairies are brilliant with wild flowers which make Uruguay known as the Purple Land.

ARGENTINA

South America's second largest nation. **Area** • 1,084,359 sq. m. **Population** • 21,762,000. **Language** • Spanish. **Government** • Republic. **Monetary Unit** • Peso (= about 0.005½ U.S. $). **Chief Cities** • Buenos Aires, capital and largest city of South America (over 3 and a half million people), Rosario, and Córdoba. **Religion** • Roman Catholic. **Mountains** • Aconcagua (22,385 ft.), highest mountain in the Western Hemisphere; Mercedario (21,885 ft.). **Rivers** • Río de la Plata, Uruguay, Paraná, Pilcomayo, Colorado.

Also found in the United States, the hornero (oven bird) builds its very solid home on anything that stands; it is a rare telephone pole that does not have one.

As our plane prepares to land at Buenos Aires, a quick glance at our atlas reveals that Argentina is the second largest country in South America. It is equal in size to all the land of the United States east of the Mississippi River plus Louisiana and Texas. Almost as long as Chile, but many times wider, Argentina is shaped like a huge leg of lamb.

Our plane lands at Ezeiza Airport in Buenos Aires. When Captain Sancho del Campo landed here by ship many centuries ago, he exclaimed, "How good is the fresh and healthy air one breathes in this place!" This marked the birth of the new city and established its name. Buenos Aires is Spanish for "good air." This name fits the Argentine capital, for, besides being the largest city of South America, it is one of the most healthful and pleasant places in which to live. It has about the same number of people as the city of Chicago and is in many ways like it. Both cities are important because they are great trading centers for the surrounding farm land, and both are the heart of the railroad systems of their lands.

Our tour of this Argentinian city starts at the beautiful Plaza de Mayo which is in the center of the city. At one end of the square is the Casa Rosada or "Rose-Colored House," which, like our White House, is the home of the President of Argentina. Nearby is the Hall of Congress. This building, with its great dome, resembles the Capitol Building in Washington, D. C. A tall monument, which was erected to honor the four hundredth anniversary of the founding of Buenos Aires, is located in the Plaza and looks very much like the Washington Monument in the United States capital. A short distance from the Plaza is the cathedral in which we visit the tomb of José de San Martín. San Martín was the leader who helped Argentina gain its independence. Like George Washington, he has often been called the "Father of His Country." In front of San Martín's

354

At left, the Plaza Congreso (Congress Square) in Buenos Aires, with the Congress building at the far end. Below, folkdancing on the patio of an old colonial home in Buenos Aires during a fiesta.

tomb are soldiers in uniforms of red, white and blue. Our driver tells us that these soldiers wear the same type of uniforms as those who fought under San Martín against the Spaniards.

Next the taxi takes us to the harbor part of Buenos Aires. This harbor is crowded with ships that fly flags of many nations. Among the flags seen are those of the United States, France, Japan, Great Britain, Norway, Italy and Greece. These ships have brought many types of manufactured items to Argentina. On their return trips, they carry frozen meat, hides, wool, corn, wheat and flour from Argentina.

Buenos Aires is not an ocean port. It is some hundred and seventy miles up the Plata River. Plata is the Spanish word for "silver," but the river does not get its name because its waters are shining and silvery. Instead, it has the yellow muddy color of most fast-moving rivers.

Our taxi driver tells us how the Plata got its name. It seems that when Sebastian Cabot and his crew were looking for a passageway to the Far East, they sailed far up this river. Along the river banks, Cabot found Indians wearing crude silver ornaments. He took some of the jewelry back with him, being quite aware that his Spanish king was very much interested in acquiring silver. He named the river Río de la Plata, which is Spanish for "River of Silver."

355

A gaucho and his son.

Iguassú Falls at the junction of Brazil and Argentina.

"Did you know that the name Argentina also means silver?" asks the driver. "It comes from the Latin word for silver. But very little silver has been found in my country. The early Indians must have obtained their silver ornaments from the land of the Incas."

There are many interesting side trips that could be taken while in Argentina. We could drive to El Tigre, a vacation land of almost countless small islands, or we could go to one of the national parks, or to an Indian reservation. One sight we really would like to see is Iguassú Falls, which are higher and wider than Niagara Falls. But a boat trip up the Paraná River to the Falls takes almost a week, and according to our trip schedule, we do not have the time.

On the way to the airport, we pass a field where two teams of mounted horsemen are riding back and forth. "They are playing *pato,*" our driver explains. "*Pato* means duck in Spanish." He continues by telling us that the object of the game is to try to make goals, as in basketball. The players pass a leather object back and forth while they gallop down the field toward the goal, a large basket perched on a pole, but having no backboard. The leather object looks somewhat like a ball with handles. "When the game was played in colonial days," the driver says with a smile, "they used real ducks!"

Leaving the airport at Buenos Aires, our airplane flies west across Argentina's great pampas region. Pampa is an Indian word meaning "a plain." Thousands of cattle are grazing in the tall grass below. Here and there, ranch houses, or *estancia,* as they are called in Argentina, and a cluster of trees break the monotony of the flat plains. Our pilot flies low to let us see the cowboys, called "gauchos," herding thousands of cattle. At certain seasons they round up their animals, rope and brand the calves. Like our own cowboys, they are famous for their skill as horseback riders. Gauchos generally wear baggy trousers tucked inside the tops of their high cowboy boots, short jackets, flat hats with wide brims,

356

and bright-colored kerchiefs tied around their necks. Girls and boys in Argentina like to hear stories of the gauchos, just as we like to hear about our own cowboys.

As our flight continues westward, the green, grassy pampas turns to the dry plains and brown foothills of western Argentina. The plane starts to climb as it gets ready to cross "the hill," as the Andes Mountains are familiarly known in this part of the world. For centuries the high mountains of the Andes (the second highest mountains in the world, after the Himalayas) have formed an effective barrier between the Atlantic and the Pacific coasts. Mount Aconcagua is the highest mountain peak in the Americas.

Our plane will fly over the famous Uspallata Pass, a route through the mountains near Mount Aconcagua which has been used for hundreds of years — first by the Indians and then by the Spanish conquerors. Later, a railroad and then a highway was built through it. And now we fly over it. A radio station in the pass keeps airplanes continually informed of weather conditions in the mountains. Our stewardess points out a sight that we have been waiting to see. Below us, on the border between Chile and Argentina, is the famous statue called the "Christ of the Andes."

Erected on the border between Chile and Argentina as a shrine dedicated to peace between the two countries, the Christ of the Andes Statue has become a sightseeing "must" on the itinerary of tourists.

In 1903, after the King of England helped Chile and Argentina to settle their boundary dispute, the cannons that had been used for possible warfare were cast into a statue of Christ. Mules pulled this statue up the mountains as far as the beasts could travel. Then thousands of Chilean and Argentine sailors and soldiers lifted the statue by ropes to a point above Uspallata Pass. There it has stood ever since.

Our stewardess tells us that at the base of the statue are the following words: "May these mountains crumble into dust before the people of Argentina and Chile break the peace which they have sworn to maintain at the feet of Christ the Redeemer."

Once west of the statue, we are in Chile, the next stop of our tour around the world.

357

Santiago, Chile. View of Calle (Avenue) Bernardo O'Higgins, showing the San Francisco Church at the far end.

17
CHAPTER

Home by Way of the Andes

CHILE

A long, narrow strip of land lying between the Pacific and the Andes. **Area** • 286,396 sq. m. **Population** • 8,222,000. **Language** • Spanish. **Government** • Republic. **Monetary Unit** • Escudo (= 0.27 U.S. $). **Chief Cities** • Santiago (capital), Valparaiso, Concepción. **Religion** • Roman Catholic. **Mountains** • Ojos del Salado (22,550 ft.), second highest peak in the Western Hemisphere, Llullaillaco (22,015 ft.), Tupungatito (18,500 ft.) — all on Argentina - Chile border. **Rivers** • Maipo, Maule, Nuble. **Lakes** • Llanquihue, Ranco, Puyehue.

Glancing at our map, we realize at once why Chile is often called the "Stringbean Republic." It is a long mountainous country shaped like a stringbean. The country's average width is only a hundred miles, which is less than the distance between Washington, D. C. and Philadelphia. On the other hand, the length of Chile is more than the mileage of our trip from Washington to San Francisco — its total area slightly exceeds that of our state of Texas. Chile has three distinct climates — warm and dry in the north; mild and moderately dry in its central part; and rainy in the forests of its cold south. And it has three corresponding regions — a northern desert where many minerals are found; a long central valley lying between two ranges of the Andes mountains; and a forested area to the south.

Although Chile is mainly an agricultural country, it has untold wealth buried deep in its mountains. Chile's copper mines rank second in the world's production. Only the United States produces more. Other minerals such as lead, silver, gold, manganese and molybdenum are also here.

358

After our plane lands at Las Cerrillos Airport, a taxi takes us to Santiago, the capital and largest city in Chile. It is a bustling, modern city that is both the manufacturing and commercial center of the country. Valparaíso, about sixty-five miles west of Santiago, is Chile's leading seaport. As in Argentina, Spanish is the official language of Chile.

An interesting vantage point in Santiago is a high hill at the center of the city. Years ago, during their wars with the Araucanian Indians, the Spaniards fortified this hill and used it as their headquarters. Today, the hill is called Santa Lucia Park.

After climbing up this hilltop park, Santiago's modern office buildings and apartment houses of ten stories look even higher in contrast to the low one- and two-story homes. To the north and south of Santiago are the fertile plains of the Central Valley where farmers grow corn, beans, wheat, oats, potatoes, tobacco, grapes, apricots, oranges and other kinds of fruit. To the west, we see the iron bridges over the Mapocho River, which divides the city in half. To the east, the snow-capped Andes loom on the horizon. Snow from the Andes was once brought into the city in containers by donkeys. Children delighted in mixing fruit flavorings with the snow to make a cooling, tasty treat.

The chicken-vendor brings his ware to the customer for selection in Valparaiso, Chile's chief port.

Ox carts form a picturesque foreground for the kind of mountain scenery that is typical of the Chilean lake district. Called the "Switzerland of South America," the lake district is actually larger than the tiny European republic.

BOLIVIA

One of the two inland South American countries. **Area** • 412,777 sq. m. **Population** • 3,596,000. **Language** • Spanish. **Government** • Republic. **Monetary Unit** • Peso (= about 0.08 U.S. $). **Chief Cities** • La Paz (seat of government and world's highest city, 11,909 ft.), Cochabamba, Oruro, and Sucre (legal capital). **Religion** • Roman Catholic. **Mountains** • some of the highest in the world in the Bolivian Andes: Illampú (21,185 ft.), Ancohuma (21,490 ft.), Illimani (21,185 ft.). **Rivers** • Paraguay, Guaporé, Beni. **Lakes** • Lake Titicaca, largest inland lake in South America, on Bolivia-Peru border.

Llamas are Bolivia's chief beasts of burden.

The next morning our airplane heads north along the coast to the next stop, La Paz, capital of Bolivia. Going northward, the green of the Central Valley gradually turns to gray. This is the beginning of the desert region in northern Chile. Here the land is without trees, grass, or even cactus. Our plane is now flying over the driest region known to man. It is even drier than the Sahara Desert. There is one part of this Chilean desert where no rain has fallen in twenty-five years. But this desert is one place where rain is not wanted, since it could destroy the nitrate industry there. Chile is the only country in the world where sodium nitrate, a mineral salt used in manufacturing fertilizers and explosives, is found in large quantities. Copper, borax and sulphur are also mined in the desert region of Chile.

Our map reveals that Bolivia has no seacoast. It is about the same size as Texas and New Mexico combined, and is the highest civilized country in the world. The cities, railroads, farms and mines are on a plateau which is more than two miles above the sea. For this reason Bolivia is sometimes called the "Switzerland of South America," but it would be more appropriate to call Switzerland the Bolivia of Europe, for the elevations at which people live in Switzerland are far below those of Bolivia.

Our stewardess tells us that Bolivia received its name from Simón Bolívar, the leader who helped free Bolivia from Spanish rule in 1825. The Spanish had controlled this country for about three hundred years. We also learn that La Paz means "peace." It was taken from the Spanish name for the city which meant "The City of Our Lady of Peace." Spanish is the official language of Bolivia.

After landing at La Paz, a taxi takes us through the city. It is one of contrasts. Many streets are narrow and steep, while others are broad, smoothly paved highways. There are old Spanish-styled houses, as well as modern public buildings, new hotels, schools and theaters. Beside the little

360

cave-like open-front shops of the past are fine modern stores. There is an old cathedral near the handsome new sports stadium. La Paz is the center of all the railways, roads and airlines in Bolivia. The little manufacturing done in this country takes place in and around La Paz. It is the gateway to the rich mining region, too.

Bolivia has much mineral wealth. Tin, silver, gold, zinc, lead, tungsten, copper and other minerals are found here. Farming is done in the highlands and the lower valley. The main crops are coffee, wheat, tobacco, corn, peanuts, and coca, from which the painkiller, cocaine, is made. But old methods of farming are employed by most farmers, so the farms are not too efficient. Peace Corps workers are helping the farmers of Bolivia to increase their output by using more modern methods.

Half the people of Bolivia are pure Indians. Riding about La Paz, we see many of them. The Indian women are dressed in blouses and bright-colored bell-shaped skirts made of hand-woven wool. Actually, they wear several skirts, one on top of another. Most women are barefooted, but they all seem to wear a hat that looks something like a felt derby.

The Indian men wear jackets and short-legged trousers. Their shoes are sandals and they wear woolen caps with earflaps. A few men wear a felt derby or fedora over the woolen cap. All the men wear or carry a poncho, a blanket with a hole in the center. Put over the head, the poncho serves as a cloak for extra warmth, or it may be used as a cover while sleeping at night.

View of the exclusive residential section of La Paz, Bolivia's capital, the highest capital in the world.

Most of Bolivia's population is Indian. These Indian women are at a meat market in Tarija.

Indians trudging along a highway near the Andean village of Viloco in the highlands of Bolivia.

PERU

Third largest country in South America. **Area** • 514,059 sq. m. **Population** • 11,511,000. **Language** • Spanish and the Indian languages of Quechua and Aymara. **Government** • Republic. **Monetary Unit** • Sol (= about 0.03 ½ U.S. $). **Chief Cities** • Lima (capital), Callao, Arequipa. **Religion** • Roman Catholic. **Mountains** • Huascarán (22,305 ft.), El Misti (19,166 ft.), Chachani (19,960 ft.) are some of the many Andean mountains. **Rivers** • Marañon and Ucayali (headstreams of the Amazon). **Lakes** • Lake Titicaca is shared with Bolivia.

Unfortunately, our stay in the highest capital of the world is a short one, since our plane is ready to take off for Cusco, Peru. Shortly after the plane is airborne, our pilot flies low over Lake Titicaca — which belongs half to Peru and half to Bolivia. It is the largest lake in South America and is believed to be the world's highest fresh-water lake. As our plane approaches it, we see that nothing but reeds and rushes grow along its shores; it is too cold for trees to grow here.

The water, too, is so cold that only one kind of fish, named the boga, can live in it, but we do see a large lake steamer chugging across the clear water. This steamer was carried piece by piece up the mountains and assembled on the shore of Lake Titicaca. There are also many small boats, called "balsas," on the water. These are built by the Indians out of reeds and rushes. Balsa means "raft" in Spanish, and these small craft are used for fishing and for traveling about the large lake.

Peru, our next stop, is a country that is often called the Land of the Incas. Centuries ago, the Incas were the most civilized Indians in South America. The area comprising Peru today was only a small part of the Inca empire. It is still one of the larger countries of South America, however — about three times the size of the state of California — but it does not have nearly as many people.

Once our plane has landed in Cusco, we shall be in the former capital of the Incas. The Incas were not a single tribe or group of related Indian tribes; instead, the Inca empire was made up of many different tribes. The ruler of the empire was called the Inca and it was from the Inca that his people got their name.

The Inca ruler was believed by his people to be a descendant of the Sun God. According to an old legend, when the Sun God sent the first Inca Emperor, Manco Capac, to rule the Indians, he gave him a golden rod and said, "Where

Scene on Lake Titicaca:
Indians in a balsa boat.

this staff, of itself, sinks into the ground, there build your capital city!"

Manco Capac's rod must have given the magic sign here, 11,000 feet above sea level, because this is where he built the Inca city of Cusco.

Roaming about this city, we find a mixture of Spanish and Inca civilizations. There are Spanish cathedrals on Inca foundations. Carved stones that are definitely Inca are built into Spanish buildings. Ancient Inca walls, too solid for the Spaniards to tear down, are still standing. Except for a few new hotels, fortunately built in Spanish colonial style, there are no modern-looking buildings in sight. The city seems to have been unchanged from the days of the early Spanish conquerors. It is very easy to imagine that the people in the streets and market places have stepped out of a history book. The exception is the airport outside the city.

Near Cusco is Machu Picchu, one of the great fortresses that guarded the Inca capital. At the railway station we board an autocarril, a bus that runs on a railroad track, and at the end of the autocarril tracks we transfer to a truck filled with benches. After driving around many hairpin

Ancient Inca sundial in Cusco, Peru.

The famous ruins of Machu Picchu.

curves, the truck finally reaches the top of a mountain. Machu Picchu's vast stone temples, houses and walls lie before us.

Machu Picchu was built in terraces on a cliff high above the Urubamba River, which eventually flows into the Amazon. This "Lost City" on its sky-high mountain was rediscovered in 1911 by archeologists. An old Indian legend tells how the Priestess and the Maids of the Sun God fled from Cusco when the Spaniards were conquering the country, hiding in this remote fortress, from which they never returned. The finding of many women's skeletons here at Machu Picchu by archeologists leads them to believe this Indian tale.

The Incas were excellent builders. They constructed many miles of highways to all parts of their empire, some of which are still in use today. They also erected strong footbridges across deep mountain canyons and some of these also can still be seen. They built walls and terraces on the steep mountainside for growing crops. Most of their cities were of stone, but the secret of their massive construction, such as we see at Machu Picchu, has been lost. Some of the stone blocks they used are about twenty feet high and almost as thick. The walls of the building fit together so tightly that not even the blade of a knife can be inserted between the stone blocks.

It is a mystery how these stones were moved and cut. The Incas did not have strong tools of steel such as we have today. They brought these giant stones long distances, yet the Incas had no mules or horses, nor did they have any carts. These Indians did not have the secret of the wheel, nor did they know about pulleys and cranes.

On our return to Cusco, we see flocks of goats, sheep and strange-looking animals resembling long-necked sheep. These are alpacas, raised for their wool, which is extra long and fine. We see herds of llamas, too. These animals, which look like camels without humps, are the most valuable creatures in all the Andean countries, since they are used to carry burdens. They also furnish wool, hides and meat.

Vicuña sometimes run across the autocarril tracks. These animals look something like an alpaca, except they are smaller and have a fawn-colored wool. The vicuña moves at a swift, easy gallop, like a deer. Unlike the llama and alpaca, which can be domesticated, the vicuña has always remained wild. These three types of animals are found only in the Andes Mountains.

The Church of San Marcello in Lima was built by the Spanish in 1584.

After a pleasant night's stay in Cusco, we leave by plane for Lima, the capital of Peru. Below us is the Peruvian plateau where the majority of the people live, and where most of Peru's mineral riches are found. In this area, too, were located the gold and silver mines which supplied the Incas and Spanish Kings with their riches. While gold and silver are still mined in this region today, the copper and lead mines are considered more important.

On the higher plateau region, sheep, cattle, llamas and alpacas are grazed, while in the lower area, potatoes, corn, wheat and barley are grown. In the valley between the Andes, sugar cane, cotton and some rice are grown. Sugar and cotton are also the main exports of Peru.

Patio of the University of San Marcos in Lima, Peru.

After our airplane has landed at a modern airport, we get off and take a taxi to Lima. Our driver tells us the story of how the Spanish conquered the Incas. "In 1535," he says, "Francisco Pizarro and a small Spanish army reached the land you are now visiting. He tricked Atahualpa, the Inca Emperor, into believing that he and his men came in peace. During the welcome that the Indians gave the Spaniards, Pizarro gave a signal. A cannon was fired and Spanish soldiers on horseback charged the helpless Indians, killing them left and right. In a short time, the Indians were defeated and Atahualpa was captured.

"Atahualpa," our driver continues, "offered the greedy Spaniards a large room filled with gold and silver if they would set him free. Pizarro agreed, but after the ransom was

Inca pottery figure of a musician.

A native woman displays various exotic fruits for sale.

paid, Atahualpa was killed and the proud empire of the Incas was at an end." He also tells us that Pizarro then built a city that he named the "City of Kings." For more than three centuries, this city, which we now call Lima, was the center of Spanish power in the New World.

Our driver stops his taxi at the Plaza de Armas, in the heart of downtown Lima. A big statue of Pizarro looks out on this central square. The government palace now facing the square once served the site of Pizzaro's fortress. Later the present palace was rebuilt for the men who ruled this wealthiest, most important of all of Spain's colonies. A fig tree planted by Pizarro still produces fruit in the palace patio. Near the square is the University of San Marcos, founded in 1551, one of the oldest universities in all the Americas, older than Harvard University by eighty-five years.

The twelve-to-two closing time for lunch is almost everywhere in Lima. This is siesta time. Everyone takes a nap or relaxes after the noonday meal. After a few disappointments in trying to shop or visit public buildings during these hours, we nap and adopt the custom of the country, just as we did in Spain and Portugal.

Speaking of customs, the Indians follow the ways of their ancestors in their dress, in their dancing, and in their music. We must remember that about one out of every two persons in Peru is a full-blooded Indian. In addition, one-third of the people are a mixture of Indian and white (*mestizos* is the Spanish word for them). Less than one in ten persons is white. There are some Negroes and a few Orientals. Spanish is the official language of Peru, but many of the Indians still speak the language of the ancient Incas. In the cities, English is also spoken by many people.

The Indians of Peru dress in the same manner as those of Bolivia, except that women wear hats of different styles. Some of the hats are tall-crowned, wide-brimmed straw hats and others are flat felt derbies. The shape and style depends on the region of Peru.

366

As we fly up the coast toward Quito, the capital of Ecuador, the barren shoreline is hidden by fog in many places. It seems strange that there should be fogs in such a dry desert, but along this part of the coast a cold ocean current, called the Humboldt Current, flows north from the icy Antarctic Ocean. Just as winter's cold often turns our breath to moisture, so the Humboldt Current chills the moist air above it, forming these thick fogs.

As our plane turns away from the seacoast, inland toward the Andes, our stewardess points out the cone of the famous sleeping volcano of Cayambe. "According to an old legend," she says, "it was deep in Cayambe's side that the powerful Incas hid the fair maids of the Sun God from Quito and also their treasures, when the Spanish conquerors came. Cayambe guards them well, since no one has ever found them. And many of the Indians who live at the base of the mountain still believe that if the fair maids or the treasure are disturbed, the volcano will come to life again and spit its fire and death upon all those who live at its base." She continues, "Although most of the South American volcanoes are now dead, a few are still active. Now and then they send streams of fiery lava up into the air."

A quick glance at our map reveals that Ecuador is a small country, about twice as large as the state of Arkansas. We also see that the equator runs across this fan-shaped country. In fact, Ecuador is the Spanish word for "land of the equator."

A short while later our airplane lands at an airport high in the Andes, a few miles from the city of Quito. This city, named after the Quito Indians, is believed to be the oldest city in the Western Hemisphere. It was the center of an ancient Indian empire before the Incas made it their northern capital. After the conquest of the Incan empire in the early 1500's, the Spaniards made this city one of their most important centers of learning and art in the New World.

Bordering on Colombia and Peru, Ecuador lies on the Northern Pacific coast of South America. **Area** • 108,478 sq. m. **Population** • 4,726,000. **Language** • Spanish, Quechua (Indian language). **Government** • Republic. **Monetary Unit** • Sucre (= about 0.05 U.S. $). **Chief Cities** • Guayaquil, Quito (capital). **Religion** • Roman Catholic. **Mountains** • Chimborazo (20,577 ft.); more than 20 active volcanoes, including the world's highest, Cotopaxi (19,344 ft.). **Rivers** • Guayas, Napo, Pastaza.

Church of San Francisco in Quito.

The streets of Quito are all steep, since the city is built on the slopes of Mount Pichincha. In the older parts of the city, some streets are so narrow that the overhanging balconies of the houses almost meet overhead. The newer sections of the city are quite modern, but all the streets, whether in the new or the old parts of the city, seem to meet at the beautiful Plaza Independencia, where a big monument commemorates the independence of Ecuador. Although Quito and other cities had been struggling with Spanish forces for many years, the final battle of independence was fought by General Antonio José de Sucre and his small army on the slopes of Pichincha. Since May 29, 1822, the country has been free from Spain and has ruled itself.

Near the plaza is the market place where Indians are selling pottery dishes, souvenirs of vegetable ivory, or hand-woven mats made of palm fiber. Others are selling leaves and roots that are used as medicines and beverages. Still others are selling woolen shawls, blankets and ponchos.

It is cool and comfortable during our stay. Even though we are less than fifteen miles from the equator, Quito has springlike temperatures throughout the year, because the city is almost two miles above sea level. The higher the altitude above sea level, anywhere on the earth, the cooler the air tends to be. That is why the snow does not melt on high mountain peaks in summer months or even on the equator. Just think — we could have a snowball fight on the equator here in Ecuador!

But not all of Ecuador is cool, as it is in the highland and mountainous region. The western part of the country, along the Pacific Coast, is hot and humid. In these hot lowland regions, people grow the cacao beans and bananas for which Ecuador is famous. One-third of all the bananas shipped into the United States come from this country. Much of the chocolate eaten and drunk come from Ecuador's cacao beans. Coffee, which is grown in the hilly regions that border the lowlands, is also exported to the United States. Other

Ecuadorian Indian mother with child bundled close to her in native fashion.

368

items exported include balsa wood, kapok, Panama hats, tagua (used in making buttons), and cinchona.

The eastern part of Ecuador is hot and humid. It is the home of several fierce Indian tribes. The Colorados (or "Red Ones," because they paint their bodies with red dye), the Aucas and the Jivaros are among the most feared savages in the world. The head-hunting Jivaros shrink the heads of their slain foes to the size of a man's fist and hang up these trophies by their hair as proof of their victories. This is a custom similar to the one observed by the American Indians who used to cut off a man's scalp for the same reason. The warrior in Ecuador who has the greatest number of heads is considered the best fighter. Instead of using bows and arrows, as our American Indians did, these barbarians employ blowguns and poison darts. The blowguns are hollow tubes eight to ten feet long. Holding the long, light tube, an Indian looks as if he were about to blow soap bubbles. But this weapon can kill men and animals. Some of these tribes live only about one hundred miles from Quito. Fortunately, they never come near the capital city.

Boy serenades girl on an instrument similar to a recorder.

In the morning, on our way back to the airport, we pass the Guayaquil-Quito railroad station. This railroad connects the two largest cities in Ecuador. Few railroads in the world have been more difficult and more expensive to build. It took ten years and the lives of hundreds of workmen to lay the 170 miles of track. The railroad begins in the low level land around the city of Guayaquil. To get to Quito, it must climb the western slopes of the Andes. The rails go through tunnels, cross fast-moving mountain streams, and creep around cuts in the face of rocky cliffs. Unfortunately, we do not have time to take this adventurous train ride. Our airplane is waiting for us back at the airport. The next stop is Panama City, capital of Panama.

Girl demonstrates the weaving of a Panama hat. This type of hat actually originates in Ecuador, not in Panama.

369

PANAMA

Connecting Central and South America, Panama is located on the narrowest strip of land between the Atlantic and Pacific Oceans. **Area** • 28,575 sq. m. **Population** • 1,177,000. **Language** • Spanish. **Government** • Republic. **Monetary Unit** • Balboa (= 1.00 U.S. $). **Chief Cities** • Panama (capital), Colón. **Religion** • Roman Catholic. **Mountains** • Chiriquí (11,410 ft.), the highest. **Rivers** • Chagres.

The Republic of Panama is located on the narrow bridge of land that joins North America with South America, and for centuries it separated the Atlantic Ocean from the Pacific. This tiny country is mostly unexplored jungle in which few people live. It is often called the "Crossroads of the New World." In fact, the fate of fortunes and empires of the Americas has depended on this narrow stretch of jungle now known as Panama.

When Spain ruled most of the Americas, a simple trail through the jungle linked the oceans, but over it passed the great treasures of gold and silver captured by the Spanish conquerors. Centuries later, gold was again the reason for building a railroad across the narrow stretch of land. It carried prospectors to California during the "gold rush" in 1849. But trade, not gold or silver, was the main reason the United States government finished the building of a canal begun by a French company. In 1914, ten years after work was started, the first ships passed through the Panama Canal. The two greatest oceans of the world were united and the North and South American continents were cut in two. With the opening of the Canal, ships sailing between the east and west coasts no longer had to make the long voyage around South America. The sailing distance between New York and San Francisco was shortened by more than 7,800 miles.

Arriving at Panama City after landing at Tocumen Airport, we find old Spanish Colonial buildings interspersed

Central Avenue, Panama City, one of the country's main shopping districts.

with modern structures. The older part of the city is crowded and the streets are narrow. But it is here that we find the most interesting sights. While walking on the Avenida Central, the main street in Panama City, we see the Presidential Palace, the Plaza Independencia — where the people of Panama once declared their independence — and the San José Church. Inside the church is the beautiful Altar of Gold. This altar was painted to look like wood by the people of the city, in order to hide it from Henry Morgan and his band of pirates when they plundered and burned the city in 1671. Near this church is the beautiful Romanesque Cathedral and its twin towers of mother-of-pearl. We also visit a high sea wall which at one time was part of the fort that protected the city. Underneath the wall were prison cells. Through the grated doors we see the rusted balls and chains along the walls. On top of this wall is a wide walkway, where people stroll to enjoy the breeze. From here, overlooking the blue Pacific, the city with its colored tiled roofs lies below.

The girl in front of the ruins of the Cathedral of Old Panama City wears a Panamanian fiesta costume.

Walking about this largest and capital city of the Republic of Panama, we find people of all races on the streets. Many are the sons and daughters of the workers who came here from over fifty different nations to help build the Canal. Others belong to families who came later. Still others are tourists, like ourselves. Spanish is the official language of the country, but English is used frequently in the cities near the Canal.

PANAMA CANAL ZONE

Of course, no trip to Panama would be complete without seeing the Panama Canal in operation. To do this, we take a taxi to the city of Balboa, near the Pacific side. On our ride there, we go into the Canal Zone. This is a strip of land extending about five miles on either side of the canal itself. This portion of land is controlled by the Canal Zone

Government, headed by a Governor appointed by the President of the United States, with the advice and consent of the Senate. Most Americans who work at the Panama Canal itself live here.

Balboa is quite different from Panama City. The streets are wide and straight, shaded by trees, and the houses and apartments all seem alike. There are stores, hotels, schools, churches and clubs, as in the United States. Our driver steers clear of the great warehouses and the vast docks crowded with steamers from many parts of the world, and soon the Miraflores Locks come into view.

Since most of the Panama Canal is higher than sea level, ships have to be lifted eighty-five feet above sea level, and then lowered eighty-five feet again. To do this, a series of steps, or locks, are built in the Canal. The ships do not climb up and down, but the "stairs of water" rise or fall, according to whether the ship is to be raised or lowered.

Standing in the lock's control tower, we watch a large ship approaching the lock and then come to a stop. The gates near the ship open while the other gates remain closed to hold back the water which is at a higher level. Small electric locomotives with cables on them pull the ship into the lock. After the ship is in place, the gates behind it are closed and water is allowed to pour back into the lock. It seems as if a giant faucet has been turned on. As the water swirls and rises, the ship rises with it. When the water is the same level on both sides of the lock, the front gates are opened and the ship is moved by the locomotives to the next lock. To lower the ship, the water is brought to the level of the lock ahead. In this way, the ship "walks" downstairs. An employee of the Canal tells us that ships must pass through six locks in the "Big Ditch," as the Panama Canal is often called, before it reaches the east coast. The locks are built in pairs, so that a ship can go toward the Pacific Ocean while another can move toward the Atlantic Ocean.

After a good night's rest in a modern hotel in Panama

PANAMA CANAL ZONE
United States territory, extending 5 miles on either side of the Panama Canal. **Area** • 558 sq. m. (including inland waterways). **Population** • 45,000. **Language** • English, Spanish. **Government** • Administered by United States Governor. **Monetary Unit** • U.S. Dollar ($). **Chief Cities** • Balboa, Balboa Heights (seat of administration), Cristobal. **Rivers** • Chagres, largely used by the Panama Canal. The Canal, linking the Atlantic and Pacific, is 40 miles long from shore to shore and 50 miles between two channel entrances. **Lakes** • Man-made Gatun and Madden Lakes are used to maintain water level in the Canal.

City, we take a taxi back to the airport, board an airplane, and take off for our next stop — Mexico City, capital of Mexico. Our course is to the northwest, as we fly on and on over Central America. There are five different independent countries in this part of the North American continent in addition to Panama: Costa Rica, Nicaragua, Honduras, El Salvador and Guatemala. In addition, there is British Honduras, which belongs to Great Britain. These Central American countries have hot lowlands on their coastlines, and rising between them, cooler highlands, where most of the people live. Bananas are one of the two main exports of the lowlands of Central America. Hardwoods, used to make fine furniture, are the other. On the gentle slopes of the rising highlands, coffee and cacao are the important products.

MEXICO

Mexico is the United States' closest neighbor to the South. The great segment of the Western Hemisphere called Latin American begins at the Mexican boundary. That is, the nations south of the United States border in the Western Hemisphere are known as the Latin-American countries. Mexico is the third largest Latin-American republic in land area, almost three times as large as Texas. Only Brazil and Argentina are larger. The land of this country is varied. Along its coasts are low plains and jungles. Rising from the coasts are great ranges of rugged mountains. Between the mountain ranges is a high, wide plateau. Mexico City is built upon this plateau region.

After being informed that our plane will be landing at Mexico City in a few minutes, we glance through the window and notice that high, green mountains seem to encircle the city like a ring. Our stewardess tells us that Mexico City, in addition to being Mexico's largest city, is the oldest capital city in North America. It is built on the spot where the Aztec Indian capital once stood.

Driving from the airport to the heart of the city, we see that, like most Latin-American countries, Mexico is a mixture of the old and the new. In the older portions there are some narrow streets, with their open-air markets. Here we can watch Mexican farmers and merchants buy and sell fresh fruits, vegetables and other foodstuffs, as well as home-made pottery and other household items. Only about one-tenth of the people of Mexico belong to the white race. The other nine-tenths are pure Indians, or else *mestizos*.

The newer parts of Mexico City remind us of big cities in the United States or in Europe. There are modern office buildings, apartment houses, shops, hotels and markets. While several skyscrapers can be seen, most of the buildings are only a few stories high. The wide streets are crowded with automobiles, streetcars, taxis and buses. On the streets

At left, the cathedral on El Zócalo, Mexico City's central square. The cathedral is centuries old and is beautifully constructed in the interior. Below, the Palace of Fine Arts in Mexico City, one of the most lavishly decorated of all modern museums.

of this portion of the city we find businessmen, workers, shoppers and tourists.

There are few large factories in Mexico City. However, manufacturing industries in Mexico are growing rapidly. The leading industries of this country are now textiles, paper, iron and steel, chemical products, fertilizers, glass, and leather goods. These industries are located in such cities as León, Puebla, Guadalajara, Monterrey, San Luis Potosí and Veracruz. Mexico has a good supply of resources, which include silver, petroleum, lead, zinc, sulfur and copper. This country also has a good supply of iron ore, coal and manganese, which permits it to produce large quantities of steel. The iron and steel center which often is called the "Pittsburgh of Mexico," is Monterrey in the northeast.

The major farm crops in Mexico are corn, rice, sugar cane, peppers, wheat, cotton, barley, potatoes, tobacco, coconuts, alfalfa, bananas and citrus fruits. For many years the farmers of Mexico did not raise enough food to feed the people well. In the last few years, however, modern farming methods and machinery have increased Mexico's farm out-

Fiesta dancers in Tasco, Mexico's center of the silver industry.

The great Aztec Temple of Tenochtitlan as it must have looked when the Spaniards entered Mexico. The picture is an artist's conception, provided from descriptive records and ruins still standing.

put to meet the needs of the people. Cattle, sheep, pigs and goats are also being raised in increased numbers.

Our taxi stops at the beautiful central plaza, which the Mexicans call Zócalo. On the north side of the plaza, or square, is a great National Cathedral of Mexico which was built on the ruins of the main temple of the Aztecs. Human sacrifices were once made here. This church is one of the oldest and largest in North America. On the east side of Zócalo, where the place of the Aztec emperors stood, is the large National Palace, built around an open court and containing government offices. Near the main entrance to the National Palace hangs Mexico's "Liberty Bell," rung by Miguel Hidalgo y Castilla on September 15, 1810, when he called upon the people to follow him in a revolt that overthrew Spanish rule. On every anniversary of this event, at midnight, the bell is rung by the president.

Later, we visit the National University, oldest university on the North American continent, and then our tour takes us to Lake Xochimilco to view the famous Floating Gardens. Our guide explains that the name of the lake, "Xochimilco," was derived from the Aztec word meaning the "place

of the flowers." Xochitl was their goddess of flowers. During the time of the Aztecs, the Indians constructed rafts of reeds, filled them with thin layers of soil and planted flowers. These rafts were floated on the lake they called Xochimilco. The Aztec emperors would then come to the lake to be rowed about in boats among the beautiful floating gardens. As time went by, the roots of the flowers became anchored in the mud at the bottom of the lake. Thus the floating gardens of the Aztecs became permanent.

As our automobile stops at a small dock on the lake, we notice several flat-bottomed boats lined up in rows waiting for people to board them. Each boat has a canopy over it to protect the passengers from the sun. Over the framework on the front of each boat is an arch of flowers with a girl's name cleverly arranged in a floral pattern. The boat of our choice has the name "Josefina."

We get aboard the craft and the boatman begins to pole it out into the main canal, while we sit comfortably in small chairs. Our boat goes down the Grand Canal de la Viga, which is the largest canal. Lake Xochimilco is often called the "Venice of Mexico," because people travel about in small boats on the many canals to see the gardens. Our guide tells us, "When the floating rafts anchored themselves on the lake's bottom, soil began to gather on top of the rafts. Eventually, land formed in great blocks with small canals dividing the gardens as you see it now." Most of the flowers sold in Mexico City are grown along the canals of Lake Xochimilco.

When we tell our guide that we are hungry, he hails a woman on a nearby boat. With a few rapid paddle strokes, she brings her boat next to ours. In the center of her boat there is a small charcoal stove full of hot coals, and on top of the stove is a metal plate, upon which she places pieces of chicken to fry. While the chicken is cooking, she also heats a dish of red beans and prepares something that looks like pancakes.

There are so many volcanos in Mexico that the Aztecs drew a picture of one when they wanted to depict a mountain. Here is a relatively new volcano named Paricutín, "born" in 1943.

"Those are tortillas," explains our guide, "and while they may look like pancakes, they taste a bit different." He informs us that to make tortillas, the Mexican cook soaks corn in lime water. Then she grinds corn by crushing it on a flat stone with another stone that is shaped like a rolling pin. Next, she takes some of this ground corn and shapes it until it is flat, like a pancake. The Aztecs had corn, or maize, long before the Spanish came. It is still the principal food of the native Mexicans.

When the tortillas are done, the woman places one on each plate along with a piece of chicken and some beans. She adds another native food which the guide explains is a green pepper, or chile, stuffed with cheese and bits of meat. The woman then covers the chicken with a sauce that contains small pieces of red peppers. Mexican food is hot and spicy, similar to the dishes we sampled in Spain.

Riding out to the airport in the evening, we remark upon how pleasant the weather is in Mexico City. Our taxi driver informs us that the climate is generally pleasing throughout the year. The days are warm, while the nights are cool. Boarding the plane, we say "Adios, México! Adios! Hello, U. S. A.! Hello!"

Awakening from our sleep aboard the jet airliner, we look out the plane's window and see the dome of the United States Capitol gleaming brightly in the dawn's early light. This is possibly the most beautiful sight we have seen on our entire trip around the world — because it is "home, sweet home!"

View of Red Square in Moscow.

Epilogue

We hope you have enjoyed your trip around the world. As we promised you in the first chapter of this book, we visited all the continents except Antarctica. As we wanted to make our trip with as little backtracking as possible, we passed through only a few countries on each continent. There are many lands — full of interesting people and places — that we weren't able to see. Perhaps we can go to these places another time. Or, one day, you may really go around the world — not just with book in hand and finger on globe, in pursuit of an author's itinerary.

It is unfortunate that our route did not permit even brief sojourns in the countries behind the so-called Iron and Bamboo curtains. Russia and China are nations of great cultural and political importance. We have, so as not to bypass these giants, given you "a glimpse behind the curtains" by including a summary and a few pictures for each.

The figures and facts for all the summaries in *Geography of the World for Young Readers* are based on research in two greatly respected books in this field of reference: the latest *Demographic Yearbook of the United Nations* and *The Columbia Lippincott Gazetteer of the World*.

UNION OF SOVIET SOCIALIST REPUBLICS (Russia)

Covering one-sixth of the earth's surface — in Europe and Asia — the U.S.S.R. is the world's largest state. **Area** • about 8,600,000 sq. m. **Population** • 224,764,000. **Language** • Russian is the chief language, but also Turkish, Finnish, Lithuanian, Armenian, Mongolian, and others. **Government** • federal state, consisting of 16 Union Republics; the largest and most important of these — over 50% of total population and 76% of land area — is the Russian Republic (Russia). **Monetary Unit** • Ruble (= 1.11 U.S. $). **Chief Cities** • Moscow (capital), Leningrad, Kiev, Gorki, Kharkov, Baku, Novosibirsk, Tashkent — all with one million or more population. **Religion** • Russian Orthodox, majority; Moslem, second largest; also Jewish, Roman Catholic, Protestant (mostly Lutheran). **Mountains** • in Asia, Communism Peak is the highest (24,590 ft.); in Europe, Mt. Elbrus (18,481 ft.). **Rivers** • Volga, Ural, Dnieper, Don, Ob-Irtysh, Lena, Amur. **Lakes** • Caspian Sea, Aral Sea, Ladoga, Baikal.

379

The Church of the Redeemer (picture above), overlooking the Moskva River, is perhaps the finest piece of architecture in all Moscow, if not Russia. Constructed in the period 1837-1883, it has a capacity of 10,000 people.

The Lunacharsky State Academic Theater in Odessa is one of the best equipped theaters in Europe (photo left).

Settlers in front of their hut at Yurta, Siberia (below left).

Oil fields in Baku, Azerbaidzhan Province, have been an important source of oil for Russia (below right).

CHINA

Second largest country, with the world's largest population. **Area** • 3,800,000 sq. m. **Population** • about 686,400,000. **Language** • Chinese. **Government** • Republic, officially known as Chinese People's Republic. **Monetary Unit** • Yuan (no established rate of exchange). **Chief Cities** • Shanghai, Peking (capital), Tientsin, Shenyang, Wuhan, Chungking, Canton, Sian, Nanking, Dairen — all with over one million people. **Religion** • Confucianism, Buddhism, Taoism are the chief religions; some Moslems and Christians (mostly Roman Catholic). **Mountains** • Tahsüeh (highest peak, Minya Konka, 24,900 ft.), Kunlun, Tien Shan, and Tsinling mountain ranges. **Rivers** • Yangtze, Hwang-Ho (Yellow), Si-Kiang (West), Pei Kiang (North), Pai, Canton. **Lakes** • largest are Tungting and Poyang.

A vista of pailous in the old part of Canton, one of Communist China's major cities (top photo).

The busy Bund, main street of Shanghai, the metropolis of China and the gateway to central and northern China.

Young girls of Peking.

Arctic Ocean

Barrow • • Pt. Barrow

UNITED
STATES
ALASKA • Fairbanks
• Nome
• Anchorage
• Whitehorse
• Yellowknife
Victoria
Island
Ba[

NORT

Mackenzie

• Juneau
Gulf of Alaska
Kodiak
I.
CANAD
AMERI

Hudson
Bay

Rocky Mountains

UNION OF SOVIET
SOCIALIST
REPUBLICS
Siberia

Lena

• Verkhoyansk

• Yakutsk

• Magadan

Kamchatka Pen.

Sea of
Okhotsk

Bering
Sea

• Vancouver
• Seattle
• Edmonton
• Regina
• Winnipeg

Great
Lakes

• Chita
MONGOLIA
Manchuria
• Khabarovsk
Sakhalin
Island
Aleutian Islands

• Portland
UNITE
• Minneapolis
To
Torc
• Chicago • Detroit
STATES
• Denver St. Louis
Washingt
• San Francisco
• Los Angeles
• Dallas
Atlan
• Houston
Mississippi
New
Orleans
Rio Grande
MEXICO
Gulf of Mexico
Havana
CU

• Mukden
KOREA
• Vladivostok
Inner
Mongolia
• Peking
• Seoul
JAPAN
• Tokyo
• Osaka
MONDAY
SUNDAY
Pacific

CHINA
Yangtze
• Shanghai
• Iwo Jima
Midway Is.
(U.S.)
UNITED
STATES
HAWAII
• Honolulu

• Canton
HONG
KONG
(Br.)
Taiwan
(Formosa)
Wake I.
(U.S.)
• Mexico City
BR.
HOND.
JAMAIC
GUA HOND.
EL SA NIC.
C.R.
PAN.

• Manila
PHILIPPINES
Guam
(U.S.)
Mariana Is.
Marshall
Is.
INTERNATIONAL DATE LINE

BRUNEI
Sabah
Sarawak
Borneo
Celebes
CAROLINE ISLANDS
Gilbert
Is.
(Br.)
Galápagos Is.
(Ecuador)
Quito
ECUAD

INDONESIA
Java
TERR. OF
NEW
GUINEA
New West
IRIAN Guinea
(Indon. Adm.) PAPUA
Ellice Is.
(Br.)
Solomon
Is. (Br.)
W. SAMOA
• Timor
• Darwin
New Hebrides
Fiji Is.
(Br.)
Tongal
(Br.)
Tuamotu Arch.
(Fr.)
Ocean
Coral
Sea
New
Caledonia
(Fr.)
Cook
Islands
(N.Z.)
Tahiti
(Fr.)

AUSTRALIA
• Perth
• Brisbane
• Sydney
• Canberra
• Adelaide
• Melbourne
Tasmania
Tasman
Sea
• Auckland
NEW ZEALAND
• Wellington